AF600133

THE PUBLIC PAPERS OF
THE GOVERNORS OF KENTUCKY

Robert F. Sexton
General Editor

SPONSORED BY THE
Kentucky Advisory Commission
on Public Documents
AND THE
Kentucky Historical Society

THE PUBLIC PAPERS OF

GOVERNOR LAWRENCE W. WETHERBY

1950-1955

John E. Kleber, *Editor*

THE UNIVERSITY PRESS OF KENTUCKY

Library of Congress Cataloging in Publication Data

Wetherby, Lawrence W. (Lawrence Winchester), 1908–
The Public papers of Governor Lawrence W. Wetherby, 1950–1955.

(The Public papers of the Governors of Kentucky)
Includes index.
1. Kentucky—Politics and government—1951– —Sources. I. Kleber, John E., 1941– . II. Kentucky. Governor (1950–1955 : Wetherby) III. Title. IV. Series.
F456.2.W47 1983 976.9'043 82-40182
ISBN 0-8131-0606-0

Scholarly publisher for the Commonwealth,
serving Berea College, Centre College of Kentucky,
Eastern Kentucky University, The Filson Club,
Georgetown College, Kentucky Historical Society,
Kentucky State University, Morehead State University,
Murray State University, Northern Kentucky University,
Transylvania University, University of Kentucky,
University of Louisville, and Western Kentucky University.

Editorial and Sales Offices: Lexington, Kentucky 40506-0024

CONTENTS

CONTENTS

CONTENTS

CONTENTS

AGRICULTURE [191]

KENTUCKY & THE NATION [206]

CONTENTS

REORGANIZATION [223]

EDUCATION [232]

CONTENTS

CONTENTS

CONTENTS

FOREWORD

THE editor of this collection of Lawrence Wetherby's public papers says that the Wetherby administration has yet to be fully appreciated even by historians and political scientists. I agree. Lawrence was not a good press agent for himself. He has little of the ego that causes most politicians to publicize and sometimes exaggerate their good deeds. He was less controversial than the hard-driving Earle Clements who preceded him or the flamboyant Happy Chandler who followed him. He was like the all-star infielder who made difficult plays look easy. The news media thus failed to highlight the solid accomplishments of his administration.

His public papers are crisp and well-reasoned, but like most such papers, when looked at in cold print, they are impersonal and stiff. They portray the highlights of the Wetherby administration, but reveal very little of the character, personality, and philosophy of the man behind them. They fail to project the intellectual honesty of the man and the camaraderie that he had with the people of the state. They do not project the image of open-door administration and people-oriented programs that were the hallmarks of his administration. A governor sets the tone of his administration and Lawrence made it clear early on that, although he had no aversion to politics, he would not permit the spoils system to interfere with honest, efficient government.

Lawrence was something of a paradox in Kentucky politics. Although he was born and raised in Jefferson County and practiced law in Louisville, he could speak the language of rural Kentucky. A product of Louisville machine politics, he was a reformer and idealist who exhibited a courageous independence of mind. Wetherby was one of the first governors in the nation, and a Southerner at that, to speak out in the 1950s on the subject of civil liberties for minority groups and, indeed, for all Americans. Two examples come to mind:

When the Supreme Court mandated the integration of public schools in 1954, Wetherby immediately proclaimed that Kentucky would follow the Supreme Court decision and that Kentucky's schools would be integrated.

When McCarthyism ran rampant in this country and the civil liberties of American citizens were being ruthlessly violated, Lawrence made no secret of his disdain for McCarthy's tactics; and when McCarthy attended the Kentucky Derby the press noted that Governor Wetherby found a convenient way to avoid being photographed with him.

Lawrence was outstanding in athletics as well as the political game, and in both pursuits he garnered a number of sobriquets. His teammates at the University of Louisville, where he was a star end on the football team, called him Chink. He has been inducted into the University of Louisville Football Hall of Fame along with such legendary football heroes as Johnny Unitas and Lennie Liles. During his political career Happy Chandler tagged him with the name Wetherbine to identify him as an ally of Clementine, which was Happy's name for Clements.

The linking of Wetherby and Clements is not without justification. Lawrence was elected lieutenant governor in 1947 largely because Earle Clements, who was the successful candidate for governor that year, threw his support to him in the Democratic primary. At that time the lieutenant governor's office was not as important, nor as costly to the taxpayers, as it is now. The lieutenant governor's only statutory function was to preside over the State Senate when it was in session and the only compensation he received was a modest per diem for performing those duties. The state did not provide a residence for the lieutenant governor in Frankfort, and Lawrence commuted to Frankfort from his home in Middletown.

Governor Clements had confidence in his ability and integrity, and gave him assignments seldom given to earlier lieutenant governors. Lawrence worked closely with the Legislative Research Commission, became knowledgeable about state government, and acted as a liason between the governor and the legislature.

When he sought a full term as governor in 1951, he won the Democratic primary by a record-breaking majority. Emerson "Doc" Beauchamp won the Democratic nomination for lieutenant governor that year. They both won handily in November 1951. They were an interesting study in contrasts. Lawrence was tall and rangy, with the courtly manners of a Southern gentleman. Doc was rotund and gregarious and usually was a little disheveled. Lawrence cared little for the nuances and subtleties of political manipulation. To him, most things were either black or white, and when a problem came along, he looked at the pros and cons, made up his mind and openly stated his position. Beauchamp, on the other hand, was the epitome of Kentucky's rural politician. The ebb and flow of practical politics was a way of life to him. It seemed sometimes that it was the game itself which interested him, and that victory and defeat were not as important as playing the game. Lawrence and Doc had great fondness for each other. Both were scrupulously honest and no breath of dishonesty or scandal touched the Wetherby administration. But a close observer could detect that Lawrence thought Doc was too political and Doc thought Lawrence was too interested in governmental reform. He frequently referred to Lawrence good-humoredly as the man on the white horse. He was a team player, however, and strongly supported the Wetherby programs.

When Lawrence ran for office his address was always listed as Middletown rather than Louisville. This was done for more than mere political expediency, since it exemplified Lawrence's fondness for the opportunities afforded by rural life. From boyhood he has been an avid sportsman, and although he is now past seventy he continues to hunt and fish and is a vocal supporter of his favorite athletic teams. He is regarded as one of the best wing-shots in the state, and can catch fish when the average fisherman cannot get a nibble. When he was governor he liked to serve wild game at informal meetings of his political cronies. These meetings were dubbed by a political wag "varmint suppers." The term caught on and has become part of the political lingo of Kentucky. He is a lover of the soil and always tends in season a vegetable and flower garden at his home in Frankfort.

It is not within my purview in this foreword to list the tangible accomplishments of the Wetherby administration, but when a definitive history of recent Kentucky is written, Lawrence Wetherby will be ranked as one of Kentucky's most forward looking and progressive governors.

BERT T. COMBS

GENERAL EDITOR'S PREFACE

THE Public Papers of the Governors of Kentucky is a series of volumes which preserves and disseminates the public record of Kentucky's chief executives. The need to make these records available was articulated by a number of persons interested in Kentucky history, government, and politics. In 1971 the Kentucky Advisory Commission on Public Documents, created by executive order, recommended the publication of the Public Papers of the Governors of Kentucky. The commission oversees and manages all aspects of the project in cooperation with the Kentucky Historical Society.

While the organization of the material may vary from volume to volume with differences in the styles of the governors, available materials, and historical circumstances, the volumes share an overall guiding philosophy and general format.

It is our hope that the series will prove useful to all those interested in Kentucky government, including citizens, scholars, journalists, and public servants. Not in themselves interpretations of Kentucky government and history, the volumes in this series will be the basis for serious analysis by future historians.

R. F. S.

EDITOR'S PREFACE

THIS volume preserves the public papers and letters from the five-year period when Lawrence W. Wetherby was governor of the Commonwealth of Kentucky. Relatively little of this material has been available heretofore to the general public. And its inaccessibility may explain why the Wetherby administration has yet to be fully appreciated even by historians and political scientists.

Today concerted action is taken to preserve the public papers of a sitting governor, but no such effort was made during Wetherby's administration. Nevertheless, more documents remain than might have been expected under the circumstances. Cattie Lou Miller and Addie Dean Stokley, who assisted and filed for Governor Wetherby, displayed a sense of history that was fortunate if not uncanny; their contribution to posterity is invaluable.

Despite the valiant deeds of Miller and Stokley, many of Wetherby's papers were lost in the transition from office. Hence, there remain relatively few letters addressed to him. Still two filing cabinets of material were saved. One may find in this collection a potpourri that includes public speeches, executive orders, veto messages, newspaper clippings, photographs, campaign materials, appointments diaries, pardons, budget materials, department materials, a progress report, and a copy of each public letter sent by the governor. Wetherby kept this collection in his personal possession after vacating the office. However, during the course of my research, he decided to deposit it in the Margaret I. King Library at the University of Kentucky. It is to be hoped that the donation, when combined with the publication of this volume, will shed light on an interesting but neglected period in Kentucky's history.

In retrospect the years 1950 through 1955 offered problems and opportunities that made being governor both a challenge and a joy. It was a period of economic growth fostered by the artificial stimulus of the Korean War, and sudden economic readjustment when the war ended, that resulted in financial problems for Kentucky's government. There was a depression in the important coal industry that caused a mass exodus of people from eastern Kentucky. A brief drought impaired agricultural production. While President Harry Truman had been quite solicitous of the state's needs, the new Republican administration in Washington was less so. Yet, of a positive nature, there were an influx of tourists, a concerted effort to diversify the state's economic base through industrialization, and an attempt to mitigate a characteristic isolation both within and without through the construction of toll roads and rural highways. The papers in this volume reflect the thought of Kentucky's executive branch on all of these issues.

From the inception of my research it was evident that I could not present the desired comprehensive view of the Wetherby administration if I relied solely upon the use of formal speeches. Whereas the editors of other volumes in this series were presented with an excess of material, I had to search for additional sources. After reading the fifty-five formal speeches, I decided to include them all and to supplement them with 101 letters. Fortunately, there were copies of 20,000 of the governor's letters. The time needed to read and make a selection delayed an anticipated completion date. But I believe the effort was repaid not only by achieving the comprehensive view, but through a presentation of the personal qualities of Lawrence Wetherby altogether missing from his formal speeches. Indeed, I used the dual criteria of comprehension and insight in selecting the letters.

The letters here were addressed to both public and private individuals, but the content was always of a public nature. While some of them contain additional information others repeat ideas already expressed in the formal speeches. I chose to use the latter for the sake of emphasis and to portray Wetherby's personal feelings. Each letter has been titled and an attempt was made to identify the recipient. Unfortunately, it was often impossible to identify these lesser-known individuals, and thus many letter recipients lack vitas. My use of the letters is not intended to be either a criticism of earlier editors who omitted them or a pattern for their inclusion in subsequent volumes. But I am certain that they do provide a unique view of the Wetherby administration.

The material is arranged by topic rather than by chronology. Within each topical section chronology is used, with the formal speeches preceding the letters. It will be noted that a disproportionate number of the speeches come from Wetherby's first year in office. This may be due to his need to establish and to publicize himself as governor in his own right after the resignation of Earle Clements. It certainly reflects Wetherby's decision to seek a full term in 1951. The formally written speeches were a means of protection against being misquoted during the campaign. Wetherby seldom made handwritten changes to his formal speeches, but where he did they are included here.

Because no calendar of engagements was preserved, it is difficult to determine with certainty just where and when Wetherby delivered speeches. No doubt he spoke more often than the selection included here would indicate, sometimes from formal speeches now lost and again extemporaneously or from brief notes. Indeed, as he developed an ease and confidence in the office, Wetherby spoke more frequently in an offhand manner. Yet, I believe that the major number of his formal written speeches is preserved here. A governor in the early fifties lacked the mobility of subsequent holders of the office. Wetherby, who sometimes drove himself, was curtailed by inclement weather that made the poor roads and undeveloped airfields hazardous to travel. Therefore, a formal address by the governor was a major event, and chances are that if it was written out it was preserved with the appropriate place and date noted.

As in previous volumes, I have chosen not to include other sources of information that are available elsewhere. Veto messages can be found in the Senate and House Journals, while proclamations and executive orders are preserved at the Secretary of State's Office, the Kentucky Historical Society, and the State Archives and Record Center. Newspaper accounts can be found by consulting major papers, such as the *Louisville Courier-Journal* and the *Lexington Herald.* Whenever the governor visited a town, his presence and speech would be published in the local press. Included in the Wetherby papers to be deposited at the University of Kentucky are several large scrapbooks filled with newspaper clippings, although most of them are taken from the *Louisville Courier-Journal* and the *Louisville Times.* I did incorporate one letter written by Edward A. Farris, Chief Executive Assistant to the governor, because it provided an excellent account of Wetherby's administrative accomplishments. Unlike earlier volumes, I did not include an appendix listing the date, location, and title of each speech. Lack of documentation precluded this admittedly valuable tool of the researcher.

Once I had selected the material to be included, an effort was made to clarify it through explanation. I attempted to identify each individual person who was mentioned, with the exception of presidents of the United States. The biographical sketches include dates, occupations, place of birth, and residence. Each piece of legislation is linked to its location in the *Acts of the General Assembly of the Commonwealth of Kentucky.* On occasion, I supplied expository sentences in order to place a speech or letter in proper perspective or to provide additional facts. Where the papers made only brief mention of a significant point, I directed the reader to where it is more fully explained. I made but slight attempt to verify the facts as stated in the speeches or letters of the governor.

The administration of Morehead State University was quite supportive of my endeavors and assisted me in a most pertinent manner to complete this project. One graduate student at Morehead State University, Virginia Ritchie, helped me with the typing. Professor James Hammack of Murray State University put me onto the opportunity, and now I can thank him. Robert F. Sexton provided me with direction at the inception and continued encouragement. Elizabeth Hough Geisler, my aunt, provided me with a warm congenial place to work, and Emma Carol Brown helped with the proofreading. The librarians at the Louisville Free Public Library amiably received my numerous requests for information and provided invaluable assistance. Finally, I must note that a great personal benefit resulted from my acquaintance with former Governor Wetherby. This most courtly gentleman welcomed me into his home to work, to talk, and to learn much of Kentucky politics, while Mrs. Wetherby's lunches sustained me through those 20,000 letters.

Objectivity is the watchword of the historian, and I have endeavored to be ever cognizant of it while selecting and editing these papers. Conscious of the future historian's need to know the facts, I have also attempted to exhibit the important accomplishments of Kentucky's chief executive between 1950 and 1955, and in a comprehensive yet intimate format. Naturally, I assume responsibility for the contents and herewith apologize for the errors that were committed.

J. E. K.

GOVERNOR LAWRENCE W. WETHERBY
November 27, 1950, to December 13, 1955

THE forty-eighth governor of the Commonwealth of Kentucky, Lawrence Winchester Wetherby, was born on January 2, 1908, in Middletown, Kentucky. The son of Samuel David, a physician, and Fanny Yenowine Wetherby, he was the first governor to be born in Jefferson County, but was one of many Methodists to hold the office.

Even though Middletown was located only a short distance to the east of Louisville, Wetherby grew up in a rural environment. As a youth, he worked on his father's farm and was an active member of the Junior Agricultural Club, a forerunner of 4-H Clubs. He attended Middletown Grade School, and in 1925 he graduated from Anchorage High School.

One might have expected Wetherby to pursue the profession of medicine, since he descended from a line of physicians, his grandfather serving as one in the Civil War. Indeed, the young boy occasionally accompanied his father on his rounds. However, Wetherby chose instead to enter the field of law, enrolling in the University of Louisville College of Arts and Science for prelegal training. He graduated from the University of Louisville School of Law in 1929 with his LL.B. degree.

Wetherby's graduation nearly coincided with the onset of the Great Depression. Nevertheless, he found immediate employment with Judge Henry J. Tilford in Louisville. Tilford had a great influence upon the future governor, instilling in him a sense of political astuteness, and they continued their legal association until November 1950.

During the years of our nation's austerity, Wetherby had many small cases. But he was not too busy to meet, court, and marry on April 24, 1930, Helen Dwyer, daughter of Dr. and Mrs. William M. Dwyer of Louisville. They had three children: Lawrence, Jr., in 1931, Suzanne in 1932, and Barbara Juel in 1935.

Throughout his life Wetherby maintained an interest in the welfare of young people. The fact that he established a new Youth Authority while he was governor gives evidence of that concern. And it was a concern that began in 1933 when Wetherby became an attorney for the Jefferson County Juvenile Court, a position he held until 1937 and again in 1942. This earlier work resulted in his appointment as the first trial commissioner of the Jefferson County Juvenile Court in March 1943. Wetherby served as a judge until March 1947, at which time he resigned to make the race for lieutenant governor.

While practicing law and working with the Juvenile Court Wetherby was a member of the Mental Hygiene Clinic Board, Board of Governors of Mary Hurst School for Girls, Health and Welfare Council Childrens Agency; and he was active in Community Chest and War Fund campaigns. He served as a member of the Board of Bar Examiners from 1946 until 1948.

During the Great Depression, Wetherby, already a Democrat, became a supporter of the New Deal policies of Franklin Roosevelt. From that time, and particularly during his years as governor, one can find vestiges of the influence in values held and decisions rendered. It was as a New Dealer that Wetherby campaigned for lieutenant governor in a six-man primary race. With the backing of the Jefferson County machine and the tacit support of Earle C. Clements, Wetherby won in August 1947. In November, on a ticket headed by Clements, Wetherby was elected lieutenant governor over Republican Orville M. Howard by a vote of 367,836 to 271,893. His election aligned him with the "regular" faction of the Democratic party, while it separated him from his fellow Democrat Albert B. "Happy" Chandler.

After his election, Wetherby continued to reside at Anchorage, Kentucky, commuting to Frankfort when responsibilities required it. He developed an intimate working relationship with Governor Clements, who gave him assignments rarely afforded earlier lieutenant governors. Hence Wetherby worked closely with the Legislative Research Commission and on the state budget, acted as a liaison with the legislators, and helped to organize the Southern Regional Education Board. He also served as Secretary of the Democratic Central Committee from 1948 unitl November 1950.

In 1950 Governor Clements ran for the United States Senate seat left vacant by Alben Barkley, who became vice president, and by the resignation of Garrett L. Withers, who had temporarily filled the seat. He was elected to a full term and vacated the governorship on November 27, 1950, when Wetherby assumed the office.

Four months later, Wetherby himself toyed with the idea of going to the Senate when a vacancy occurred upon the death of Virgil Chapman on March 8, 1951. However, bowing to commitment and family wishes, he decided instead to seek a full term as governor. He won the Democratic primary in August 1951 by a record-breaking majority. During the following campaign he was aided by having Emerson Beauchamp, a popular western Kentucky politico, as his candidate for lieutenant governor. Helped by state police raids on gambling establishments in northern Kentucky, the Weatherby-Beauchamp ticket defeated Republican Eugene V. Siler by 58,000 votes in the general election.

Governor Wetherby's legislative accomplishments included a call for one extraordinary session of the General Assembly in order to increase both teachers' salaries and benefits to the needy and government employees. Later, he created a separate Department of Mental Health, had enacted the first anti-strip mining law, and began the construction of toll roads and a new state fair grounds. Improvements in education came with an amendment permitting the allocation of educational funds to school districts on the basis of need rather than the number of pupils. In 1954 and 1955 as governor and chairman of the Southern Governors' Conference, Wetherby supported the Supreme Court's school desegregation order and urged its peaceful implementation as the law of the land.

In 1955 Wetherby supported Judge Bert T. Combs for governor. In a classic example of party factionalism, Combs lost to A. B. Chandler in one of the most bitterly contested primary campaigns in Kentucky's tumultuous political history. Chandler was elected governor; and Wetherby turned over the office to him on December 13, 1955.

With the completion of his term, Wetherby returned to Anchorage. But in 1956 he was selected to represent the party in a race for the Senate seat left vacant by the death of Alben Barkley. His Republican opponent was John Sherman Cooper. That same year, Senator Clements ran for reelection against Thruston B. Morton. Both Democrats lost, partly as a result of the Eisenhower landslide vote and partly because Governor Chandler bolted his party to support the Republican candidates.

In 1960 Wetherby moved to Frankfort, where he became a consultant to Brighton Engineering Company and practiced private law. In 1964-1966 he was a member of the State Constitution Assembly. In 1965, at the request of the Franklin County Committee, he ran for the Kentucky State Senate against a candidate supported by Chandler, and won. He was President Pro Tempore of the Senate from 1966 to 1968. He left the State Senate in 1969 and held no elective office afterwards.

In later years, Wetherby continued his practice of law. He served as a director in several corporations, including the Lincoln Income Life Insurance Company, retiring from its board in 1978. He was president of the Frankfort Country Club and was active in raising funds for the YMCA.

OATH OF OFFICE
Frankfort / November 27, 1950

GREATER honor falls to the lot of no man than to be permitted to serve his fellowmen, whether it be in the realm of government or another chosen field of endeavor. I am both proud and humble as I undertake the duties of governor of the Commonwealth of Kentucky, proud to follow in the illustrious footsteps of Governor Clements[1] and other great Kentuckians, yet humble before the Almighty Father of us all as I seek to properly discharge the duties of the office to which I have been called under the constitution.

Advancements have been made during the past three years in the field of state government. These will be carried forward. A proper course has been chartered that will make our task easier. I have played a part—a somewhat minor one—in many of these improvements and am not entirely unfamiliar with what has transpired.

The leadership which has been supplied for these many forward steps has not always come from the ranks of government. Much of it has come from the impetus of public-spirited citizens whose interest in the welfare and advancement of Kentucky is as great as that manifested by those in the public service.

In a democratic society, all men are equal. Those entrusted with authority do not rule; they serve. One entrusted with high public office should seek the cooperation and guidance of the best talent available, wherever it may be found, for therein lies our strength and security. In our society, power and responsibility alike are shared. Fortunately, it is not concentrated in the hands of a few. And that is as it should be. Your public officials are mere symbols through which your collective wishes are executed.

In Kentucky there is now less sectional feeling than there has ever been. The reason is simple. All people of Kentucky are better acquainted with their neighbors, and Kentuckians of all sections are beginning to learn and understand the common problems of all their fellow citizens. They are realizing that just as a man cannot be healthy if there is sickness in any area of his body, a Commonwealth cannot be wholly prosperous if the economy of any section languishes. No chain stretches mightier than its weakest link, and removal of sectional barriers improves the lot of all our people. Our program has for its aim a better understanding on the part of all the people of the problems confronting other sections of the state.

A cursory review of the record of the past three years is appropriate upon this occasion. We review some of the past that we may set our sights higher for greater achievement. We promise continuing improvements in public education, agriculture, health, and the many other fields in which government plays a vital role. Such is the aim of leadership that may well be provided by the Committee on Functions and Resources of State Government,[2] a fine group of nonpartisan, public-spirited Kentuckians whose efforts are deserving of wide commendation. Through this agency, we hope to find the correct answers to many perplexing problems, answers that will point to the dawn of a new day for many.

Kentucky is proud of the record made during the last three years in the field of road building. More than $85 million have been invested in improvements to our road system, embracing more than 7,000 miles of new construction, a figure twice the amount built during any previous four-year administration. This program is for the betterment of the city and country folk alike.

More than twenty-five hundred miles of rural highways have been constructed—represented by an investment of more than $24 million—making it easier for the mud-bound child to attend school; for the ill to obtain the services of physician; for the farmer to get his products to market. Such a forward-looking program must and shall be continued with greater momentum.

The progress that has been made in road building, with its aids to education, travel, and marketing, also has aided materially in extension of rural electric lines to our rural folk. Here again, the facilities of government have been most helpful. The Public Service Commission[3] has given every encouragement to the extension of these facilities. It has approved every application for extension of facilities, whether made by a private or public utility. Three years ago, less than half of Kentucky farmers enjoyed electricity. Today, the figure is nearly 80 percent. We expect to see the job completed before many moons, when electricity will be in the reach of all.

Akin to these programs, yet separate, is the continued useful development of our park and recreational areas. Kentucky is a regular tourists' mecca, with more natural attractions to offer than any other state in the union. We shall continue this worthwhile program.

In 1948 the legislature authorized the reorganization of the Highway Patrol into a State Police Department. This has been done and today we have an excellent department. It has been taken out of politics and is supplementing local law-enforcement agencies.

In the field of industrial relations, nothing is more important than the promotion of harmonious relations between employer and employee. We have sought to achieve such a goal. The machinery has been overhauled to make certain that speedy hearings are held in industrial injury and that these are decided with promptness. Both workmen's compensation and unemployment benefits have been increased to a level consistent with payments being made in surrounding states.

Our coal mines must be made safe places in which to work, as must other industrial establishments. A continued downward record in the field of fatalities in industrial accidents is commendable. Any steps taken to enforce rigidly the safety rules have the hearty approval and support of all forward-looking citizens. It shall be our policy to do everything to achieve that end.

Health standards have been raised materially in the last three years. Facilities for treatment of diseases have been both increased and improved. Three of five new tuberculosis hospitals have already been opened; two more will be opened shortly. And a new tuberculosis hospital is planned for the mentally ill at Central State Hospital, Lakeland.[4] Through the Hill-Burton Act[5], we have extended financial aid to hospitals in both urban and rural centers and, as a result, more than two thousand additional hospital beds have been made available in rural areas where doctors are scarce. Through an appropriation for medical research, we have taken a step that will gradually mean new doctors for rural areas.

The mental health program in Kentucky requires both new treatment facilities and additional housing. Along both fronts, material progress has been made. Our facilities for treatment are gradually being raised, and we propose to make them sufficient so that many mentally ill may be cured and returned to their homes without long confinement within the institutions. The proper care and treatment of these patients require the continued sympathetic understanding and services of well-qualified personnel. We intend to procure as rapidly as possible the services of the best experts in the field of mental health. Our staffs have shown marked improvement in recent years, and with your continued support, they can become second to none.

Equally important it is that there be decent housing facilities for the unfortunates committed to our care. There has been initiated a program of construction and rehabilitation of the institutions that will, when present contracts are completed, eliminate the blight of overcrowding at the mental hospitals. State farms are producing more of the institutional food requirements than ever. Production has been increased to a point where we will soon have available additional funds to spend to improve treatment facilities.

Industry has been encouraged to locate here through wise and proper steps. During the past four years, more than 250 new industries, employing more than 40,000 people and with an annual payroll of more than $60 million have located here, a welcome addition to our economy.

I could speak to you of accomplishments in many fields—conservation, agriculture, industrial activity, the National Guard, and others—but time does not permit; an efficient job has been done in many fields. Both the Insurance Department and the Department of Motor Transportation[6] have been reorganized and a new code has been written for each of them so that they can now meet the needs in their fields of government.

These are trying times in our nation's history,[7] and we in Kentucky will make every effort to assist in the defense work, and Kentuckians will, as always, rally to the forefront. I ask all of you state employees to return to your positions tomorrow morning—you may have the rest of the day off duty—and to render to the public the same loyal service that you have been rendering during the past three years.

Here in Kentucky, we have some of the greatest talent to be found anywhere, whether in the field of government or in private endeavor. Kentuckians are ever equal to meet any crisis. I covet for all Kentucky success and pray God to give me wisdom and strength to carry out the task which has been assigned me. Mr. Chief Justice,[8] I am now ready to take the oath of office as governor of the Commonwealth.

---

1. Earle C. Clements (1896-), Sheriff, county clerk, Union County judge (1921-1941); state senator (1941-1944); member, United States House of Representatives (1944-1947); governor of Kentucky (1947-1950); member, United States Senate (1950-1957); Kentucky highway commissioner (1959-1960); born in Morganfield and resident of Washington, D.C. Robert Sobel and John Raimo, eds., *Biographical Directory of the Governors of the United States, 1789-1978* (Westport, Conn., 1978), 2:545-46.

2. The Committee on Functions and Resources of State Government consisted of not more than twenty-five members appointed by the governor. They were selected from areas of industry, agriculture, labor, the professions, small business, etc., and were interested in the welfare and advancement of the state. The committee was not to serve beyond December 31, 1951.

In Conjunction with the Legislative Research Commission, the committee made a comprehensive study and survey of the requirements, needs, and responsibilities of the state government, a survey of the existing tax structure, and the prospective and potential tax sources available to the state. The study and survey was to inform the governor and the General Assembly as to the most feasible, equitable, and economically sound program of government of the state.

See *Acts of the General Assembly of the Commonwealth of Kentucky*, 1950, Chapter 124 (H. B. 449), pp. 541-43.

3. The Public Service Commission is composed of a chairman and two other members appointed by the governor and approved by the senate. They are authorized to fix and change rates and services of public utilities that operate electric, gas, water, telephone, and certain types of pipeline services in Kentucky. John Estill Reeves, *Kentucky Government* (Lexington, 1966), p. 105.

4. Eventually six tuberculosis hospitals were built and located at Ashland, Glasgow, London, Louisville, Madisonville, and Paris. Reeves, *Kentucky Government*, p. 85.

5. The Hill-Burton Act, entitled the Hospital Survey and Construction Act (Public Law 79-725, Title VI of Public Health Service Act, August 1946), authorized grants to the states for surveying needs and developing plans for construction of facilities; assisting in the construction and equipping of needed public and voluntary nonprofit general, mental, tuberculosis, and chronic disease hospitals, and public health centers. A 1949 amendment to the Hospital Survey and Construction Act (Public Law 81-380, October 1949) authorized the Public Health Service to conduct and provide grants for research, experiments, and demonstrations relating to the development, effective use, and coordination of hospital services, facilities, and resources. Funds were not appropriated until the 1956 Appropriation Act. See "Hill-Burton Program Progress Report July 1, 1947-June 30, 1968," (Silver Spring, Maryland, 1968), pp. 3-5.

6. The Department of Insurance was created in 1950 by removing the Division of Insurance from the Department of Business Regulation. It functions to administer insurance laws and regulate the conduct of the insurance business, license company agents and representatives, administer insurance taxes, and purchase the insurance required by state agencies. Reeves, *Kentucky Government*, p. 112.

The Department of Motor Transportation was created in 1950 when the Division of Motor Transportation was removed from the Department of Business Regulation. It is responsible for the regulation and taxation of all motor vehicles for hire, and it regulates the fares, rates, services, and charges of motor carriers. *Ibid.*, p. 114.

7. Governor Wetherby was referring to the Korean War (June 25, 1950, to July 27, 1953).

8. Porter D. Sims (1887-), city attorney of Bowling Green for eight years; circuit judge of the Eighth Judicial District (1928-1938); appointed commissioner of appeals (1938-1942); elected judge of the Court of Appeals in 1942 and 1951, chief justice (1947-1951). Frank K. Kavanaugh, *Kentucky Directory* (Frankfort, 1952), p. 175.

INAUGURAL ADDRESS
Frankfort / December 11, 1951

THE course of events in Kentucky's history makes this an important and memorable day. One chapter ends and another begins in the exciting history that extends from the Isaac Shelby[1] inauguration through all the 159 years of this Commonwealth. Time has shown the importance of that first inauguration which launched Kentucky's statehood in 1792. In contrast to today's spectacle it was marked with simplicity, and the lone newspaper of the new Commonwealth devoted only a few words to describe the proceedings.

With the population growth and pride of the people in having a state government of their own, Kentuckians attached increasing significance to succeeding inaugural ceremonies. Beginning with the inauguration of James Garrard[2] in 1796, the first one held in Frankfort, the people of this city and county have shown boundless hospitality and devoted much time and attention to seeing that those who come here on Inauguration Day find a warm welcome and a joyful occasion. The 1951 Inaugural Committee and all those working with them have spent days and weeks planning, arranging, and directing the countless details that are involved in developing the various inaugural ceremonies. I know all who are enjoying this day join me in thanking the people of Frankfort and Franklin County for all you have done to make this a wonderful day.

I want also to say to our hosts that Mrs. Wetherby, our children,[3] and I have enjoyed the year we have already spent in your community, and we are looking forward to an equally pleasant stay during the coming four years. We thank you for accepting us into your town, and we shall endeavor in every possible way to return the friendship the people of Kentucky's capital city have shown us.

Every county in the state is represented here today. Your presence is personally gratifying to me, and I am confident the local citizens and the Inaugural Committee are very pleased that this enthusiastic throng is gathered. The friendly spirit of Kentuckians, so strongly evidenced here today, gives meaning to our state's motto[4] and makes it the living rule of our people's loyalty and patriotism. I am personally thankful that ours is a tradition of unity. I have faith that we will continue this tradition and that the members of both parties which sought offices in the recent election will combine in a spirit of friendly cooperation their efforts toward building a greater Kentucky.

Forty-five fortunate Kentuckians have been accorded the honor of taking the oath of office as governor. Of that number, I am the seventh to have had the privilege of taking the oath twice. I took the oath of office last November with a deep sense of the solemnity of the occasion. I anticipated the wide range of duties and the responsibilites reposed in the office. But the year I have served as governor has deepened my understanding of the high order of public service required to execute the contract I reenter with you today.

To fulfill the obligations of an office of public trust and to render the type of public service the citizens of Kentucky are entitled to precludes any compromise of the strict standards of ethics our constitution and laws invoke. Perfection in government may never be attained, but the democratic form of government is the most nearly perfect governing device that has ever been developed. The administration we usher in today will be based on concepts of morality and honesty consistent with the best ideals of our American democratic form of government.

I have the utmost confidence in the integrity of these officials whom you have selected to serve with us for the next four years. I have the same confidence in the men and women who will head the appointive agencies of state government. Serious blows have been struck at the confidence of the American people in their government. Corruption and mismanagement have been laid at the doorstep of many in responsible positions in public life. Those serving in a public-policy role must renew with determination their efforts to insure that public service is characterized by efficiency, economy, and honesty. These elements will receive first consideration in the administration of every program carried out in the state government while I am governor.

There is also a demand today for progressive government. While serving as governor I have had the opportunity to study in careful detail every activity of state government. My administrative program and the recommendations which will be made to the approaching legislature are the result of careful analysis, and they are designed to give the people of Kentucky progressive and efficient government for the next four years.

The entire program, of course, will have to be tailored to available resources and the will of the people expressed through the General Assembly to provide the funds required to meet the costs. Included in this program will be features pointing toward new achievements on both short- and long-term bases. Substantial parts of the overall program will be carried over from the administration just ended and will be continued along sound, progressive lines. Among others, these in clude construction and improvement in our road system, continued expansion of public utility services for the benefit of city and rural residents alike, and the continued development of our state parks and promotion of the tourist industry. Education and social welfare services will receive continued support with concerted effort to effect noteworthy improvements in each field. We shall continue to encourage industrial expansion and, measured by the degrees of success thus far achieved, industrial expansion during the coming four years should go a long way toward reaching the much-needed balance between agriculture and industry in Kentucky.

Because the machinery for further progress in these and other fields is already in operation, no new administration ever had a better foundation on which to build. There are other fields, however, in which improvements must be initiated. A year ago, I requested the Legislative Research Commission[5] to study the registration and purgation laws of our state with a view to making recommendations to the 1952 legislature. That group, aided by a citizens' advisory committee, has spent much time in drawing a model law to safeguard the integrity of the ballot and assure fair elections throughout the state. A stringent yet workable registration and purgation law will help assure clean, honest elections. Such a law will also tend to maintain the people's confidence in their government.

We also plan improvement in our welfare institutions. The state's mental hospitals have long given little more than custodial care to those committed to them. It is my belief that these institutions have a real duty to provide the treatment that will return as many patients as possible to useful lives. We have started a treatment program, and we have great hope for and confidence in it success.

Another project of the Legislative Research Commission is the study of the laws dealing with child welfare. Again aided by an advisory committee, the commission will suggest to the legislature a comprehensive code embracing the best thinking and the most modern techniques dealing with children's problems. I will endorse and recommend this proposed legislation.

I am convinced that the proposals which I have mentioned and the others that I shall submit to the legislature are sound, constructive plans which will make for a businesslike operation of our state. However, without the cooperation and friendly assistance of the legislature, state officials, employees, and the general public my efforts as governor will fall short of the high goal we seek. Your presence here today shows that you have an interest in this administration as it gets under way. I invite and sincerely hope that you will retain the same degree of interest you now demonstrate.

No man can approach the duties of being governor without a feeling of deep humility. This is my most humble moment. It is also a moment filled with pride in being tendered the highest honor you can bestow upon a fellow Kentuckian. I do not accept that honor lightly. Mindful of the faith that you have shown in me and confident of God's guidance, I shall perform my duties as governor to the best of my ability. I am now ready, Mr. Chief Justice,[6] to take the oath of office as governor of the Commonwealth.

---

1. Isaac Shelby (1750-1826), member, Virginia legislature (1779); trustee, Transylvania Seminary (1783); member, Kentucky Constitutional Convention (1792); governor of Kentucky (1792-1796, 1812-1816); chairman, board of trustees, Centre College (1819-1826). *Who Was Who in America, 1607-1896* (Chicago, 1967), H:550.

2. James Garrard (1749-1822), member, Virginia House of Delegates (1779) and from Fayette County (1785); represented Fayette and Bourbon counties in the convention for the establishment of Kentucky as a state (1784-1790); governor of Kentucky (1796-1804). *Who Was Who in America, 1607-1896* (Chicago, 1967), H:268.

3. Helen Dwyer Wetherby (1907-), born in Louisville, the daughter of Dr. William Dwyer and Juel Kelly Dwyer. She married Lawrence W. Wetherby on April 24, 1930. Oral interview with Helen Wetherby.

Lawrence W. Wetherby, Jr. (1931-1978), born in Louisville, married Jane Wheatley in 1963; Suzanne Wetherby (1932-), born in Louisville and resides in Frankfort; Barbara Juel Wetherby Perry (1935-), born in Louisville, married George Perry in 1954 and resides in Mt. Vernon, Ohio. Oral interview with Lawrence W. Wetherby.

4. Kentucky's state motto: "United We Stand, Divided We Fall."

5. The Legislative Research Commission, formerly the Legislative Council, was reorganized in 1948 to consist of the lieutenant governor as chairman, the president pro tempore of the senate, the Speaker of the House, and the majority and minority leaders of the two houses. It publishes many studies of great value to the legislature, the citizens of Kentucky, and students of Kentucky government. As provided for by Kentucky law, its primary functions consist of legislative research, bill planning and drafting, and revision of statutes. It is responsible for Kentucky's participation in the Council of State Governments, for interstate cooperation generally, and for prescribing the form and manner in which administrative regulations shall be prepared, and maintaining a file and distributing copies of rules and regulations issued by the administrative agencies. John Estill Reeves, *Kentucky Government* (Lexington, 1966), p. 66.

6. James William Cammack, Jr. (1902-1958), teacher (1924-1930); Kentucky Department of Education (1930-1934); state National Recovery Administration director (1935); member, Public Safety Commission (1935-1938); appointed judge of the Court of Appeals in 1938 and elected in 1939; became chief justice of the Court of Appeals in January 1951, born in Owenton. *Who's Who in America, 1952-1953,* 27th ed. (Chicago, 1952), p. 379.

LEGISLATIVE MESSAGES & STATEMENTS

CALL FOR AN EXTRAORDINARY SESSION
Frankfort / February 21, 1951

BECAUSE of emergency conditions which have developed, I have today decided to issue a call for the General Assembly to meet in an extraordinary session on Monday, March 5, 1951. The purpose would be to consider appropriating for schools, public assistance, and welfare additional funds which apparently will be available for expenditure during the coming fiscal year and for the further purpose to enable governmental employees in Kentucky to come under the new Social Security Act.[1]

It is possible to make the increased appropriations without new tax levies because it has become apparent that the state's general fund will have approximately a $10 million surplus on July 1, 1951. Accordingly, I am confident that the General Assembly at this special session can make additional appropriations for the schools, public assistance, welfare, and social security in a total amount of $9,250,000 without imposing new taxes or endangering the state's financial structure.

Based on that forecast, I will ask the General Assembly to consider the following four subjects at the special session:

1. An appropriation of not to exceed the amount of $6 million for the fiscal year of 1951-1952 as an increase in state funds for the payment of teacher salaries in the common school system.

2. An appropriation of not to exceed the amount of $2 million for the fiscal year of 1951-1952 as an increase in state funds for the public assistance program, including old-age assistance payments, aid to the needy blind, and aid to dependent children.

3. An appropriation of not to exceed the amount of $250,000 for the fiscal year of 1950-1951, and an appropriation not to exceed $750,000 for the fiscal year 1951-1952 as an increase in the amount available for the care and maintenance of those unfortunates who are housed in the state welfare institutions.

4. Legislation making it possible for the employees of the state, the counties, the cities, and other governmental subdivisions and agencies to be brought under the provisions of the United States Social Security Act so that they may qualify for its old-age and survivors-benefit program, and an appropriation not to exceed $250,000 to pay the state's share of this program.

There are extraordinary circumstances which have developed that justify consideration of these subjects at a special session. Inflation throughout the nation has continued upward, increasing the cost of living to schoolteachers, the aged needy, and recipients of needy-blind and dependent-children payments. It has also increased the cost of providing for the inmates of the state welfare institutions. Common decency demands that these people be given increased assistance, especially since it appears that additional state funds will be available for this purpose. State government is charged with responsibility for the welfare of its citizens, particularly the public charges, and to ignore that responsibility when the means to help meet the challenge are available would be an inhuman disregard for duty.

The cold, hard facts of economic life confront the common school system of Kentucky. Once again this nation has been plunged into a preparedness program that dips deeply into the manpower pool. Armament plants have been reopened, and new ones are being built. The location of the Atomic Energy Commission plant near Paducah, the reopening of defense factories, the calling of additional men to the armed forces, all these and other factors have increased the difficulty of securing an adequate number of qualified teachers for the school system and persuading those now teaching to remain in their jobs. The schools are losing teachers to the armed forces, to the defense plants, and to higher paying jobs in private industry. If the state will have funds during the coming school year which can be used to raise teacher salaries, it is right and proper that the state legislature should appropriate such funds for that purpose.

Since the regular session of the General Assembly last year, the United States Congress has passed an act which makes possible coverage of employees of the state, the counties, cities, and other governmental subdivisions under the Social Security Act. In these days of doubt and confusion, security is becoming increasingly an objective toward which most individuals are striving. Provisions should be made for retirement benefits for the governmental employees who heretofore have been barred from such a program.

There is a pressing need now for the schoolteachers and the school administrators to know what state money will be available for them during the forthcoming school year. Under state law, school boards during March must offer contracts to teachers for the next year, and teachers must indicate before May 1 whether they will accept those contracts. There will be many teachers who will stay with their jobs if they can secure an even moderate increase in salary. The welfare of the school students, the future citizens of Kentucky, our hope for tomorrow, depends upon keeping competent teachers in the schools, and demands that we take action where action is possible.

The foregoing facts demonstrate conclusively that there is real justification for action by the state legislature now. It is my honest conviction that appropriations within the limits outlined will be possible because of the anticipated surplus.

The General Assembly went as far as it could at the 1950 regular session in appropriating all funds that were within sight. In fact, when Governor Earle C. Clements proposed a budget to the legislature on January 9, 1950, he stated: "The anticipated revenue of the state, under our present tax structure, based on not a conservative but a liberal estimate, will not exceed $115 million. This estimate is predicated on the assumption that there will be little, if any, change in present prosperous conditions."

Actually, Governor Clements was willing to go beyond what the Department of Revenue told him he could reasonably anticipate from taxes during the year, although at the time there were those who charged that state expenditures under that budget would exceed revenue. When that estimate was made, there was no indication that the national economy would be subjected to the artificial uplift that always accompanies a war-preparedness program such as that now under way. That program has had a sharp upward effect on the economy of Kentucky and has helped to bring new revenue into the state treasury. Inflation, boosting the cost of things, has boosted receipts from certain taxes, too.

I will ask the General Assembly to consider appropriations within the limits set forth in my call for the special session. These four subjects are the only ones under consideration which demand emergency attention.

Although Governor Wetherby initially opposed an extraordinary session, when he was made aware of the revenue surplus he felt the financial crisis in certain areas warranted a call for the General Assembly to meet.

1. The United States Congress broadened social security coverage through an amendment to the U.S. Social Security Act on August 26, 1950. (Chapter 803, H.R. 7439, Public Law 733.) Section 106, entitled "Voluntary Agreements for Coverage of State and Local Employees," said states could extend the insurance system to services performed by individuals in their employment if the state requested such. *United States Statutes at Large,* 81st Congress, 1950-1951, Vol. 64, Pt. I, pp. 476-524.

EXTRAORDINARY SESSION OF THE GENERAL ASSEMBLY
Frankfort / March 6, 1951

DURING the past three years on several occasions I have had the opportunity of appearing before the General Assembly for the purpose of calling the joint session into order.[1] However, this is the first oportunity I have had to address the Assembly in the capacity as chief executive. I, therefore, would like to welcome all of you to Frankfort and extend to you, the legislative branch, greetings and good wishes from the executive branch and to ask for your cooperation in the job which we are about to undertake.

Since you adjourned on March 17, 1950, our nation has again been called upon to defend our way of life. The defense preparation incident thereto has necessarily entailed the reopening of defense plants, and the policies of the national government reflect the gravity of world conditions. Old defense plants are being reopened and new ones are being built. The federal government has located within our Commonwealth an Atomic Energy Commission plant near Paducah. In short, our whole economic pattern has changed since January 1950 from a peacetime to a war mobilization economy. Inflation throughout the nation has increased the cost of living, working special hardship on the straight salaried employees in both public and private employment. The schools are losing teachers to the armed forces, to the defense plants, and to higher paying jobs in private industry. The decreased purchasing power of the dollar has placed the aged needy, recipients of needy blind assistance, and children receiving dependent payments in an increasingly unfavorable position.

These same circumstances have also increased the cost of providing for the inmates of the state welfare institutions. The cost of clothing, food, and other services to the inmates has increased to such an extent that it is impossible for the Welfare Department to meet its needs under the present budget.

Along with this economic spiral upward, which is working added hardships on the aforementioned groups, has come increased and unanticipated revenue into the state treasury. According to the most accurate predictions of the state's two chief fiscal agencies, the Department of Revenue and the Department of Finance, the Commonwealth will have on July 1, 1951, an accumulated surplus of approximately ten million dollars.

Recognizing the emergency conditions as above outlined and assuming on the best available authority that an unencumbered balance of approximately $10 million will be available, for whatever use the legislative and executive branches of the state government deem proper, I felt it incumbent upon me to call the General Assembly for the purpose of considering the emergencies in these respective fields and ask you to take action thereon.

I have studied at great length and in great detail the financial picture of the state government. I invite all of you to confer with the officials of the Department of Revenue and the Department of Finance, so that you might become acquainted with the present status of the general revenue fund and the entire financial structure of your state government. After making a study of the financial picture of the state, I am prepared to recommend to the members of the legislature, as outlined in my call,[2] the following appropriations:

1. To pass an act appropriating a sum not to exceed $6 million to the common school per capita fund for the payment of increased salaries of teachers for the school year 1951-1952, said fund to be used for the salaries of teachers and for no other purpose, and without the levying of any additional tax. An appropriation of $6 million to the per capita fund will increase the per capita per child by $8.78—or from $29.59 to $38.36. This amount of money, distributed to the 232 school districts, will provide for an annual average increase in salary amounting to approximately $300 per teacher. Of course, the annual increase in salary will vary in school districts, because the pupil–teacher ratio is much higher in some school districts than in others. Also, some school districts

have a greater percentage of their pupils attending private and parochial schools than do other school districts.

2. To pass an act appropriating to the Department of Economic Security for the fiscal year 1951–1952 a sum not to exceed $2 million for old-age assistance payments, aid to the needy blind, and aid to dependent children. This appropriation to be made without the levying of any additional tax.

3. To pass an act appropriating to the Department of Welfare a sum not to exceed $250,000 for the fiscal year 1950-1951, and an appropriation not to exceed $750,000 for the fiscal year 1951-1952 as an increase in the amount available for expenses of operation of said department. These appropriations to be made without the levying of any additional tax.

Under the budget bill adopted in 1950,[3] our Welfare Department is unable to make proper provision for the increased number of wards under its care. I have, therefore, asked that you supplement their appropriation for this fiscal year to the extent of $250,000.

During the past eleven years we have made real progress in the building program as it affects the penal and mental institutions.[4] However, we have fallen behind in a treatment program for those confined in our mental hospitals. In my opinion we are now ready and should devote more of our resources toward the treatment and rehabilitation of our mental patients, so that many more of them can be returned to their homes to lead useful lives.

We have neglected to provide adequate treatment facilities for our patients. It has been conclusively demonstrated in some of the mental institutions of other states that by proper treatment and care many, many cases, which in the past have been given up as hopeless, can be cured. I believe in, and have always advocated, the treatment approach to mental health problems. Doctors and psychiatrists are now available to carry out such a program. Let's not delay further in making the money available for this purpose. I am sure that under the reorganization which is now taking place in the Welfare Department, and in the Division of Hospitals and Mental Hygiene in particular, much good can be done with this appropriation.[5]

There is also another item which I consider merits your attention and is worthy of being classified of an emergency nature. This relates to the need for legislation whereby officials and employees of the state, counties, cities, and governmental subdivisions and agencies might be covered under the provisions of the Social Security Act. This broadened social security coverage was made possible through an amendment to the United States Social Security Act by the federal Congress in August

1950. In these days of doubt and confusion, security is becoming increasingly an objective toward which most individuals are striving. Provisions should be made for retirement benefits for governmental employees who, heretofore, have been barred from such a program. By enacting this legislation, you will place the employees of your state government on a more equitable basis with those engaged in private industry, who are now enjoying the benefits of the Social Security Act.

In this connection, I should like to recommend your consideration and action upon legislation enabling the officers and employees of the state, counties, municipalities, political subdivisions and agencies thereof to be covered under the old-age and survivors insurance system of the United States Social Security Act under Public Law No. 734, 81st Congress, and to appropriate a sum not to exceed $250,000 to finance the state's share of this program for the fiscal year 1951-1952. This appropriation to be made without the levying of any additional tax.

The bill which will be presented to you this afternoon has been thoroughly studied and has been drafted with the help and cooperation of the federal agencies dealing with this subject and is a revised draft of the model act fitted to meet the requirements of the Kentucky Constitution.

In the 1950 session of the legislature, you appropriated all of the revenue then in sight. In fact, there were those who charged that you were guilty of deficit spending. However, as I have related, the revenue has exceeded all estimates, and I am confident that under present conditions these appropriations can be safely made without additional tax measures. In the 1950 session of the legislature you created for the purpose of determining the needs and methods of meeting the needs the Functions and Resources Committee, which is now in the process of carrying out your mandate. This committee will report in December of this year its findings and recommendations.

This report and the recommendations made will afford the basis upon which the 1952 General Assembly may act, in order to meet the future needs of Kentucky's government. The recommendations which I am making should be treated as I am treating them—solely for the purpose of meeting present critical emergencies.

I am willing to share with you the responsibilities called for in passing the two bills which will be submitted to you today. I believe that you can secure all of the information which you deem necessary to act upon this proposed legislation immediately. From the responses I have had from many members of the General Assembly, I believe that a substantial majority of you favor these proposals. All legislation sessions are an expense to the taxpayers. Let's hold the expenses of this session to a minimum, and I would ask you to try to complete this job within a period of two weeks.

I urge you to follow these recommendations and to enact into law both of these measures. Upon the passage of these two bills you will be able to return to your homes with the satisfaction of knowing that you have made a real contribution to the welfare of our great state.[6]

The special session of the General Assembly approved, with only one dissenting vote, the four appropriations of funds for emergency measures as requested by Governor Wetherby. The legislators completed their task in ten days.

1. Lawrence W. Wetherby was elected lieutenant governor on a ticket headed by Earle C. Clements on November 4, 1947. He called three joint sessions into order: the regular sessions of 1948 and 1950 and an extraordinary session in 1949.

2. For a text of the governor's call see speech from February 21, 1951, in this section.

3. Governor Clements had recommended the following budget in 1950-1951: Department of Welfare, $6 million; Department of Economic Security, $9.13 million; Department of Health, $1.415 million; Tuberculosis Sanitoria Commission, $1.350 million. The total welfare budget was $18,065,000. This amount was 31.45 percent of the total 1950-1951 budget. See *Journal of the Kentucky Senate of the Commonwealth of Kentucky* (Louisville, 1950), 1:96.

4. The state of Kentucky operated the following penal and mental institutions: house of reform at Lexington; state reformitory at La Grange; state penitentiary at Eddyville; women's prison at Pee Wee Valley; Western State Hospital at Hopkinsville; Eastern State Hospital at Lexington; Central State Hospital at Louisville; Kentucky State Hospital at Danville; Kentucky Training Home at Frankfort.

5. In 1951 a Division of Hospitals and Mental Hygiene was created within the Department of Welfare. For more information see letter of February 9, 1951, in the Health and Welfare section.

6. For the enactments of the extraordinary session, see *Acts of the General Assembly of the Commonwealth of Kentucky,* March 5, 1951-March 14, 1951.

REPORT ON THE EXTRAORDINARY SESSION
Cincinnati, Ohio / March 18, 1951

DURING the portion of the program allotted to me, I should like to discuss the extraordinary session of the Kentucky General Assembly, which adjourned last Wednesday.[1] I should like to approach this matter in the form of a report. First, the subjects which I asked the legislature to consider. Second, a brief outline on the action taken by the legislature upon the recommendations made. Third, the meaning of the benefits of the legislation enacted.

My recommendations were as follows: $6 million to be appropriated to the common school per capita fund for the payment of increased salaries of teachers. Appropriate $2 million for old-age assistance payments, aid to the needy blind, and aid to dependent children. Appropriate $250,000 for the fiscal year 1950-1951 and $750,000 for the fiscal year 1951-1952 as an increase in the amount available for expenses of operation of the Department of Welfare and legislation enabling officials and employees of the state, counties, cities, and governmental subdivisions and agencies to be covered under the provisions of the Social Security Act. This broadened social security coverage was made possible through an amendment to the United States Social Security Act by the federal Congress in August 1950.[2]

During the extraordinary session, which lasted only ten days, all of the program was approved as recommended, with only one dissenting vote, evidencing a degree of accord seldom seen in the Kentucky General Assembly. Accordingly, it is now possible for an advanced program in all of these fields.

An appropriation of $6 million to the common school per capita fund will increase the per capita per child by $8.78, or from $29.59 to $38.36. This amount of money distributed to the 232 school districts will provide for an annual average increase in salary amounting to approximately $300 per teacher.

It is estimated that the appropriation of $2 million to the Department of Economic Security will increase old-age assistance payments from the present monthly average of $20.58 to $30.00, aid to dependent children payments from the present monthly average of $37.17 per family to $42.00 per family, and aid to needy blind payments from the present monthly average of $22.11 to $32.00.

Under the budget bill adopted in 1950 our Welfare Department[3] was unable to make proper provision for the increased number of wards under its care. The supplemental appropriation for this fiscal year of $250,000 and an appropriation of $750,000 for the fiscal year 1951-1952 will enable the department to initiate a comprehensive treatment program for those confined in our mental hospitals. Real progress has been made in the building program of our mental institutions during the past eleven years. I feel we are now ready and should devote our efforts toward the treatment and rehabilitation of our mental patients so that many more of them can be returned to their homes to lead useful lives. Doctors and psychiatrists are now available to carry out such a program, and with sufficient funds for proper treatment and care it is my belief that many, many cases, which in the past have been given up as hopeless, can be cured.

Provisions are being made for retirement benefits for governmental employees who, heretofore, have been barred from such a program, placing these employees on a more equitable basis with those engaged in private industry and giving them security, a goal toward which most individuals are striving.

The 1950 legislature provided for the creation of the Functions and Resources Committee, whose membership is composed of twenty-three responsible citizens representing agriculture, business, labor, education, and the various professions. The legislature charged this group with the responsibility of determining through study, research, and compilation of data the needs of our state and the means whereby those needs can best be met. This committee is now in the process of carrying out that mandate and will report this year its findings and recommendations. This report and the recommendations made will afford the basis upon which the 1952 General Assembly may act, in order to meet the future needs of Kentucky's government. Everyone acquainted with the work of this committee is highly encouraged over the prospects that its findings will point to a long-range development program which will place education, social welfare services, and all other fields of government in Kentucky on a level favorable to other states with comparable population, resources, and taxable wealth.

---

1. The Extraordinary Session of the Kentucky General Assembly was called by Governor Wetherby on February 21, 1951. It convened in Frankfort on March 6, 1951. Its purpose was to appropriate a $10 million revenue surplus.

2. For more information see speech of February 21, 1951, in this section.

3. The budget proposal of the Welfare Department can be found in the footnotes of the speech of March 6, 1951, in this section.

STATE OF THE COMMONWEALTH ADDRESS
Frankfort / January 15, 1952

IN compliance with the Constitution, I requested this opportunity to appear before you so that I might report on the general operations of state government, its finances, and my recommendations dealing with the state's fiscal policy during the next two-year period. From time to time during this session, I shall make additional recommendations, either by personal appearance or through the duly elected leaders of the House and Senate. Today, I shall discuss the general operations of state government for the past four years, make certain specific recommendations, and submit a budget covering the next two-year period.

I am fully aware of the tremendous job that lies ahead which requires our attention. You are invited, individually and collectively, to consult and discuss with me, at any and all times, any problems or subjects which affect you, me, or the people of Kentucky.

It is gratifying to report much progress in the operations of state government. Many advances can be accredited to the sound legislative programs that the General Assembly enacted in the regular session of 1948, the special session of 1949, the regular session of 1950, and the special session of 1951. This report will be a brief summary of what has been done during this period. Brevity decrees that many items of progress be left out. Some of the agencies will be omitted, but an examination of the records of every department indicates progress. The departments I will discuss are those that touch directly and affect the welfare of thousands of Kentucky's citizens.

Department of Highways. This department has inaugurated a balanced construction and maintenance program including both primary highways and rural roads and bridges. The construction figures show 8,602 miles of roads completed or under contract. From the two-cent road tax enacted by the 1948 General Assembly, the department has constructed or contracted for nearly 4,000 miles of rural roads at a cost of $36,623, 237. The department's expanded program has contributed greatly to the promotion of the tourist industry. Recently, a reorganization of the department, as recommended by the Public Administration Service and the Committee on Functions and Resources, has been undertaken.[1] A five-year plan of major highway improvement has been adopted.

Department of Welfare. During the past year this department has been reorganized.[2] A trained psychiatrist now heads its Division of Hospitals and Mental Hygiene, and greater emphasis is being placed on treatment.

The special session of 1951 gave the Welfare Department an additional $750,000. In 1948 Kentucky spent $0.99 a day for each patient in its mental hospitals. Today, $1.60 is being spent. Both figures exclude food produced by the department.

An extensive building program is under way at Central, Eastern, and Western State hospitals. Additional medical equipment has been supplied to all of them. We are progressing, and the additional recommendations I shall make will, I believe, give Kentucky an adequate mental health program. Concerted efforts have been made to raise the standards at both houses of reform at Greendale.

The Division of Agricultural Production was established in the Welfare Department in 1950. Food produced on the farms during the last fiscal year was valued at $827,000.

Agricultural and Industrial Development Board. In 1948 the General Assembly established this board to study Kentucky's potentials and to encourage increased use of our resources. It has made community surveys of forty-two cities; these surveys are available to industries seeking Kentucky locations. It has been instrumental in bringing more than $70 million worth of new plants to the state. The board has published a land capability map showing where industries depending largely upon the soil can profitably locate.

Department of Conservation. Attendance at state parks jumped from 373,589 during the 1947-1948 fiscal year to 2,041,743 in 1950-1951. Four new parks—Kentucky Dam Village, Kentucky Lake, Cherokee, and Carter Caves—have been built since 1947. One of the country's finest hotels will be opened at Kentucky Lake in March. Our entire park system has been improved. It is now one of the best in the nation and largely accounts for the tremendous increase in our tourist business, which exceeded $300 million last year.

Also in this department are the Divisions of Soil and Water Resources, Forestry, and Flood Control and Water Usage. The Soil and Water Resources Division has assisted in the organization of twenty-five soil conservation districts since 1947. The Division of Forestry now provides organized forest-fire protection for 4,254,000 acres of state and private forest land, and the Division of Flood Control and Water Usage has reviewed and approved reports on proposed improvements on the Upper Cumberland, Lower Cumberland, Fernbank, and Greenup dams.

Department of Economic Security. This department was established in 1948. Under it, old-age assistance grants have been increased from an average of $17.30 monthly in January 1948 to $29.77 at the present. Aid to the needy blind has increased from an average grant of $18.44 to

$31.82. Aid to dependent children has increased from $34.25 a family to $41.96. Maximum payments for needy blind and old-age assistance are now $50.00 a month, and maximum payments for dependent children have been raised to $27.00 for a parent, $27.00 for the first child, and $18.00 for each additional child.

The 1951 special session of the General Assembly enacted legislation making possible social security coverage for state and local governmental employees, which programs are administered by this department.[3] Practically all state employees have been covered, and agreements have been made with more than seventy-eight political subdivisions to cover their employees.

Department of Health. This department has adopted a policy of local control for local health departments. A formula for fair and equitable distribution of state and federal funds to local health departments was instituted. Seven additional counties opened local health departments, making a total of 111. Three mobile health units were placed in service for local health departments to use in remote areas. Trained administrators were placed in nineteen counties where there are no full-time medical health officers. Twenty-five new community hospitals and thirteen additions to existing hospitals have been completed since 1947. Federal Hill-Burton construction funds brought to Kentucky under this program total $20,546,828.

State Tuberculosis Sanatoria Commission. This commission was created by the 1949 General Assembly. Five new hospitals for tuberculosis treatment have been accepted, and the state now has 500 more beds. New techniques of care are giving the hospitals a greater record of service through a larger turnover of patients. Kentucky's death rate from tuberculosis has been reduced from 58.2 to 36.6 per 100,000 population. More than three times as many people were X-rayed by mobile units under the Department of Health than in the previous five years.

Department of Education. The level of financial support for public education is higher today than at any time in the history of the Commonwealth. The common school fund during the past four years has been increased from $19,501,245 to $30,500,000 or 56.4 percent. At the same time local school districts have increased their tax revenue from $21,795,333 to $36,963,034, an increase of 69.6 percent. The per capita fund has been increased by 49.3 percent.

As a result of the $6 million appropriation by the special session of 1951, the per capita reached $38.40 and teachers received an average salary increase of $300. The number of emergency teachers employed has been decreased from about 5,300 to approximately 2,900 for the year 1951-1952. Teachers' salaries have been increased from an average of $1,555 in 1946-1947 to an average of $2,350 in 1951-1952.

Department of Finance. This department is better organized, staffed, and equipped to meet the demands made upon it by all other agencies of state government than at any time since its creation. It now has a full-time budget director, streamlined accounting methods, and a new program for recruiting and training state employees. The Division of Purchases has improved its operations by spreading its buying assignments among qualified buyers who specialize in certain items. It has established a central store to furnish supplies to various agencies. By this method, $54,000 was saved during the fiscal year 1950-1951.

Department of Revenue. The department has sought to eliminate tax evaders through a policy of education and enforcement by the use of federal income tax records. The number of pay returns since 1948 has increased approximately 125 percent. Local property assessments have had the attention of the department since 1948. The general property tax calendar from assessment to collection has been shortened from eighteen to twelve months. Taxes are now collected in the same year assessment is made. The cost of administration is one of the lowest in the nation. It takes only a little more than one cent of each tax dollar to pay for collecting it.

Department of State Police. The State Police Force was activated July 1, 1948, as the law-enforcement arm of the state to replace the old Highway Patrol. This department of state government has made rapid strides since its organization. It has been able to recruit some of the highest type young men in Kentucky. It now has the respect and confidence of the public generally and serves as a supplement to local law-enforcement agencies in all sections of the Commonwealth. The department has made a fine contribution toward the development of a highway safety program.

Department of Alcoholic Beverage Control. The department has tightened controls and adopted a much stricter enforcement policy. The department has recently adopted a regulation designed to cut down juvenile delinquency by strictly enforcing a ban on minors in taverns. Later in this message I will recommend specific legislation concerning this department.

Division of Game and Fish. Last year, the Wildlife Management Institute ranked Kentucky seventh among the states. Kentucky has the best Junior Club Educational Program in the nation. There are now about

25,000 Kentucky boys in Junior Conservation Clubs in all counties of the state. The clubs own two camps and will soon have a third.

Department of Industrial Relations. This department administers a Workmen's Compensation Act that gives more protection to the working man and his family than any similar act Kentucky has had. Maximum family benefits have been increased from $15.00 a week to $23.00. The maximum compensation payable to a totally disabled employee has been increased from $18.00 a week to $24.00.

Legislative Research Commission.[4] This commission was created by the 1948 General Assembly as a continuing arm of the legislature. Since 1950 it has worked on numerous projects upon which it will report during this session. It also worked with the Committee on Functions and Resources of State Government and their report, I am sure, will be submitted soon.

At this point, I would like to make some specific recommendations to you upon legislation which I consider essential to the welfare and advancement of Kentucky and which the people have endorsed during recent months.

First, I recommend that you enact into law a new Registration and Purgation Act. In December 1950 I requested the Legislative Research Commission to appoint a group of officials and citizens to study the registration and purgation law of the state and to prepare a bill designed to remedy the defects in our existing law. The committee has devoted much time and study to this problem and has prepared what they consider a good law. The bill will be introduced by the majority leader of the House of Representatives,[5] and I ask you to enact it into law. The enactment of such a law will encourage our citizens to exercise one of their most precious rights and will encourage more of them to participate in elections.

Second, I recommend that you enact into law a Child Welfare Code which will recodify the laws pertaining to children and will establish a State Youth Authority. The Legislative Research Commission, aided by an advisory committee of interested citizens, has devoted much time and study to this problem. The bill which they have drafted will be introduced by the majority leader of the House of Representatives, and I ask you to enact it into law. The enactment of this bill will go a long way toward remedying some of the evils now existing in our state under present law. It will give to the Youth Authority the right to determine the needs and protect the children committed to it.

Third, I recommend that you enact into law an act creating a Department of Mental Health. During the last year we have reorganized the Department of Welfare and have secured as the head of the Division of Mental Hygiene a competent psychiatrist[6] who has demonstrated during this period that it is possible, through a treatment program, to return many unfortunate citizens to useful lives. All functions of our Welfare Department have shown tremendous improvement. Under present organization, however, the vast scope of the department's responsibilities complicates its administration and operation. The separation of mental and penal institutions into two departments will allow for the improvement of each and will permit increased emphasis on the mental health treatment program. With one man heading each department, much closer supervision will be possible. It is for these reasons that I recommend that you remove the Division of Hospitals and the Mental Hygiene from the Department of Welfare and create a separate Department of Mental Health. This bill will be introduced by the majority leader of the House of Representatives, and I ask you to enact it into law.

Fourth, I recommend that you enact into láw an act providing for the mandatory suspension or revocation of the license to sell alcoholic beverages, upon conviction of the licensee or his agent of gambling on the premises. A question has been raised as to the power of the alcoholic Beverage Control Board to revoke such a license or permit on these grounds. In order to clarify the law and to enable the Alcoholic Beverage Control Board to follow a stricter law-enforcement policy, I deem it advisable to have such a law enacted. This bill will be introduced by the majority leader of the House of Representatives, and I ask you to enact it into law.

Fifth, I recommend that you enact into law an act which makes the fixing of athletic contests a felony. Our Commonwealth has been shocked in recent months by the basketball scandals,[7] and in order to deter any such future actions in our state I believe such legislation advisable. The majority leader of the Senate[8] has therefore introduced such a bill, and I ask you to enact it into law.

Sixth, I recommend that you enact into law an act increasing the penalties for the illegal sale and distribution of narcotics. The illegal use of narcotics has rapidly increased, and in recent months the sale and distribution of narcotics to children has increased throughout the country. In order to prohibit such occurrences in Kentucky it seems advisable that a stiffer penalty should be provided for the punishment of those illegally selling or distributing narcotics. The State Department of Health is preparing such legislation at this time, and upon its introduction I ask you to enact it into law.

Seventh, I recommend that you enact into law an act which will remove the University of Kentucky, and all of the state colleges of the

Commonwealth, from the control of the Personnel Division of the Department of Finance. Since the passage of the Reorganization Act, technically but not by practice, the employees of the university and state colleges have been under the Division of Personnel. The bill will be introduced by the majority leader of the Senate, and I ask you to enact it into law.

These are specific recommendations which I make at this time. You will notice that I have not mentioned one of the most involved problems facing this session of the legislature—that of redistricting Kentucky. I have omitted this purposely. I believe that if all of us will give our immediate attention to the budget bill, these specific recommendations, and your own bills, we can then give our undivided attention to the passage of a redistricting bill and in so doing assure a more orderly business schedule.

So that the various agencies of state government may plan their programs during the next two-year period, it is necessary for you first to enact a budget law. In preparing this budget the principal aim has been to allocate equitably the general fund revenues to provide for essential functions of government. This budget allocates every dollar in hand and in sight, all anticipated revenue for recurring types of expenditure, and all anticipated surplus as of June 30, 1952, for capital outlay and other nonrecurring expenses.

Requests for general fund support from the state's agencies and departments, exclusive of capital outlay, totaled approximately $212 million for the next biennium. The commissioner of revenue estimates that the present tax structure will yield $159 million during the next biennium. The estimate is based on the assumption that the legislature will reenact the existing income tax rates, and the current inflationary trend will continue during the next two-year period.

We recognize that many agencies of state government could wisely use more money than is proposed by this budget. However, the estimated general fund expenditure for this year 1951-1952 is $72,500,000. To continue this rate of expenditure for the next two years will require a total of $145 million, leaving a difference between the present rate of expenditure and anticipated revenue of $14 million for allocation.

This budget recommends that the General Assembly appropriate $7,900,000 of the $14 million for educational purposes, $4,200,000 for health and welfare, and $1,900,000 for all other governmental activities.

Expenditures this year for education are estimated at $39,800,000. To continue this rate, appropriations for the next two years would be $79,600,000. This budget recommends appropriations for education totaling $87,500,000, an increase of $7,900,000. The major portion of the educational increase goes to the common school fund. The recommended appropriation for the biennium is $64,588,500, which is $15, 588,500 more than was appropriated to the fund by the 1950 General Assembly. The appropriation by the General Assembly to the common school fund in 1950 was $49 million for the 1950-1952 biennium. The 1951 special session of the General Assembly appropriated an additional $6 million, which was to meet an emergency. An examination of this budget will show that we have been able to continue this increase for each of the next two years and to add an additional sum of $3,588, 500 for the biennium. Over the three-year period, including the current fiscal year and the coming biennium, the increase over the 1950 appropriation to the common school fund is $21,588,500.

The increase recommended in this budget is for the equalization portion of the fund. At present the equalization is 14.05 percent of the common school fund. The recommended appropriation will bring this figure to 17.53 percent for 1952-1953 and to 20.08 percent for the fiscal year 1953-1954.

Proposed appropriations for mental health services for the biennium are $9,942,000. This is an increase of $1,100,000. During recent years Kentucky has steadily improved and expanded the physical plants of our mental hospitals. Mere custodial care, however, does little to reduce population of our institutions, because it does not discharge patients rapidly enough to stabilize hospital population. The recommended appropriation for mental hospitals will provide for an intensive treatment program. The cost of mental health will rise but at a far lower rate than would result from custodial care without additional treatment. Thus, in the long run, a treatment program, aside from the humanitarian aspects, will result in economy.

This budget proposes $2,250,000 to enable the Health Department to establish units in all counties and bring them to an economical operating level. This is an increase of $844,800. The county health department is the basic unit in the state's program of providing health services to its citizens. Many of these departments are understaffed and inadequately equipped and do not give the state full value for each dollar expended or serve their communities effectively.

The additional appropriations to health and welfare will be found in the tuberculosis hospital program, Welfare Department for the penal institutions, and other health and welfare services.

The distribution of the $1,900,000 proposed increase under this budget for all other governmental activities is shown by your budget document. Many factors, such as price increases, increased cost of personal services, loss of federal funds, and cost of replacing equipment have been considered in reviewing the needs and distributing funds for support of all agencies. The commissioner of Finance[9] estimates that the available surplus as of June 30, 1952, will be $12,894,720. I recommend appropriation of the entire amount for nonrecurring expenditures.

The proposed budget appropriates from surplus $10,600,000 to the State Property and Buildings Commission. This amount will enable the state to continue a planned building program in an orderly, systematic manner.

This budget also recommends appropriation of $348,220 from the general fund surplus to the Teachers' Retirement Fund. This meets a need which is a result of legislative action imposing additional obligation against the fund. Also recommended is an appropriation of $40,000 to the Department of Education to complete the survey of school facilities.

Other appropriations recommended go to the Agricultural and Industrial Development Board to continue the mapping program, to the Airport Development Account, and to the Department of Finance and Statute Revision Commission to establish working funds.

There is a further consideration in regard to surplus. In the event revenues do not reach expectations, the commissioner of finance will have the authority to reduce allotments. It is also necessary that we have flexibility should revenues exceed the estimate. To take care of such a contingency, an escalator clause is included in the budget which appropriates to a special emergency fund any revenues up to $3 million in excess of the first year's estimate of $78 million. Should any revenue accrue to this fund, it may be allocated by the governor during the second year of the biennium.

This budget was prepared to distribute all available and anticipated funds under the existing revenue laws. In its preparation we have not anticipated any new tax measures. If you should make any additional appropriations it will be necessary for you to enact revenue measures to support such appropriations.

---

1. As a result of the reorganization, the General Assembly in 1954 enacted a bill creating a Highway Authority to foster, promote, and expedite the construction, maintenance, and improvements of a modern and adequate system of roads, in the interests of the public safety and general welfare. The authority was directed by a corporate and political body constituting a public corporation and governmental instrumentality and agency of the Commonwealth. It consisted of the governor, lieutenant governor, attorney general, secretary of state,

state treasurer, commissioner of finance, commissioner of highways, the state highway engineer, and eight citizens appointed by the governor.

Section 9 of the bill states that the purpose of the act is to acquire, construct, reconstruct, improve, equip, furnish, maintain, operate, lease, and finance public highways, bridges, viaducts, tunnels, traffic circles, grade separations, maintenance sheds, offices, garages, and roadside rests. The authority was given the power to raise funds by selling bonds. *Acts of the General Assembly of the Commonwealth of Kentucky,* 1954, Chapter 39 (S. B. 137), pp. 99-119.

2. In 1951 a Division of Hospitals and Mental Hygiene was created within the Department of Health.

3. For more information see the footnotes to the speech from February 21, 1951, in this section.

4. For a description of the Kentucky Legislative Research Commission see the footnotes to the Inaugural Address, December 11, 1951.

5. Harry King Lowman (1913-1977), educated at Morehead State Teachers College and the University of Kentucky; teacher and army veteran; state representative (1942-1944, 1946-1964), Speaker, (1960-1963); born in Boyd County. Frank K. Kavanaugh, *Kentucky Directory* (Franfort, 1952), p. 150.

6. Frank Macfarland Gaines (1916-), state commissioner of mental health (1952-1956); chariman, Council on Mental Health Training and Research of the Southern Regional Board (1955-1957); chairman of five-member citizens advisory committee on personnel administration (1960-1964); born in Carrollton and resides in Louisville. Hambleton Tapp, ed., *Kentucky Lives: The Blue Grass States Who's Who* (Hopkinsville, Ky., 1966), pp. 189-90. For more information on the reforms in mental health see letter from February 9, 1951, in the Health and Welfare section.

7. For more information see letter from December 27, 1951, in the Reorganization section.

8. Richard P. Moloney (1902-1963), lawyer, educated at the University of Kentucky; probate commissioner, Fayette County court; state senator (1946-1956); state representative (1960-1963), majority leader (1962-1963); born in Lexington. Kavanaugh, *Kentucky Directory,* p. 141.

9. Clifford R. Barnes (1913-), administrator in the federal government (1935-1948); director of budget (1948-1951); commissioner of finance (1951-1955); educated at Asbury College and American University; he was born in Montevideo, Minnesota. Kavanaugh, *Kentucky Directory,* p. 172.

COUNTY OFFICIALS CONVENTION
Louisville / December 10, 1952

THIS is a convention and, recognizing that there are many other things vastly more interesting to do than listen to my speech, I shall hold my remarks very brief. Not only in deference to what I know your wishes to be will I be brief, but the formidable array of subjects and problems with which we are somewhat jointly or mutually concerned confines me to a restricted list.

I say we view these matters from a common basis. On the one hand, all of us are public officials and, I am sure, personally dedicated to doing the best possible job of which we are capable. On the other, though your functions are of county or district scope and those of us in Frankfort find our scope of activity statewide, we are working together, sometimes directly, sometimes indirectly. But, regardless of the policies followed and the actions taken, the kind of job done has a way of reflecting on all of us.

From a selfish standpoint, working at the task of running our county and state governments ought to make us, as a collective group, strive to cast rays of sunshine instead of gusty shadows. There is, of course, even a more important and compelling reason and need for maintaining our respective performance records. I am referring to the inherent right of the people of every county throughout the entire state to the best, most efficient and economic government possible. This assignment is not an easy one. It taxes the strength, the ingenuity, and the will. There must be a more than ordinary degree of interest and even zealousness on our part as public officials if we are to measure up to the high standards to which we give lip service and which the public rightly expects.

If I seem to belabor the fact that a county or state official can be negligent in his duites and unresponsive to legitimate requests or pleas for action, it is prompted by the fact that the governor's office is the ultimate repository of the citizens' and taxpayers' expression of grief, dismay, and indignation. When all goes well with the service that is furnished our citizens, the office does not hear about it, except in a general way of course, and I would not have you think that I would attempt to appraise the job you or any other group of officials might be doing only on the basis of negative comments. I do think that where we have information that might help us improve our service to the public, we should share it with each other. Certainly I am continually interested in improving the quality of the job I am trying to do, and I know you are as interested as I am in maintaining service to the public from all levels of our government at the highest possible quality.

In the field of state government there are current problems with which I am confronted. I feel there is no finer opportunity, nor a more appropriate group with which to discuss them informally, than is the one here tonight. The problems being of major importance and statewide in scope lend themselves especially at this time to general public discussion. Any ideas or suggestions you have relating to any or all of them are encouraged and welcomed.

Budget: We are confronting a problem before it confronts us.

Eastern and southeastern Kentucky: An area that is becoming unpopular with its young people. The Agricultural and Industrial Development Board will undertake a survey early next year in an attempt to attract new industry to that section which is the state's number one economic problem. This is reflected by the large amount of public assistance, unemployment compensation, and school equalization funds being distributed in that area.

Lien law:[1] Good legislation that has drawn a tremendous amount of criticism and bitterness. It may develop into the most rugged issue in the next legislature. I support the law and believe that is has ridded the public assistance rolls of many persons who did not belong there in the first place.

Speed traps or, better still, traffic traps: Their number is increasing in the state. Several communities have become horrible to motorists. It is a shame, for instance, for a family from Michigan to enjoy two weeks vacation in Kentucky and recall it chiefly by some rude, uncalled-for arrest on their way home, thus destroying all the goodwill the state has built up with them.

---

1. In 1952 the General Assembly enacted a bill that related to public assistance and welfare of needy aged, needy blind, and needy children, amending and repealing part of the Kentucky Revised Statutes. (It amended sections 205.010, 205.200, 205.210, 205.240, 205.990, and repealed subsection 3 of section 205.170.) The act allowed the Commonwealth to have a lien upon all real estate and rights to real estate belonging to, or thereafter acquired by, any recipient of public assistance as a needy aged or needy blind. The lien became effective upon the first payment of assistance to the recipient and continued until it was satisfied or became unenforceable. The 1954 General Assembly did not rescind or alter the 1952 act. *Acts of the General Assembly of the Commonwealth of Kentucky,* 1952, Chapter 33 (S. B. 101), pp. 51-59.

FISCAL CRISIS IN THE STATES
Louisville / September 29, 1953

IT is indeed an honor to be on the program of a conference such as this, and I am grateful to your program committee for the privilege of speaking to you today. Your committee asked me to talk about how a governor looks at fiscal problems faced by the states today. More specifically, the subject chosen is "Fiscal Crisis in the States."

This reminds me of the story of the colored preacher who announced his next sermon would be on "The Great Crisis," and one of his deacons promptly inquired, "What is a crisis?" To which the parson replied, "Why dat's de hell of a mess we's in!"

There is a fiscal crisis in the states. Let me describe briefly what I mean by it and how I interpret some of its implications. The fiscal world we live in has literally turned upside down during the last generation. Every governor is aware of it, and tax specialists like yourselves are well aware of it. But most citizens are not.

Several outstanding facts impress me as descriptive of fiscal problems in the period since 1932. These are as follows: 1) great growth of government expenditures at all levels accompanied by higher taxes and increased debt; 2) shifting emphasis in taxes from local to state to federal government; 3) increase in overlapping taxation, duplication, and triplication of some tax sources; 4) relative decline of property tax at state-local level accompanied by increase of income and sales taxes; 5) rapid rise of the grants-in-aid system federal to state and state to local government.

Time does not permit us to analyze all these issues, and even if it did, frankly, I have no ready-made prescription to offer for their solution. Other speakers undoubtedly will deal with some of these matters. I can only skim the surface. My purpose essentially is to focus on an issue which cuts across all the above intergovernmental relations and the prospects for a better balance in expenditure and tax programs among the federal, state, and local governments.

The fiscal crisis, if we can call it that, like the growth of cancer, is a development that has been in motion for many years for the most part. Let us see what has happened. In 1932 local government dominated the tax collection field with 56 percent of the total for all government in the United States. The states took in 22 percent, and the federal government took in an equal share. By 1937 the federal became dominant with 39 percent, the local next with 38 percent, and the states got 23 percent of the total. By 1952 it is estimated that the federal had jumped to 75 (it had been 82 at the height of World War II) and the state percentage overshadowed the local by 13 to 12.

These simple facts reflect a remarkable shift in governmental activity in our federal system. We are just beginning to wake up to what they mean. The main causes are not hard to find—depression, war, increased population, and demands for more and higher standards of governmental services, particularly education, welfare, and highways.

In the face of these developments each level of government has struggled to meet its problems generally without any reference to the effects on the others. The actions during the last twenty years, for the most part, have been marked by an absence of orderly intergovernmental coordination. The fiscal systems have grown like a patch-work quilt, and they look pretty threadbare in many spots today.

Numerous studies, private and public, have been conducted; shelves are literally stacked with reports and recommendations and yet little, if anything, constructive has been accomplished to produce a more rational fiscal relationship among the various levels of government.

The Conference of Governors in recent years has given much consideration to the problem. Last year the conference unanimously recommended that the federal government begin to bring order out of chaos by getting out of the gasoline tax field and leaving road construction and maintenance to the states. Other proposals have been considered by the governors. There is a general feeling that the states are closer to the people and are, therefore, more responsive to the people than is the federal government. That is why the federal government ought to get out of as many programs as possible and turn them over to the states. Obviously, there are limits to such cutbacks. The national safety and welfare must, of necessity, require continuation of much federal assistance and participation with the states.

Through the efforts of your governors, working through the Council of State Government, Congress has enacted a bill creating a new Commission on Intergovernmental Relations.[1] Just a few days ago the president announced the completion of the selection of members for the twenty-five-man commission. A report is due by March 1954. There is very little time for deliberation and study. Lack of time may prevent much more than a beginning toward constructive recommendations.

Another type of problem has appeared which illustrates the importance of securing better coordination. Interest rates were suddenly raised this year by the federal government, and the states were not consulted. As a result, many state and local bond issues are going begging. We have city and school bonds shelved in Kentucky as elsewhere.

The relative decline of the property tax at the state-local level also has had a marked effect on state finances. While the general property tax remains the chief source of local tax revenue, this tax has been extremely sluggish in its behavior. The valuations placed on property by local tax assessors have failed to keep pace with rising property values. As a direct consequence of fractional valuation many cities, counties, and school districts have been squeezed between a falling effective tax rate and rising costs.

Confronted with this frozen property tax base and tax rate limitations, local governments are constantly turning to the states for greater financial assistance or permission to broaden their tax powers. In recent years several states, including Kentucky, have launched programs designed to make the property tax more efficient and equitable as a revenue instrument for local governments. While progress has been made in equalizing the assessments made by local assessors, few states have succeeded in raising local assessment levels high enough to relieve the financial distress of local governments and school districts.

In addition to the problems of intergovernmental relations there are serious problems concerning budget machinery facing every governor. Foremost of these problems is the recent trend toward increased legislative participation in the preparation of the executive budget.

Between 1911 and 1926 every state adopted some type of formal budget procedure. In forty of the states the responsibility of formulating an integrated financial plan for presentation to the legislature rests squarely on the governor. This trend has important implications which should be carefully considered because of the fundamental problems inherent in the maintenance of a proper balance of power between the legislative and executive branches of government.

During the development of the executive budget there has arisen a widespread but undefined feeling that somehow the legislature and the people were losing control of their government. Many contend that there is a dangerous concentration of power in the hands of the chief executive. There is a sense of frustration on the part of the legislature and the average citizen. They feel that the budget is too complicated for adequate control or comprehension.

The trend toward more extensive participation in the formulation process by the legislature is partly a result of this frustration. It seems to offer a technique by which the all-important fiscal affairs can be returned to the people. That this is an appealing slogan is evidenced by the fact that in the past twenty years the legislature of nineteen states, in varying degrees, have entered the budget preparation process. One state has a permanent staff responsible to the legislature which prepares a budget proposal of its own. It constitutes an alternative to the proposed budget which is still required and presented by the governor. In several other states, legislators participate in the formulation of a fiscal program prior to the governor's submission of the document to the legislature. This is done chiefly by the legislators or their staff members taking part in hearings conducted by the executive branch.

The need for a well-informed legislature and citizenry is genuine. On the whole the danger of arbitrary action on the part of the executive should not be minimized. It is doubtful, however, that the creation of legislative budget agencies is the tool which will accomplish the desired results.

The movement is indeed a movement backward. Beginning about 1900 the effort to draw clear lines of responsibility at the state level between the legislative and the executive branches resulted in a general strengthening of the chief executive. As a rule the governor was specifically given the responsibility of budget formulation and the initiatory power of the legislatures was restricted.

The basic factor in the executive budget idea is that there is presented an integrated program by a politically responsible official. Expenditure proposals are most meaningful when all requests for funds are presented for simultaneous review. To the extent that the legislative branch influences the preparation phase of the budget, the essential unity of the chief executive's financial plan is lost.

In terms of political responsibility, the legislature is not constituted to formulate a statewide program with unity and coherence. Each legislator represents his particular county, his particular economic group, or his particular interest. The governor can claim to represent the entire state. Moreover, he has submitted a program to the people upon which they have passed judgment at the ballot box. He is the governor because the majority of the voters approve that program.

The answer to this aspect of legislative-executive relationship does not lie in increased participation by the legislature in what is essentially an executive function. Piecemeal review of the budget as it is in the process of formulation accomplishes no real good. The time for legislative evaluation and action is after the governor has presented his program.

All of the results by those seeking information and interpretation of the governor's proposal can be obtained without weakening the executive budget structure. The results can be obtained by legislative insistence that the governor's plan be clear and comprehensive. The legislature has every right, indeed an obligation to the people, to insist that the governor fully explain and defend his financial program.

Another major issue confronting governors is the shortage of revenue to meet current needs. The economy appears to be slowing down. The states are spending more than they are taking in. Surpluses have all but vanished. Several observations can be made in light of the experience in Kentucky.

First, Kentucky is limited by its constitution to a bonded debt limit of $500,000. Therefore, any consideration of borrowing and direct deficit spending as a fiscal policy is purely academic in this state.

Second, with the express purpose of preventing a deficit in any fiscal year, the Kentucky General Assembly, as a part of the general appropriations bill, enacted provisions designed to keep expenditures from exceeding income. The commissioner of Finance, with the approval of the governor, is obliged to reduce allocations of funds to the various state agencies when it appears that revenue estimates will not be met.

Policy decisions must, of course, be made in light of the specific nature of the deficit problem. If the revenue loss appears to be temporary, should recurring costs be reduced or should the brunt be borne by nonrecurring budget items? When it first becamed evident in Kentucky that our income for the first year of the 1952-1954 biennium would be less than the revenue estimate, it also appeared that revenue for the second year, although below the estimate, would still be higher that our receipts had ever been before. It did not appear wise, in this event, to curtail services and dismiss personnel to the extent of the reduction when we could maintain our programs at the going level throughout the biennium by reducing certain nonrecurring appropriations.

At a later date it was obvious that the revenue losses were more than temporary and that the current spending programs could not be maintained. Then a major relook at all expenditure programs, recurring and nonrecurring, had to be examined.

Policy decisions had to be made in light of the intent of the legislature as reflected in the approved budget. In addition, the policies arrived at should not bind the people nor the legislature to a tax and expenditure program which they have not clearly demonstrated a willingness to accept.

Basically different techniques of reduction can be used dependent upon whether the reduction is to be large or small. A relatively minor reduction can be accomplished by a belt-tightening or postponement program under the overall surveillance of the governor's budget staff. Our first reduction effort in Kentucky was of this type. Personnel complements were frozen, and the purchase of capital outlay items was postponed. Agencies were instructed to cut inventories to the lowest possible operating level.

Major reductions cannot effectively be accomplished in the same manner. The policies and procedural controls exercised in the first instance imposed undesirable obstacles in the program planning of agencies and were difficult to execute equitably. Furthermore, the imposition of these controls would not have provided the dollar deductions necessary.

We accomplished the job in Kentucky by approaching the problem in the same manner as formulation of the initial budget. Agencies prepared budget estimates which included alternative reductions. These cutbacks were based on an examination of every aspect of the services offered and an evaluation of whether these services should be reduced or abolished. These estimates were tabulated and reviewed by the budget staff. Budget hearings with the individual agencies and the governor's cabinet were held. And finally, a revised fiscal plan for the 1953-1954 fiscal year was drafted.

I have described our budgetary difficulties in order to underscore the serious administrative problems posed by declining revenues. Implicit but not stated in a review of these budget reductions are such problems as disruption and dislocation of program planning and harmful effects on employee morale. Many persons, for example, misread newspaper stories and believed that these jobs were to be abolished.

Because it now appears that the good old days of steadily rising tax collections may be at an end, and with no surplus to cushion the shock, the role of the tax administrator becomes even more crucial. He must use his best judgment in forecasting tax collections and maximizing tax compliance.

In describing the fiscal crisis of the states, I have outlined certain fiscal and budgetary issues confronting a governor. But in a larger sense the state fiscal crisis is but another manifestation of a much deeper crisis. It is the struggle of the Free World under American leadership to halt the extension of Soviet dominion over mankind. In this awful conflict our traditional concepts of federalism and states' rights must be subordinated to the stark demands of national survival. As long as our cities live under the constant threat of annihilation, the major share of governmental expenditures must be for defense and military aid. As long as we remain a garrison state, our most productive tax sources must be channeled to the federal government. Just a few days ago President Eisenhower stated, "There is no sacrifice, no labor, no tax, no service too hard for us to bear to support a logical and necessary defense of our freedom."

In reexamining our federal, state, and local governmental relationships, therefore, the most pressing need is to be realistic. If we allow our deliberations on intergovernmental relationships to be infected with narrow partisan, economic, or sectional aspirations, only harm can be done to the democratic institutions which we are attempting to strengthen. Our federal, state, and local relationships must be viewed steadily and soberly against the larger backdrop of the hard demands we must face in a world where human freedom itself can be quickly lost.

This speech was delivered at the forty-sixth National Tax Association Conference held at the Kentucky Hotel in Louisville. Governor Wetherby saw in the federal government's costly military spending the cause for at least a part of Kentucky's financial plight. He agreed with an earlier speaker, Rowland R. Hughes, deputy director of the United States budget, who defended a reduction in military expenditures. Hughes warned of the danger that we might spend ourselves into defeat. *Louisville Courier-Journal,* September 30, 1953.

1. This twenty-five-member commission was created by Congress. President Dwight Eisenhower named the members in late September 1953.

STATE OF THE COMMONWEALTH ADDRESS
Frankfort / January 12, 1954

MY mission here is to advise you of the condition of Kentucky. In these sixty days we must do the planning for two years. You are working for Kentucky, and I assure you it is an honorable duty. This will be one of the occasions in our lifetime to recognize and meet the demands of public service.

As prescribed by the Constitution, legislatures of the Commonwealth have met with regularity since 1792. The record of their proceedings has contributed much to Kentucky's glorious history and tradition. As each governor and the membership of each General Assembly grappled with the problems common to their era, the pen of history has acclaimed their accomplishments, decried their failures, or scorned their record of mediocrity.

In offering this report I am not unmindful of the oft-repeated statement that the second legislative session of a governor's administration is labeled as a standpat or do-nothing assemblage. This has largely resulted from political races of the future dominating the deliberations and action on matters coming before the Assembly. Let us resolve today that progress and advancement for Kentucky shall be our theme rather than running future political races, whether they be Democratic or Republican. I know we all share the same determination to escape this censure.

Since November 27, 1950, on which date I became governor, few if any individuals have traveled this state more extensively than I. On these journeys to every corner of the state, my eyes have been focused and my ears trained to what people are thinking and desiring. I have confirmed my long-standing opinion that the people are always ahead of political leaders in their thinking on public affairs. The people are aware of Kentucky's problems and needs. They are anxious that something be done about them, and we are the people they selected to do the job.

Having a direct bearing on these questions is the general economic picture of our state. While the average per capita income of our citizens has steadily risen, I regret to report that the coal-producing counties of eastern Kentucky are in a serious economic crisis. This administration through its agencies is coordinating its efforts and working with community organizations of that section in an attempt to reverse this trend. We are endeavoring to attract new industry, provide new tourist and recreational facilities, and otherwise lay a firm foundation on which a more diversified economy can be built.

In the agricultural sections of the state a severe drought and unstable cattle prices have worked hardships on many farm families. However, the overall situation points to medium-level prosperity.

Since World War II our urban centers have experienced an almost phenomenal growth. Along with this increased population has come new industrial expansion, bringing job opportunities for many thousands and investments in excess of $2 billion.

In the past two years your state government has operated with a flattering minimum of public criticism. Every unit has performed efficiently with the public's interest serving as their chief guidepost. Parallel to good public service during the current fiscal year has been the successful determination of the administration to live within Kentucky's revenue means. To do this, progressive programs envisioned by the administration and endorsed by the 1952 legislature had to be reexamined and pared down. A reduction in the number of state employees became necessary. These actions were difficult and painful, but the state will not be in debt at the end of this fiscal year, and nowhere among state services has a breakdown occurred. This was accomplished without reducing our support to elementary education. Full information on the operation of each department is available in reports which have been filed as required by law.

Before turning to a detailed review of the budget proposals, an important fact should be noted. The General Fund represents less than one-half of the state's annual expenditures. This fact creates considerable confusion and wide misunderstanding. There are three distinct parts of the state's fiscal pattern. First is the General Fund which receives all moneys not earmarked for special purposes by the Constitution or statutes of the Commonwealth. The General Fund constitutes the major financial support for education, health and welfare, conservation and agriculture, and general government. Second is the Road Fund which by constitutional provision receives motor fuel and vehicle taxes which are devoted to the road program of the State. Third are the various trust and agency funds which receive funds that can be spent only for designated functions. For instance, funds received from the sale of hunting and fishing licenses can be used only by the Department of Fish and Wildlife Resources. College tuitions can be spent only by the college receiving them. At this time we must concern ourselves primarily with the General Fund income and expenditures and consider the other funds as they relate to the General Fund.

Before presenting any proposals for the next biennium let me review with you the financial developments of the past two years. The budget which the last General Assembly approved was based upon the expectation of the General Fund tax collections of $78 million and $81 million for the two fiscal years to follow.

Some of you will recall that I told the General Assembly at that time that the revenue estimate was optimistic. I also asked that provisions be written in law which would allow the budget to be adjusted downward should such a need arise. All of you are aware that tax collections did not meet expectations. Reductions were necessary in both the first year of the biennium and in the second, the year in which we are now operating. The nature of the reductions which we chose has a direct relationship to the budget I present to you today.

I proposed to the legislature in 1952 a budget which provided for progress in education, public health and welfare, and all programs of state government. By almost unanimous vote the General Assembly approved this program.

When revenue fell short, budget reductions were inaugurated to accomplish two things. One, to carry out as many of the agreed-upon program advancements as possible, and two, to carry them out within a balanced budget. I was determined not to present to you upon your arrival in Frankfort for this session a host of deficiency appropriation bills. Keeping the budget balanced, and we have kept it balanced, has required the curtailment of programs, but the curtailment has been on an orderly planned basis.

While reducing the budget for the present fiscal year, we have tried to maintain as many as possible of the advancements which had already been made. In addition, there are some programs in our state in which standing still actually means moving backward. I felt the state could not afford to move backward. Preserving our advancements and allowing some forward movement involved making choices. I made these choices.

The first choice involved the use of accumulated money in the revolving and trust and agency accounts of some agencies. This was money which had been accumulated prior to the present fiscal year. The agencies are using this trust and agency surplus for normal operating expenses for the current fiscal year. Many appropriations out of the General Fund were cut to the extent of the amount available in these accounts. To continue the programs being partially financed by the use of these revolving funds which will largely be depleted by the end of this fiscal year, additional support from the General Fund must be provided for the coming biennium.

The second choice was to postpone replacement of equipment and certain aspects of maintenance. Postponements of this nature over a longer period than a year or two cannot be continued. The budget I am proposing for the fiscal years 1954-1955 and 1955-1956 can be more clearly understood if I outline the major steps and decisions which went into its preparation.

First, each agency was asked to submit to me its request for funds. Most requests were conservative. I also asked that each agency estimate and justify in detail the cost of continuing present programs. From the beginning, this was one of the primary considerations in reviewing the budget requests. Every possible effort was made to apply the same factors to each agency to insure that continuation cost for one agency had the same meaning that it did for every other.

As the second step, I requested the Department of Revenue to give me a tentative estimate of the income we could expect from our present tax system. The Revenue Department estimated our income at about $76 million a year. At this point, I had to make a choice. I could present to you a budget within anticipated revenue. Such a budget would sharply reduce the present programs of the state. The alternative was to propose adjustments in our tax system to raise additional funds required. The estimated cost of continuing programs at present levels of operation is $81,200,000 a year, or $162,400,000 for the biennium. This is about $5,200,00 per year above the estimated revenue.

The need for increased dollar support to continue the present programs is attributable to several factors. I spoke of two of these in relation to present-year reductions. Four other factors are of major significance. First, new buildings and other facilities, begun during the present biennium, will be opened. The new ward building at Kentucky Training Home is an example. Provision must be made to operate these new facilities. Second, workloads in some agencies will increase due to factors beyond our control. An example of many that could be recited is the Welfare Department, which operates the Training Home, Kentucky Village, and the penal institutions. Third, personal-services costs will be higher. It is the policy of the state to award annual pay increases to employees for the first four years they occupy a position. Allowance must be made in any budget for the cost of these increases. Fourth, replacement of depleted inventories at our institutions and slight increases in prices and utility rates.

I have made two major exceptions to the policy of continuing the programs of the state at present levels. First, I have proposed an increase of $6 million for the biennium for the Common School Fund. This brings the biennial appropriation to the common schools to $69,571,000, over $20 million above the appropriation made by the 1950 session. Second, I have proposed an additional appropriation to the Department of Library and Archives of something over $200,000 for the bookmobile project. I feel that the citizens and the local governmental units of the state have indicated sufficient interest in this project to justify this increase.

To continue present programs in all fields to provide for increases in the common school fund and for the bookmobile project, I recommend an appropriation of $84,600,000 the first year, and $84 million the second year, a biennial budget for recurring costs of $168,600,000 from the general fund.

In addition to the appropriations recommended from recurring revenue, this budget proposes the appropriation of $7 million of nonrecurring revenue for capital outlay purposes. The major appropriation in this amount is to the State Property and Buildings Commission for continuation of the state's building program. This proposed appropriation for capital outlay by the Buildings Commission continues a sound and well-established policy of dedicating nonrecurring revenues to nonrecurring types of expenditures.

The general functions of education continue to receive the major share of the General Fund, 55.8 percent. Health and Welfare will receive

30.7 percent, Agriculture and Conservation 1.7 percent, and all other activities of government 11.8 percent.

In the preparation of this document all funds of the Commonwealth have been considered. You will note that agency receipts have been more clearly reviewed than in any previous budget. This budget anticipates that all of the support possible for an agency program will come from its own resources, thereby lessening as much as possible the claim against the General Fund. These estimates are based on the assumption that the federal government's participation in federal-state programs will continue on the present basis. Should this fail to materialize, our only choice will be reductions in programs in which changes are made in federal support.

The budget is not a matter of bookkeeping alone. It is a detailed plan of what your state government hopes to accomplish in the two years to come translated into dollars. The proposal I have made to you is my own evaluation of the desires of the people for state services weighed against their willingness and ability to pay for them. It has been no simple task to make this evaluation. The alternatives are seldom exact or pleasant. The job of looking two and a half years ahead is full of hazards and uncertainties.

I have attempted to present this proposal to you simply and clearly. It is my feeling that the budget document on your desks represents the best possible selection of available information to facilitate your understanding of the proposals made.

The General Fund expenditure budget submitted can be balanced by anticipated revenue from the existing tax system together with enactment of new measures which I propose as follows: 1) establish a pay-as-you-go plan for collection of the individual income tax by a system of withholding and declaration; 2) change the cigarette tax from the present rate based on price to a flat rate of three cents per pack of twenty cigarettes; 3) increase the beer consumption tax from $1.50 per barrel to $2.50 per barrel; 4) increase the wine consumption tax from twenty-five cents per gallon to fifty cents per gallon; 5) remove the pari-mutuel tax exemption and change the existing flat rate to a graduated tax.

The pay-as-you-go income tax plan is not new. The federal government started it a decade ago. The states of Delaware, Oregon, and Vermont have adopted this method of collection and report much success. This plan will make the income tax more just because it will require everyone to pay uniformly. It will be far more convenient for the average taxpayer. Pay-as-you-go will cut down tax delinquency. It insures collection of the tax before either the taxpayer or his ability to pay disappears. This method will also help the state by providing a more regular flow of money into the treasury. As it is now, the heaviest state expenditures are in the first part of the fiscal year, while income tax collections are concentrated in the last half.

The Department of Revenue has made a careful study of how the withholding plan works elsewhere. A plan of administration is ready that will be easy for employers to follow in arranging for withholding. The effective date would be July 1, 1954. The Department of Revenue estimates an additional $3 million per year as a result of this tax plan. The first year under pay-as-you-go will result in an estimated $7 million of nonrecurring revenue due to advancing payments to a current basis. I have recommended that this sum be appropriated for nonrecurring expenditures.

The second proposal dealing with the cigarette tax will produce an additional $2,700,000 annually. Kentucky's cigarette tax is now based on price. Many packs are already taxed at three cents. This proposal would establish a three-cent tax on all standard packs of twenty cigarettes. Kentucky's rate has been considerably below the average. Thirty of forty states specifically taxing cigarettes have a rate of three cents or more.

The third proposal increasing the beer tax would yield an additional $1,100,00 annually. With this increase Kentucky would still have an equivalent or more favorable rate compared with most of our neighbors. For example, the tax per barrel in Ohio is $2.50; Indiana, $2.71; Tennessee, $3.40; West Virginia, $5.50.

The fourth proposal increasing the wine tax would produce an additional $200,000 annually.

The final revenue proposal is a more equitable approach to pari-mutuel taxation. It will establish a uniform tax on all pari-mutuel bets regardless of the track where the bets are placed. It is estimated this will produce an additional $800,000.

There are many other ways to raise taxes, but we have recommended those which we believe will cause the least overall harm to the economy and to our citizens in general. I have presented a budget designed to meet Kentucky's minimum needs, and if it is approved the above measures, or others that would produce an equal amount of revenue, must be enacted.

There are several proposals with which the public, I know, is greatly concerned. I urge your serious consideration of each. The fact that Kentuckians realize that our educational system is sick was revealed by the 241,000 majority given the amendment permitting a change in the method of distributing school funds.[1] All of us hold office by popular election and must keenly respect a majority of this dimension. The action of Kentucky voters was an overwhelming expression of confidence in the desire and ability of the legislature and the elected officials to write and enact into law a sound and equitable method of distributing school money. This is the next step necessary to developing a sound educational system. Work is now under way by educational leaders, the State Department of Education, the Legislative Research Commission, and others to write such a bill for submission to you during this session.

The unregulated mining of coal by the strip or open-pit method causes soil erosion, stream pollution, increases likelihood of floods, imapirs efforts in the conservation of soil, water, and other natural resources, and otherwise destroys the value of land for agricultural purposes. Each generation must be aware of its responsibilities to the next. A generation is only temporary, but the ravages of strip-mining have mutilated the topographical face of Kentucky forever. This mining method is comparatively new and is rapidly expanding. Without control, thousands of additional acres will be destroyed. In our failure to provide for a degree of rehabilitation of these areas we are being unfaithful to posterity. The strength of local governments in these sections is being sapped by the destruction of taxable property. Strip-mine regulation is not a newcomer to the Kentucky legislature. A bill was introduced in 1948 but was not acted upon so that further study could be applied to this subject. In 1950 a similar bill was emasculated by amendment. In 1952 the hopes of all forward-looking Kentuckians were demolished by the power and influence of special interests. Again an effective but reasonable strip-mine regulation bill will be introduced. I urge its passage to the dignity of yourselves and the Commonwealth.

Man is confused enough by circumstances beyond his control. All of us can wind a clock, but few of us can tell what time it is in Kentucky during the summer months. To avoid this confusion I hope the legislature will make a full exploration of our laws dealing with time.

Under our existing law the mentally ill are described as idiots, lunatics, feeble-minded, and insane, and in the methods prescribed for the admission of such people to our mental hospitals they are treated and handled in the same manner as criminals. Since we have developed a Department of Mental Health it is now time for us to make additional advancements in this field, and we therefore propose to revise the laws dealing with the description of the mentally ill and also propose to revise the method by which such people may be committed to our mental institutions for diagnosis, care, and treatment. This department has made rapid strides during the past biennium, and we feel that the legislation which will be submitted to you dealing with this subject will provide means for additional advancement in dealing with these unfortunate citizens of Kentucky.[2]

During the past year a committee of interested citizens working with the Department of Welfare made a complete study of our laws dealing with probation and parole. They have found many outmoded provisions within the statutes and have prepared a bill which will revise and modernize the entire system of probation and parole. The bill would require the circuit courts to have an investigation conducted by a probation officer before placing any person on probation. It modernizes current procedures and corrects many inadequacies which now exist. This bill will be submitted to you during the session, and I hope you will give it your consideration and approval.

Under recent decisions of our Court of Appeals several flaws in our laws dealing with the selection of our juries, both grand and petit, have been pointed out. The Kentucky Judicial Council has made a careful study and prepared legislation which we feel would correct some of these defects and provide for a more orderly process for the selection of juries. This legislation would materially strengthen our jury system, removing some of the outmoded provisions of the present jury laws, and would give to our citizens a greater confidence in our judicial system.

During the 1952 session of the General Assembly you directed the Legislative Research Commission and the governor to appoint a commission to study the question of alcoholism. Such a study has been made and a detailed report and recommendations on that problem will be submitted to you. This report points out the seriousness of the problem. I urge you to study it carefully and give proper consideration to the recommendations offered.

The right to vote is one of our most precious rights, and during your last session you enacted into law a new Registration and Purgation Act which, I think, has been very beneficial to Kentucky. Every effort should be made to encourage our citizens to participate freely in the election process, and with this in mind we have explored the possibilities of making voting machines available to all counties desiring to adopt this method of voting. Enabling legislation will be presented to you which will aid in financing the purchase of voting machines by the counties of Kentucky that desire to use them. The enactment of this measure will further encourage our citizens to participate in elections. This proposal would be permissive and not mandatory.

One of the beauty spots of Kentucky has long been inaccessible, but during recent years a new highway has been built into the Breaks of the Sandy. The people of Virginia and eastern Kentucky are interested in the development of this natural asset. Representatives of our state and Virginia have negotiated to jointly develop this area for recreational purposes. It will be necessary, in order to do this, for the federal Congress to approve a compact between Kentucky and Virginia, and it will also be necessary for the legislative body of each state to enact enabling legislation. The Department of Conservation has prepared a bill which will be introduced by members from that area, and I urge you to pass it.

Kentucky has more animal rabies than any state in the Union. Our animal-disease reporting system has shown as many as 155 cases in Kentucky in a single month. The Department of Health has prepared legislation dealing with this problem from the health standpoint. It will be submitted to you and certainly deserves serious consideration. Kentucky should have an effective rabies control law.

I have mentioned several of the proposals which I shall make to you during the course of this session. There are additional subjects including specifically a recommendation dealing with our highway system, which I shall make when a survey now under way has been completed. I shall make additional recommendations either through your leadership or by appearance before you.

My sincere desire is to work with you harmoniously during the coming weeks for the enactment of legislation designed to advance Kentucky. The citizens of Kentucky are depending on us. Let's give them our best effort. We must not betray their trust.

---

1. This amendment, authorized by the legislature in 1952, permitted the General Assembly to prescribe the manner of distribution and use of public school funds. On November 3, 1953, voters approved the amendment. The action was supplemented in 1954 when the General Assembly approved a Minimum Foundation Program that provided for the establishment, operation, and financing of a foundation program for the public schools and for the apportionment, distribution, and use of the public school foundation program fund. It attempted to assure substantially equal public school educational opportunities by basing the amount of funding on needs. The extent of each school district's need was based on the number of pupils actually in school. It did away with the state aid approach, and the state and local school districts became partners in providing a minimum of school services for each child. Funding for local schools came from two accounts-per capita and equalization. A school district could share in the equalization funds provided it met specific requirements for operating time, single salary schedule, local tax effort, etc. *Acts of the General Assembly of the Commonwealth of Kentucky,* 1954, Chapter 214 (H.B. 365), pp. 590-603. For Governor Wetherby's assessment of the Foundation's success see speech from December 7, 1955, in this section.

2. Governor Wetherby proposed and the legislature approved acts authorizing the designation of private homes and private nursing homes for placement and family care of certain state mental hospital patients. The legislature also reorganized the Department of Mental Health in its functions, powers, and duties. It allowed the department to produce printing of any class for the use of the hospitals and the department. It established the confidential nature of certain department records and reports. It clarified the methods of hospitalization of mentally ill persons and defined the custody, support, and treatment of incompetents. Finally, the legislature proscribed the method of inquest, commitment, and discharge of incompetents.

REVIEW OF THE ADMINISTRATION'S ACCOMPLISHMENTS
Louisville / December 7, 1955

I WOULD like to express to station WHAS-TV my appreciation for the invitation to appear on this program and to present to the people of Kentucky a report on what has happened in their state government during my administration. I believe that it is right and proper that there be a review of my stewardship as your governor, not for the purpose of bragging about what may have been accomplished, but to assist in determining where we stand now and how we should move in working together for the future. I believe that it is pardonable for me to say that I am proud of the record that has been made during the eight years that I have served you in Frankfort, three years as lieutenant governor and five years as governor.

One of the great Kentucky industries has as its advertising slogan "Progress Is Our Most Important Product."[1] I am pleased to say that progress has been the most important product of the two administrations in which I have served at Frankfort. There has been progress on every front in state government. Kentucky now has many new fine buildings, and many of its older ones have been renovated. Our highway system has been improved materially. Our educational standards have been raised to much higher levels. Emphasis on the conservation, development, and utilization of our scenic and natural resources has been increased. The state has given added attention to its obligation to the mentally ill and other wards of its institutions and to the aged needy and dependent.

There have been definite objectives and a coordinated pattern behind the programs which we sought to develop during these eight years. They have been based on recognition of the fact that Kentucky is a relatively poor state. In 1948 the average per capita income of Kentuckians was only $965 per year. This meant that from that limited income a Kentucky citizen could not afford to pay state taxes in amounts sufficient to support the functions of state government as adequately as most of us want them financed.

One fundamental key to the ability of state government to provide the services which its citizens demand is per capita income. In 1954 this per capita income was $1,216. The same income in Ohio was $1,983. In Tennessee it was $1,212. The national average per capita was $1,770. The average Kentucky taxpayer in 1954 paid $70 in state taxes. His neighbor in Ohio paid $86, and his neighbor in Tennessee paid $83. The national average payment was $97.

We felt that state government ought to provide leadership in raising general economic well-being of the state and its people, and that whereever possible state funds ought to be spent in such a way that they would constitute investments which would return future dividends to the citizens of Kentucky. The making of such investments has been one of the major objectives of my administration. There have been great returns from these investments and even greater dividends can be forecast for the future.

One of the most important projects developed by your state government during the past eight years was the complete program of securing topographic maps which has been carried out through the Agricultural and Industrial Development Board. The state Highway Department has been saved many hundreds of thousands of dollars by having these topographic maps available. They are invaluable assets in attracting industries and in a multitude of other ways that constitute real values to Kentucky's people. This topographic map project cost the state a total of $3 million over a period of years, yet it constitutes an investment that will pay dividends to Kentucky for many years to come.

The same objective of raising Kentucky's economic level and increasing the income of its citizens was behind our emphasis on the development of the park system and the tourist industry. In eight years, we have invested about $9 million in capital improvements in the state parks, with the result that today we have one of the outstanding systems in the nation. We have spent about $400,000 a year advertising Kentucky, convincing tourists that this is a place to visit. Our tourist income has risen to more than half a billion dollars a year. It is estimated that the Highway Department receives $8 million a year in gasoline taxes from out-of-state tourists alone, as much annually as we spent in seven years to develop the parks.

I mentioned that in 1948 the average per capita income of Kentuckians was $965. In 1954 that average income for Kentuckians has risen to $1,216. This average income in Kentucky was increased by 26.7 percent between 1948 and 1954. The national average increase during this period was only 18.7 percent.

Another major area on which I wish to report is also in the nature of the investment. This is the investment of our resources in the education of our children and the foundation which has been laid for further progress. Kentucky can boast of many accomplishments, but in the field of education there are none more significant than the advances which have been made in the past three years. Three years ago the road to educational progress in Kentucky was blocked. The roadblock was Section 186 of the Constitution.[2] This administration took the lead in a campaign to give Kentucky a sound educational program. The first step in this movement was to amend Section 186.

The legislature in the 1952 session authorized a proposed amendment to permit the General Assembly to prescribe the manner of distribution and use of public school funds. After this amendment was submitted to the people an extensive educational campaign was conducted to give the people of Kentucky the facts. On November 3, 1953, the voters went to the polls and voted overwhelmingly for the amendment.

The next step was to see what services the people wanted for their children. Again, as a result of a grass-roots survey, the people spoke in no uncertain terms. Given the facts about overcrowded classrooms, teacher shortages, dilapidated buildings, and inadequate transportation services, they indicated a desire for a sound educational program. On the basis of what the people said a program was developed. This program is a people's program, it is a Foundation Program.

The 1954 General Assembly enacted this into law. The Foundation Program is based on educational needs. The extent of each school district's need is based on pupils actually in school. The law also provides a new concept of financing education in Kentucky. It does away with the old state aid approach, and the state and local school districts become partners in providing a minimum of school services for each child.

It is encouraging to note that after the adoption of the Foundation Program, local contributions increased $3,300,000 per year. This increase in local effort is significant. It shows that Kentuckians not only want better educational opportunities for their children but are willing to pay for them. The next step in the movement to improve education should be full financing of the Minimum Foundation by the 1956 General Assembly.

While participating in the move for a sounder basis of financing education, this administration takes pride in pointing out that appropriations to the Common School Fund have risen steadily.

The present biennial appropriation of $69,571,000, which I recommended to the 1954 General Assembly, is over $20 million above the biennial appropriation made by the 1950 session. In addition, the Teachers' Retirement System has been strengthened and benefits have been increased. These increases should prove to be an important factor in attracting and retaining competent teachers for our public schools.

Other investments in the future of Kentucky have been made in our highway system, the State Fair, and in the conservation of our natural resources.

An important point which Kentuckians must keep in mind in thinking of what they want their state government to do is that our state is in competition with the forty-seven other states and other nations. This is particularly true in connection with the highway program. The states are in competition in providing good highway transportation as a means of attracting tourists, industries, and businesses which must have such facilities. The state which does not keep pace with modern trends in highway development is going to be bypassed. We cannot kid ourselves about that. We must learn what the traveling public wants and then meet those wants. There is no secret about what the traveling public wants. The answer is that those who travel by highway demand modern roads for comfort and safety. Other states are rushing to fill those needs. We have felt that our efforts to advance Kentucky's highway system have constituted a major investment in Kentucky's future.

Kentucky's highway accomplishments during the past eight years can be measured best in terms of road constructed. Over 16,000 miles of road have been built, rebuilt, or resurfaced. Much of the construction has been in improvement of existing routes. Relocation or widening our highway system account for more than half of all construction work. In 1948 there were 10,255 miles of highway being maintained by the state. As of June 30, 1955, 18,000 miles were under state maintenance.

A major highway development is our turnpike,[3] which is necessary to avoid Kentucky becoming a detour state. In 1954 construction was started on the first modern toll road in Kentucky. The heavy volume of traffic and the high number of accidents on the section of U.S. Highway 31-W from Louisville to Elizabethtown demonstrated the need for this relief route. The turnpike will be a superhighway of latest design. All cross traffic will be carried over or under the road by bridges and underpasses. Access will be limited to points where sufficient traffic will justify it. All contracts call for completion of the road by January 1956.

Construction of the turnpike will not cost tax dollars. It is financed by a bond issue. The bonds will be retired from tolls paid by the users of the highway and by income from the leasing of service and food facilities.

The new State Fair plant is another long-range development designed to promote agriculture and industries related to agriculture. It was apparent that expansion of the old Fairgrounds was economically unsound and almost physically impossible. The State Fair Board and the state Property and Buildings Commission have approved financing and construction of a new plant which will cost approximately $15 million. The plant will include a Coliseum Building, an Exposition Building, a livestock pavilion, a sheep and swine pavilion, a restaurant, an administration building, and a multipurpose stadium. The sources of financing are proceeds from the sale of the old Fairgrounds, grants from the Building Commission, and proceeds from the sale of revenue bonds. The project is soundly financed; construction is moving ahead rapidly and should be completed for the 1956 fair.

Another investment area has been in the conservation of our natural resources. In 1954 the General Assembly enacted the Strip Mine and Reclamation Act, after efforts to pass such a law had failed in three previous sessions. The purpose of the law is to reduce the damage caused by uncontrolled acid water created by strip (open-pit) mining, reduce damaging erosion from spoil banks, and restore vegetation to denuded areas.

The effectiveness of the job done by the Reclamation Commission can be appreciated when an area that has been reclaimed is compared to sections stripped long before the act went into effect. After twenty or more years some old spoil banks are still barren of all growth except scrub brush.

Timber is one of our most valuable assets. The Division of Forestry provides organized fire protection to 5,761,000 acres of forests in the state. More than 5,000,000 trees were distributed to land owners for planting during the past years. This compares with 1,251,000 in 1948.

Our program of conserving the soil and water resources of the state has benefited every county in the Commonwealth. A statewide flood control program is being developed by the Division of Flood Control and Water Usage. Working with the federal government, we have set up four Pilot Plant Watersheds in Kentucky. These projects—Plum

Creek, Upper Green River, Red River, and Rough River—will do a complete upstream flood-control job on those watersheds in a five-year period.

I am proud of the advances which have been made in the treatment of the mentally ill. Our general public health activities have been extended. Progress has been made in our Child Welfare, Public Assistance, and all social service programs.

One of the major health and welfare problems which this administration faced was the care for the mentally ill. The problem had reached such proportions that it was necessary for us to change our hospitals from custodial institutions to treatment centers. It was recognized that a separate department of state government was needed to meet the special requirements of this new approach. The General Assembly of 1952 created the Department of Mental Health.

The department began a program of recruitment of trained medical personnel. Training programs for hospital attendants were instituted. In 1952 there were only nineteen physicians in the four mental hospitals. Today there are forty-three. The attendant group, which plays such an important role in the care of patients, is becoming better equipped daily to participate in a treatment program.

Physical facilities for treatment have been improved. In 1953 new ward buildings were completed at Western and Eastern State hospitals. Renovation and rebuiling projects increased the bed capacity of each of the hospitals. Plans have been made for construction of four additional floors to a section of the main building at Kentucky State Hospital. Contracts have been awarded for construction of a treatment center at Eastern State Hospital.

A grant from the Governor's Emergency Fund this year enabled the department to purchase newly developed drugs. Through the use of these drugs a greater number of patients have become responsive to treatment. Many patients, who in former years were considered incurables, have been returned home.

The total mental health program has required expenditures of three times as much annually as we spent eight years ago. Progress has been rapid.

The general health program has been extended to more of our citizens. Today, Kentucky has a full-time health department in every one of its 120 counties.

In 1952 the General Assembly enacted the Youth Authority Act[4] and established a central point for the administration of children's services which includes the reception and diagnosis of delinquent children and the care and placement of dependent and neglected children. As operating policy the emphasis in the children's institutions was shifted from one of correction in a penal sense to one of diagnosis, treatment, and training. This whole diagnosis and placement process culminates in a program that is child-centered. It is a program of care, treatment, and rehabilitation of the children committed to the Youth Authority and is designed to provide for the classification, segregation, and specialized treatment of children according to their respective problems and needs.

Since 1948 the average Public Assistance grant to the aged has been increased from $17.36 per month to $35.38, and the grant to the blind from $18.52 to $37.11. The average monthly grant per family in the Aid to Dependent Children program has been raised from $37.46 to $63.33. Unemployment benefit payments have increased. Today the weekly minimum is $8.00 and the maximum is $28.00

This attempt to capsule the activities of your state government in this brief report has obviously left many things unsaid, many areas of progress unmentioned. I have prepared a report in much more detail which will be issued this week in Frankfort, and to which I invite your attention.[5]

The efforts of this administration have been directed toward two overall objectives: One, we have endeavored to provide the very best governmental services possible within the available tax resources, and two, we have sought to increase the economic ability of Kentuckians to provide themselves with a higher standard of living which, in turn, enables them to buy better education, health, welfare services, and roads.

In concluding this report, I would like to take this opportunity to thank those who have headed the various departments of state government and all state employees for the contribution which they have made to this administration. I would also like to express my appreciation to the many citizens and citizen groups who have cooperated so consistently in helping us in our efforts to build a greater Kentucky and to the press and radio for the job of telling Kentuckians what is going on in Frankfort.

This speech was broadcast over television station WHAS.

1. An ad slogan used by the General Electric Company. Governor Wetherby was instrumental in getting the company to locate a major appliance plant at Louisville.

2. Section 186 stated that each county was entitled to its proportion of the school fund based on its census of pupil children for each year; and if any school district did not use its pro rata share at the end of the second school year, it reverted into the treasury and was used for the general apportionment of the

school fund the following school year. See *Constitution of the Commonwealth of Kentucky* (Frankfort, 1891), p. 46.

3. Governor Wetherby was a strong advocate of turnpike construction. Albert B. Chandler used the turnpike issue in the Democratic primary campaign of 1955 and termed the Louisville and Elizabethtown stretch a road that began nowhere and ended nowhere. For more information on turnpike construction see letter from December 7, 1953, in the Transportation and Public Safety section.

4. The Youth Authority Act related to children and their care, custody, treatment, and disposition. It included provisions as to juvenile courts and to the jurisdiction and powers of other courts concerning children, and provided for the establishment of agencies and facilities of the state for the administration of state functions regarding children. Except in stated cases, the county court of each county was given exclusive jurisdiction in proceedings concerning any child living or found within the county. The country court was, in proceedings concerning children, called the "juvenile court." No child under the age of sixteen was to be incarcerated with older felons but in a separate suitable facility for the detention of children. It provided for assistance to mentally ill, defective, or physically ill children coming before the court. A juvenile court, in the event of a felony, could transfer the case to the circuit court of the county in which the offense was committed. If found guilty there, the child could be committed to the penitentiary unless he/she was under the age of twenty, when the court could commit the child to the Youth Authority. Much of this act concerned the placement of child offenders and their supervision. The act established a Youth Authority Board consisting of a director and a governing board and officers, staff, and personnel necessary for its performance of duty. Funds were appropriated for its operation. See *Acts of the General Assembly of the Commonwealth of Kentucky*, 1952, Chapter 161 (H. B. 157), pp. 428-51.

This act indicated Governor Wetherby's intense interest in children and reflected his experience as a juvenile court judge of Jefferson County. He was personally appalled by the conditions under which children were held and punished in certain counties of the Commonwealth.

In the Democratic primary campaign of 1955, Albert B. Chandler made the Youth Authority Act a campaign issue by stating his opposition to it. The provisions of the act were altered subsequently under the Chandler administration (1955-1959). See *Acts of the General Assembly of the Commonwealth of Kentucky*, 1956, Chapter 157 (H. B. 362), pp. 285-312.

5. The report is entitled "Kentucky State Government: A Progress Report," prepared by the Department of Finance, Division of Budget, and is 163 pages in length. It is a good in-depth review of Governor Wetherby's achievements and presents the administration's view of itself. It is divided according to departments.

REGISTRATION AND PURGATION LAW

Letter / November 30, 1950

[To members of the Legislative Research Commission, Frankfort]

PERMIT me to take this opportunity to thank the members of this commission[1] for the fine cooperation which you have given to me during the past three years while I acted as chairman of the body. I have enjoyed the association tremendously and feel that we have made some real progress in putting the commission on a sound footing.

Now that I have assumed the duties of governor, I should like to designate the acting lieutenant governor, Louis Cox,[2] to preside as acting chairman since it will probably not be possible for me to attend all of the meetings of the commission. It is my hope, however, that the members will invite me to meet with you at various times during the coming years.

The registration and purgation laws of Kentucky give me a great deal of concern. I should, therefore, like to request of the commission that you authorize a project immediately for the study of the registration and purgation laws of the Commonwealth and that, after your study has been completed, you draft the best possible code of election, registration, and purgation law so that the rights of all voters may be fully guaranteed.

In making your study and codification of these laws, I would suggest that the commission authorize its acting chairman to name a committee consisting of county clerks, judges, county attorneys, and citizens who have shown an interest in the subject and have some knowledge of registration and purgation within their respective counties.

I believe that if a proper job is done on this project we will necessarily create an additional interest on behalf of the people in participating in their government by exercising their rights to register and vote.

---

1. For more information on the Legislative Research Commission see inaugural address of December 11, 1951.

2. Lewis D. Cox (1907-1971), attorney, member, Kentucky Senate (1941, 1945, 1949); president pro tem of Senate (1948, 1950, 1952). As president pro tem he was in line to succeed Governor Wetherby from November 27, 1950, until December 11, 1951, when Emerson Beauchamp became lieutenant governor. Born in Frankfort. Frank K. Kavanaugh, *Kentucky Directory* (Frankfort, 1952), p.138.

SOCIAL SECURITY FOR STATE EMPLOYEES
Letter / January 8, 1951

[To Joe Williams, Benton]

THE question of social security for public employees, about which you wrote, has given me a great deal of concern, and immediately upon assuming office as governor I asked Attorney General A. E. Funk[1] to make a thorough investigation of the laws of Kentucky to determine whether or not it was possible for our state to enter into an agreement with the Social Security administrator so as to make all public employees eligible for the benefits under the new act. After studying this matter General Funk informs me that under the present laws I cannot sign such an agreement without specific authorization from the state legislature.

I am very sympathetic with the social security program, and I deeply regret that the amendment to the social security law by the federal Congress on August 28, 1950, was not adopted before the 1950 session of the Kentucky legislature adjourned on March 17, 1950.

While it is desirable to have an enabling act immediately, I do not feel that it is of such an emergency that justifies me in calling a special session of the legislature in view of both domestic and international conditions with which we are now faced. However, I am confident that the merits of this needed legislation will be apparent immediately to the 1952 legislature and that enabling legislation will be submitted to the membership early in the session so that the various public employees in Kentucky may participate in this broadened social security program.

Subsequently, Governor Wetherby did change his mind and called on February 21, 1951, for an extraordinary session of the General Assembly to meet and consider, among other things, the question of social security for public employees. The governor altered his position when it was discovered that there would be a surplus of state revenue in 1951. For the call for the extraordinary session, see the message from February 21, 1951, in this section.

1. Alvarado Erwin Funk (1895-1954), attorney, Bullitt County (1930-1935); assistant attorney general of Kentucky (1936-1944), attorney general (1947-1951); born in Bullitt County. Frank K. Kavanaugh, *Kentucky Directory* (Frankfort, 1950), p. 119.

Joseph Williams (1913-), accountant, born in Marshall County and resides in Benton. Letter, December 24, 1980.

1951 SPECIAL SESSION OF THE GENERAL ASSEMBLY
Letter / March 2, 1951

[To J. E. Reeves, Lexington]

THIS acknowledges your February 28 letter written as chairman of the Fayette County Committee for Citizenship.

As was evidenced by the promptness with which I acknowledged and, in my opinion, met the problem of voter registration and purgation in Kentucky immediately upon becoming governor, and as I have indicated to you through previous correspondence, no subject of a public nature has longer maintained my interest, concern, and hope for improvement.

At the time a decision was reached calling for a special session of the General Assembly, I recognized and anticipated that a number of subjects other than those included in the call would be suggested and urged to be included in an amendment and expansion of the original proclamation. The validity of this anticipation is now substantiated by an even twenty-five different subject matters that have been received by the governor's office. Many of these proposals, like your own, merit consideration; however, to include all or even a substantial portion of this number would, of course, not be feasible, and to include some and exclude others would be unwarranted discrimination. For that reason you may have noted a public statement in which I took a stand against broadening the call.

Having a more specific bearing on your committee's suggestion, I should like to say that the basic reason behind the subjects which were included in the legislative call was their emergency and urgent nature. Since the existing registration and purgation law has been on the statute book for more than a decade, I cannot reconcile the mild hysterics that have been demonstrated recently with respect to this matter with the real emergency that besets those matters on which I have requested the General Assembly to act.

There is yet another point worthy of mention. This relates to the controversial aspects of a workable registration and purgation law. As you may recall, in the 1950 legislative session more than a half dozen bills were introduced, each designed for the purpose of improving and strengthening the present law, yet none of these measures reached the point in the legislative mill where it could be said that it enjoyed even small chance of being passed. Recognizing this problem, several weeks ago I asked the Legislative Research Commission to make a comprehensive study of the entire subject of voter registration and purgation. To assist in this undertaking, I am confident you know, an advisory committee, composed of a membership whose training, experience, and fitness for the assignment cannot be questioned, was appointed by the Legislative Research chairman[1] to assist in developing a sound, workable bill backed up with sufficient data and information whereby the 1952 General Assembly might enact into law a measure that will assure the citizens of Kentucky honest and incorruptible elections.

Governor Wetherby did recommend a new Registration and Purgation Act to the General Assembly in 1952. The bill was opposed by many courthouse politicians and Lieutenant Governor Emerson Beauchamp. Governor Wetherby exerted pressure in its behalf, and he called Beauchamp into a private meeting when he learned that the lieutenant governor was lobbying against the bill. The General Assembly did enact the legislation. For more information see letter of March 25, 1952, pp. 65-66.

1. Lewis Cox, acting lieutenant Governor.

John Estill Reeves (1902-1978), research assistant, Kentucky Legislative Council (1937-1938); assistant state local finance officer (1938-1939); teacher, Department of Political Science, University of Kentucky (1940-1941); administrative analyst, United States Department of War (1943-1944); executive assistant, Kentucky Department of Revenue (1944-1945); became secretary of the Fayette Committee for Citizenship (1946); president of American Society of Public Administration; born in Owenton. *Who's Who in the South and Southwest, 1959,* 6th ed. (Chicago, 1959), p. 669.

VETERANS' BONUS
Letter / July 31, 1951

[To Salley Tate Evans, Hardinsburg]

In direct answer to your inquiry on my position toward a veterans' bonus, I should like to advise that the financial condition of our state government and the taxable resources of the Commonwealth will not support a bonus to Kentucky veterans without placing one in a strain and difficult position and on a dangerous and depleting footing that would lead to dire economical consequences. In addition, considering the compelling needs of Kentucky's education and welfare programs and also that the veterans and their children would be saddled with the debt which would be largely paid by themselves, I consider it to be the best interest of both the veterans and Kentucky to oppose such a measure.

1952 GENERAL ASSEMBLY
Letter / January 28, 1952

[To Taylor Berry, Mount Olivet]

DURING the past week I have received considerable mail bearing on the four general topics discussed in your communication. In this response I should like to discuss each topic briefly and shall endeavor to make my position clear and consistent with that part of the platform on which I was elected and which was further elaborated upon in my recent message to the General Assembly.

At the time the Committee on Functions and Resources advanced the proposal of state-operated retail package liquor stores, I expressed my opposition and shall continue to oppose such a move. This is based on my belief that the state should not take over any category of private enterprise and that a large majority of the people of Kentucky do not favor the state government engaging in the direct sale and distribution of alcoholic beverages.

For some time there has been a growing alarm and concern among those interested in the welfare of our people, and especially that of our youngsters as they might be affected by the narcotic traffic and the threat of drug addicts. Some time ago, at my request, the state Department of Health began studying existing law covering this matter with a view of amending it to meet the increasing evils that are associated with these illicit operations. I shall extend my full support and exert every means to secure the enactment of the needed law.[1]

The law relating to gambling in licensed taverns and specifying it as cause for suspension or revocation of the alcoholic beverage license has been considered both indefinite and inadequate. There is now pending before the legislature a bill clarifying and strengthening the authority of the board to deny or revoke licenses on this ground, and I am supporting it to the fullest possible extent.[2]

With reference to the legislation that has been introduced providing for the restoration of the county-unit local-option arrangement in voting on the question of the legal sale of alcoholic beverages in counties containing a city of the fourth class, may I say that the subject, in my opinion, involves broad and important questions of public policy. The legislative membership, in its good judgment, will accord whatever consideration is deemed right and desirable, and while I shall not in any way endeavor to influence or direct the thinking of any member on this important subject, my own actions will be guided by whatever determination is made by the General Assembly, and if a measure of this kind is passed, I shall extend approval by signing it.[3]

---

1. Any person who sold or caused to be sold, supplied, prescribed, administered, dispensed, or furnished any narcotic drug in violation of this law to a person under twenty-one years of age was guilty of a felony and fined not more than $5,000 and confined in the penitentiary for not less than twenty years, and up to life. Lesser punishment was prescribed for a first offense. *Acts of the General Assembly of the Commonwealth of Kentucky,* 1952, Chapter 120 (H.B. 62), pp. 311-13.

2. The act said that the conducting of gambling operations in or upon premises licensed under the alcoholic beverage law was of great detriment to the welfare and morals of the public, and promoted vice and crime. An emergency situation was declared to exist, hence the need to strengthen the authority to revoke a license. In 1951 Governor Wetherby had sent the state police on gambling raids to cities in northern and western Kentucky, but the situation was still prevalent. *Acts of the General Assembly of the Commonwealth of Kentucky,* 1952, Chapter 111 (H.B. 22), pp. 304-5. For more information see letters of August 27, 1951, June 9, 1952 and November 14, 1952, in the Crime section.

3. The General Assembly in 1952 did nothing about the sale of liquor in fourth-class cities.

REGISTRATION AND PURGATION LAW
Letter / March 25, 1952

[To E. Skiles Jones, Louisville]

I APPRECIATE your March 20 letter. The further along I get into the job of being governor the higher value I place on the thinking and ideas of people over the state offering suggestions which they consider to be good from the standpoint of improving state government and the promotion of Kentucky.

By and large, the reaction to the new registration and purgation law has been very favorable and I feel that as it is better understood and is placed in action even greater support and confidence will be generated among those sincerely interested in fair and honest elections in the state.

Our most immediate task is to get the new law into the hands of all county election commissions and all county court clerks and effect a cooperative and working arrangement between both, as well as with the State Election Commission and the State Purgation Board. This is a right sizable undertaking and I anticipate will require most of the time and energy of those who would necessarily have to take a leading role in directing the activity of your proposed all-out registration drive. Nevertheless, I feel that given a year's practical operation under the new law, further attention and consideration might well be devoted to greater election participation through increased registration, and I shall be glad to keep such a proposal in mind.

E. Skiles Jones (1913-), attorney, educated at the University of Louisville and Jefferson School of Law; judge, Jefferson Circuit Court, Common Pleas Branch (1970-1976); born in Louisville and resides in Anchorage. *Kentucky State Bar Association* (Louisville, 1967), p. 280.

STATE SALES TAX
Letter / April 15, 1953

[To J. L. Bowler, Berea]

SINCE news accounts of the downward trend in state revenues caught the public's interest, I have received many letters from people expressing views and ideas on both the revenue and tax sides of the problem. I appreciate hearing from you.

Those writing in favor of a sales tax or some other revenue-producing law that would provide additional money for our schools and social welfare programs very enthusiastically feel that now is the time to start serious thinking about the possibility of securing such enactments at the next session of the General Assembly. There are others, such as yourself, just as sincerely opposed to such talk and considerations.

I have endeavored all along, and shall continue to do so, to avoid either formulating definite ideas as to what should be done in this respect or making any public announcements voicing my feelings in this regard. I have repeatedly stated that I personally did not advocate any changes in our existing tax structure until such time as a discernible majority of the people of the state felt that they were willing to support education and the social welfare programs, the two largest revenue-demanding functions of state government, either through broadening and increasing the present tax structure or through the enactment of a general sales tax. This shall continue to be my policy until the matter has received much further study and consideration.

Governor Wetherby, while he held a strong personal commitment in favor of a sales tax, took this pragmatic view of its chance for enactment. In 1954 the governor tapped other sources of revenue by increasing the taxes on alcoholic beverages, cigarettes, and pari-mutuel betting. For more information see letters from March 10, 1954 and June 29, 1954, in this section.

STATE CAPITOL RENOVATION
Letter / July 15, 1953

[To Patrick Tanner, Owensboro]

A LETTER from you in the *Courier-Journal*'s Point of View on July 11 has come to my attention.[1] Your energetic interest in state government is commendable but I fear you have slashed at me without an abundance of facts. Please permit me to offer some rebuttal to your published outcry.

About two years ago, $2 million was set aside for a renovation of the State Capitol. This money is still in the treasury and is not a serious factor in our current fiscal problems. The Capitol was constructed in the early 1900s and, in those days, there was practically nothing better. In the 1950s, with most business and governmental offices modernized, I sometimes wonder how it is possible to employ folks to work in the building. In the summer the heat in the offices all but overcomes the employees. In the winter the building is difficult to heat, simple to overheat. The lavatories facilities are wretched and the drinking fountains are antiquated. Things really can be improved and we hope to do it.

If the renovation is completed, the legislature, the Research Commission, and the Statute Revision Commission, and the press will be accommodated on the third floor. The second floor will be given over completely to the Appellate Court, whose judges, commissioners, and other officials are now scattered throughout the building. The first floor will house the attorney general and his large group of assistants, the secretary of state, and the governor's office. Skilled architects and engineers are in agreement that the interior of the Capitol should be remodeled.

This administration does not contemplate recommending the levying of a sales tax. It is a good idea, however, for our citizens to explore and understand this subject. We are trying to solve fiscal situations in 1953 with a tax program largely enacted about twenty years ago. This task is anything but easy.

The withholding of the state income tax, I will admit, has been discussed seriously by our revenue officials. The chief purpose of a withholding act would be to bring all Kentucky wage earners under the state income tax, instead of just you, me, and some 150,000 others. A withholding law would be up to the legislature and, at this point, we have done nothing but discuss the project.[2]

In 1949 a special session of the General Assembly was called to give county tax commissioners all the tools necessary to equalize property assessments. The State Revenue Department stands willing to help any county bring about a more orderly and honest assessment. What is needed is initiative at the local level. If the state government, without local request, undertook to rearrange assessments, we would be accused of making Hitler look like Cinderella.

On many occasions, bills have been introduced in the legislature to reduce the number of counties. These measures always meet crushing defeat. Legislators are not prone to abolishing county governments and courthouse groups. We should have fewer counties, but it will take more than the likes of you and me to attain this objective. I give this to you as practical advice.[3]

I am trying to inform, not ruffle, you. Your letter in the *Courier-Journal* tipped me and I thought of writing to you. Your continued support is solicited.

---

1. In his letter to the editor of the *Louisville Courier-Journal* (July 11, 1953), Tanner wrote that during a time of "critical financial deficit" it was "out of order to ask for bids to remodel the capitol." He opposed Governor Wetherby's support for a retail sales tax, payroll tax deductions, and other funding methods. Tanner suggested a state law causing equalization of local property assessments. Finally, he recommended reducing from 120 to thirty-five the number of counties in order to offset operating expenses.

2. Governor Wetherby suggested the withholding of the state income tax to the General Assembly in 1954, and the assembly enacted the bill. For more information see letter from January 27, 1954, in this section.

3. For more information on the consolidation of counties see letter from July 23, 1953, in the Reorganization section.

Patrick Tanner (1917-), district official, United States Veterans Administration (1946-1953); chairman, Owensboro City Traffic and Safety Committee (1951-1952); owner of a paint and wallpaper store in Owensboro, where he resides. *Who's Who in Kentucky* (Hopkinsville, 1955), p. 332.

INCOME WITHHOLDING TAX LEGISLATION
Letter / January 27, 1954

[To Isaac Liebschutz, Louisville]

DURING the past several days viewpoints of many Kentuckians bearing on the tax program recently adopted by the General Assembly have reached this office.

My endorsement and support of the income-withholding-tax legislation was based on the belief that there are many people in Kentucky who are failing to pay their legal and fair share of their income tax obligations. This is not only grossly unfair to those citizens who are conscientious in this regard, but our educational system and other vital public functions of state certainly need any additional revenue that is owed by the taxpayers and that can be collected only by this medium.

I am asking the Revenue Department to write you in detail outlining the merits the General Assembly saw in the proposal.

This act authorized every employer making payments of wages to deduct and withhold a tax upon such wages. *Acts of the General Assembly of the*

Commonwealth of Kentucky, 1954, Chapter 79 (H.B. 21), pp. 203-45. See section 22.

Isaac Liebschutz (1900-1957), owner and manager of a bookstore; member of the Masonic Lodge and the Filson Club; born in Louisville. Telephone interview with Mrs. Helen Liebschutz, December 26, 1980.

STATE SALES TAX
Letter / March 10, 1954

[To Talton Hall, Cumberland]

YOUR communication supporting enactment of a sales tax is acknowledged. This measure was introduced early in the current session of the General Assembly. It was discussed, debated, and publicized more than any other bill before the legislature. When its advocates attempted to have the bill taken from committee and made eligible for an open vote, the pro sales tax group was defeated and, for all practical purposes, the bill was killed by this action.

Kentucky's governmental services probably need the fiscal bolstering of a sales tax. Apparently, the legislators took the view that a sales tax enacted at this time might lead to its political destruction in forthcoming elections. I predict that a sales tax is on the horizon of Kentucky and, when it is adopted, it should remain on the law books long enough for the collectors and public to learn how to administer it and to become aware of the many benefits it will bring our citizens in the form of better schools, superior law enforcement, and progressive health and welfare programs.

The sales tax of 3 percent was enacted by the General Assembly in 1960 during the administration of Governor Bert T. Combs. Governor Wetherby believed that the state needed additional revenue to provide basic and improved services and that this was the best means to get it. He encouraged Governor Combs to support the legislation even though it would be a politically unpopular act. For provisions of this act, see *Acts of the General Assembly of the Commonwealth of Kentucky,* 1960, Chapter 5 (H.B. 75), p. 16.

Talton Hall was president of the Cumberland Parent-Teacher Association.

STATE SALES TAX
Letter / June 29, 1954

[To Mrs. Lansing Hinrichs, Louisville]

If a sales tax that Kentucky enacted in 1934 had not been erased for political advantages in 1936,[1] the Commonwealth might have reached the vanguard of progressive states by now. Kentucky was among the first states to adopt a sales tax and just about the first one to have it taken away. It was gone before the state had time to learn how to administer it efficiently and before the retail collectors learned to withhold for the government the exact amounts specified by law.

Had the sales tax been given a reasonable length of trial, it probably would have been retained, especially after the people could observe the good results, and the well-being of Kentucky would be far superior to its present health.

The recent assessment raising by the State Tax Commission stems chiefly from the fact that Kentucky does not have an across-the-board sales tax. To avert financial uncertainty in several county governments, to help school districts into the Foundation Program and to bring various types of property assessments to the state average as required by law were the reasons fortifying the program of the Tax Commission. The commission did the best it could in good conscience with what it has on the law books.

The next legislature convenes in 1956. If the majority of the people desire a sales tax, they must convince those representing them in the legislature that such a tax is necessary for the support of schools, hospitals, and government and that the people are ready to tolerate it. On great and vital issues, legislators will heed the voters.

---

1. The sales tax was repealed under the first administration of Governor Albert B. Chandler (1935-1939), who opposed the tax. For provisions of the repeal, see *Acts of the General Assembly of the Commonwealth of Kentucky, 1936*, Chapter 101, pp. 320-21.

VOTE FOR EIGHTEEN-YEAR-OLDS
Letter / December 7, 1955

[To LaVerne Chapanian, Fresno, California]

ON November 8 the voters of Kentucky amended their constitution to lower the voting age from twenty-one to eighteen years of age. The amendment carried by 85,188 votes, which is substantial.[1]

Personally, I was not inclined to favor this amendment as I think higher bracket teenagers are likely to have their minds busy with problems other than those of government and good politics. However, our people have spoken, and I shall willingly abide by their mandate.

Your request for information on this amendment is being forwarded to the Legislative Research Commission. I am sure they will be glad to forward whatever data they have available for distribution.

---

1. The constitutional amendment was approved by members of the General Assembly in 1954. See *Acts of the General Assembly of the Commonwealth of Kentucky,* 1954, Chapter 2 (S.B. 13), pp. 3-4. An account of the approval of the amendment can be found in the *Louisville Courier-Journal,* November 9, 1955.

DEMOCRATIC PARTY LEADERSHIP

JEFFERSON-JACKSON DAY DINNER
Louisville / April 21, 1951

THE assignment given me is indeed an honor, yet it hardly seems necessary to introduce one of the best-loved men in America, the greatest political campaigner of the past quarter century, and a great Democrat, a spiritual disciple of Thomas Jefferson and Andrew Jackson—the men we honor tonight—and if our welcome seems to be warmer than that we usually accord our distinguished visitors I feel sure none will be offended, for it must be remembered that we are not only honoring the vice president but an illustrious son of our own beloved Commonwealth.

Kentucky has ever been a land of liberty-loving people. In every emergency our people have rallied to the forefront in defense of decency and justice. In times of peace her citizens have been loyal to the principles that make our country great and have taken on willingly obligations to make more secure the blessing of a free land.

We are proud of our accomplishments in the fields of agriculture, labor, and industry during the past eighteen years under the humane and progressive policy of Democratic administrations, and we are equally proud of the leadership furnished by Kentucky sons and daughters to the Democratic party in prompting legislation for the benefit, not of a priviliged few or a favored class, but for all Americans.

This leadership, however, is not limited to the past two decades. It is interesting to note that three leaders of national and international fame have come from the First Congressional District in Kentucky. Matthew Lyon, one of the most enthusiastic Jeffersonians of his day as a resident of Vermont and member of Congress from the state, was probably the guiding force that brought about the election of Jefferson in the House of Representatives. Taking leave of that state he moved to Kentucky and within two years was elected to Congress from our Commonwealth.

Ollie M. James was the strong right arm of Woodrow Wilson in the stirring days of World War I.

The third statesman of this trio we are privileged to have with us tonight—the iron man who was the staunch and fearless Senate leader under the matchless Franklin Delano Roosevelt during the dark depression days of the 1930s and the perilous days of World War II, one who is today working in the people's behalf and whom Kentucky sacrifices to the nation's service—Alben W. Barkley.[1]

Fellow Kentuckians, it is my distinguished honor to present the vice president of the United States, our own Alben Barkley.

---

1. Alben William Barkley (1877-1956), prosecuting attorney, McCracken County (1905-1909); judge, McCracken County (1909-1913); member, United States House of Representatives (1913-1927); member, United States Senate (1927-1949, 1954-1956); vice president of the United States (1949-1953); born in Graves County. *Who's Who in Kentucky* (Hopkinsville, Ky., 1955), p. 20.

PRIMARY ELECTION BROADCAST
Louisville / July 24, 1951

THE 1951 primary election is less than two weeks away. On May 29, the date I formally entered as a candidate, I announced that in seeking the Democratic nomination for governor a vigorous campaign would be made. Since that time I have visited every section and most of the counties. I also announced at the beginning of this campaign that my platform was based on my record as a public official, on the program now being carried out in the state government, and on additional progressive ideas I have in mind for the further advancement of Kentucky. This I have done without resorting to wild promises or leveling charges against my opponents. I do not believe in making a political race on the weakness of my opponents but rather on what I have done and propose to do. I shall continue to conduct the remainder of this campaign on the same ethical level to which I have adhered in the past.

In 1947 the people of Kentucky elected me lieutenant governor. As the law provides, I became the presiding officer of the State Senate. While serving in this capacity I assisted in the preparation of and assumed leadership responsibility for some of the most important and far-reaching legislation which the General Assembly of Kentucky ever enacted.

The hallmark of accomplishment of that 1948 session of the General Assembly rests with the rural roads legislation.[1] During the past three years, $30 million have been expended on construction and reconstruction of 3,000 miles of farm-to-market roads. Every county in Kentucky has benefited under this new road program. I am proud to be numbered among its early advocates and to have had a very substantial part in securing its enactment. If nominated and elected I pledge continued wholehearted and unconditional support to the state's rural road program.

Another step taken by the legislature in that outstanding session was the consolidation of all social welfare agencies receiving and allocating federal funds into the new state Department of Economic Security. In this same category of improving the facilities of state government to meet current demands and needs the 1948 General Assembly wisely provided for the creation of the Legislative Research Commission.[2]

The state's record in enforcing traffic laws and performing general police functions under limited authority imposed upon the old Highway Patrol was neither satisfactory nor acceptable. In 1948 a new Department of State Police was created. Its officer and trooper personnel have been carefully screened and selected. They are indeed a credit to Kentucky.[3] I shall continue to support the program developed by our State Police Department and strive always to protect its integrity and the nonpartisan status under which it functions. With proper support and assistance it can do much to make our highways safer.

Another monumental accomplishment of the 1948 legislative session was the creation of the Agricultural and Industrial Development Board dedicated to the study of Kentucky's needs and potentialities in the fields of agriculture and industry.[4] This board, composed of nine outstanding Kentuckians representing agriculture, labor, business, and education, is doing a remarkable job in directing the work of the agency so that the long-dreamed-of balanced economy between agriculture and industry might become a reality. Working in close and successful cooperation with the Kentucky Chamber of Commerce and local community promotion organizations throughout the Commonwealth, this state agency has been a prime factor in the location of industries in Kentucky which, during the past six months, have committed themselves to spend $1 billion in Kentucky.

As governor during the next four years, I shall continue to consider the work of the Agricultural and Industrial Development Board of the highest importance to the end that more wealth may be attracted into Kentucky and that our people will find at home better employment opportunities and remain within our state.

While I have enumerated some of the high points of the record of achievement, the pendulum of progress in its sweep upward has brought with it other important advancements destined to make lasting contributions to the welfare of Kentucky and her people.

For half of a century the problem of tax assessment inequities existing between individual property owners in a county and the great assessment variations between counties had been studied and talked about without a sincere effort made by anyone to remedy the existing evils. By 1949 our whole public educational system was dangerously threatened as a result of official inaction and lethargy through the years. With an eye on the pressing needs of education and a feeling of responsibility to the property owners and taxpayers of the state, the General Assembly enacted legislation for the gradual correction of property assessment in Kentucky yet preserved all of the functions and protected the sacred principle of local self-government.

One of the most beneficial pieces of legislation to Kentucky adopted during the 1950 session was the creation of the Committee on Functions and Resources of State Government. The committee is composed of twenty-three outstanding and representative citizens. It is now making a detailed study of your government with a view of determining the needs and services for Kentucky's people and how best to meet those needs. This committee will make a report for submission to the 1952 session of the legislature and will serve as a guide for the next session.

With the experience and detailed knowledge of the affairs of state government gained during the three busy and eventful years served as lieutenant governor, I succeeded to the office of governor on November 27, 1950, not as a man without knowledge of the problems and responsibilities of the office but rather one intimately acquainted with the broad program of progress already under way and with additional plans and ideas calculated to bring the greatest possible benefits and improvements yet realized. My only resolve was to furnish the people of Kentucky the kind of leadership they expected and to see that they were provided honest, efficient, and responsible government.

The right to vote is one of the most precious freedoms enjoyed by Americans. Recognizing that our registration and purgation law contained many inconsistencies and shortcomings, almost immediately I requested the Legislative Research Commission to study this problem and make recommendations to the 1952 legislature. I expect to support the recommendations offered by this commission and to advocate the enactment of a new registration and purgation law.[5]

Motivated by the principle that action speaks louder than words, I formulated a program fashioned to meet special emergency conditions brought about by a combination of forces growing out of the national preparedness program on one hand and the increased demands and responsibilities of state government to its citizens on the other.

It became evident early this year that by frugal administration of the affairs of state government and aided by the war-inflationary economy a substantial surplus could be built up by July 1. Basing my action on the best calculations offered by the Departments of Revenue and Finance, I convened the legislature in extraordinary session for the purpose of considering supplemental appropriations of $6 million additional for teachers' salaries, $2 million additional for old-age assistance benefits, aid to the needy blind, and aid to dependent children, and $1 million additional to the Department of Welfare. In addition, I recommended that legislation be enacted enabling employees of the state, counties, cities, and other governmental subdivisions to be brought under the provisions of the federal Social Security Act so that they might qualify for its old-age and survivor benefits.[6]

The manner in which this program was received by both the membership of the legislature and a vast majority of the people of Kentucky indeed reflects most favorably on its soundness. Within a period of two weeks, and with only one dissenting vote out of a combined House-Senate membership of 138, the recommendations I offered to the General Assembly became law.

The funds earmarked solely for teachers' salaries have meant an average yearly increase of $300 per teacher. This demonstrates my interest and concern toward the problems of education in Kentucky. I advocate and am pledged to support the further improvement of our school system to the maximum of available resources.

The step taken allowing state and local governmental employees the opportunity to be included under federal Social Security coverage means retirement benefits and security in old age for thousands of loyal, conscientious Kentuckians.

In securing the additional allocation for the Welfare Department I pointed out to the members of the legislature that while real progress had been made during the last several years in the building program at our penal and mental institutions, we had fallen behind in a treatment program for those confined in our mental hospitals. With funds available and with the department and its mental health operations in the experienced and capable hands of Commissioner Luther Goheen[7] and Dr. Frank Gaines, a treatment and rehabilitation program is now being developed so that many of these people can be returned to their homes to lead useful lives. I am profoundly interested in the problems of all our welfare institutions. Through the help of doctors and trained psychiatrists we are determined to elevate the status of our mental hospitals from institutions offering largely custodial care, to hospitals affording cure and rehabilitation to those patients amenable to medical treatment. We shall not spare time, effort, or available resources in carrying out this humanitarian mission.

A part of any man's record as governor of the Commonwealth will be written by officials appointed to head the state departments and agencies as well as the many other appointments the law requires. During the past eight months I have been called upon to make as many important appointments as many governors have been required to make during a full four-year term. I am proud to call your attention to the quality and caliber of men appointed during this time. Declining the opportunity to go to the United States Senate, I selected one of the most able, well-known, and esteemed Kentuckians to represent our great state in the upper house of the federal Congress, Tom Underwood.[8] The naming of Bert Combs[9] to the Court of Appeals added an eminent attorney to Kentucky's highest court. Career engineers now direct our state Highway Department and rural road program, and the same careful consideration to merit and qualifications has been devoted to the selection of other department heads whom I have appointed. This same policy is reflected in the type of men I have named to public office whether they be a justice of the peace or United States Senator.

Remarkable results have followed our efforts in developing Kentucky's tourist industry. Last year tourists spent $290 million in Kentucky. This has benefited all Kentuckians. This was no accident. It was the result of a definite plan which we promoted and which we shall continue to promote. This plan consists of the development of a complete state park system. I believe today we have one of the finest systems of state parks in the nation. During the last three years we have invested $6 million of your money in parks. This is an investment which will through the years pay dividends by increasing the tourist business. Under the leadership of Henry Ward[10] as commissioner of conservation I am sure we will make rapid strides during the next four years, and working with public-spirited citizens who have contributed so much to this program we will attain our goal of $500 million from the tourist business by 1955.

Kentucky agriculture is progressing on a sound and profitable foundation. Its full development will receive the fullest support and cooperation from the state through the Department of Agriculture. Impressive strides are now being made in grassland farming. I believe that added emphasis can be placed on our dairy and beef cattle industry, assuring greater profits to the farmer and at the same time effecting soil conservation and a land-building program essential to this and future generations.

Time this evening will not allow a discussion of other phases of state government which I shall continue to discuss during the campaign. However, the foregoing is an outline of my record and of the platform on which I seek your support and vote. I am sincerely interested in advancing Kentucky. I offer for your consideration this record of performance and this sound constructive program.

This speech was broadcast over radio station WHAS in Louisville.

1. This legislation placed an excise tax of seven cents per gallon on all gasoline sold. Two-sevenths of all amounts received were set aside for the contruction, reconstruction, and maintenance of rural and secondary roads. The fiscal courts of each county recommended to the Department of Highways the rural highway needs of said county. For provisions of the act, see *Acts of the General Assembly of the Commonwealth of Kentucky,* 1948, Chapter 45 (H. B. 195), p. 92 and Chapter 46 (H. B. 196), pp. 93-95.

2. For more information see footnotes to Inaugural Address of December 11, 1951.

3. See an Act to provide for the public safety, by creating a Department of Kentucky State Police, *Acts of the General Assembly of the Commonwealth of Kentucky,* 1948, Chapter 80 (H. B. 291), pp. 172-84.

4. See an Act creating an Agricultural and Industrial Development Board, *Acts of the General Assembly of the Commonwealth of Kentucky,* 1948, Chapter 48 (H. B. 199), pp. 98-101.

5. For more information on the Governor's support of this law see the speech from January 15, 1952, in the Legislative Messages and Statements section.

6. For the Governor's call of an extraordinary session of the General Assembly see speech from February 21, 1951, in the Legislative Messages and Statements section.

7. Luther Thornton Goheen, Sr. (1908-1969); principal of high school, Blandville (1937-1941); superintendent of Childrens Home of Kentucky, Lyndon (1941-1947); superintendent of Masonic Home, Louisville (1947-1951); commissioner of welfare (1951-1953); executive director of Louisville and

Jefferson County Community Chest (1953-1964); executive director of Korsair Home, Louisville (1964-1969); born in Birmingham. Phone interview with Luther Goheen, Jr., December 3, 1980.

8. Thomas Rust Underwood (1898-1956), general manager, editor of the *Lexington Herald* (1931-1943); secretary of Kentucky State Racing Commission (1931-1943, 1947-1948); member, Kentucky State Planning Board (1935-1939); assistant to director of Office of Economic Stabilization (1943); member, United States House of Representatives (1949-1951); member, United States Senate (1951-1953), born in Hopkinsville. Senator Underwood was defeated in 1952 by John Sherman Cooper. *Who's Who in America, 1954-1955,* 28th ed. (Chicago, 1954), p. 2719. The Senate vacancy to which Underwood was appointed was created by the death in an automobile accident of Senator Virgil Chapman on March 8, 1951. Governor Wetherby, although intrigued by the notion of holding three different positions of government in less than a year, decided to remain as governor. His decision was influenced by his family's wishes and his commitment to the people to serve out his term as governor.

9. Bert Thomas Combs (1911-), judge of Kentucky Court of Appeals (1951-1955); governor of Kentucky (1959-1963); gubernatorial candidate (1955, 1959, 1971); judge of United States Court of Appeals (1967-1970); born in Clay County and resides in Louisville. *Who's Who in America, 1974-1975,* 38th ed. (Chicago, 1974), 1:620.

10. Henry T. Ward (1909-), member, Kentucky House of Representatives (1933-1943), majority leader (1943); member, Kentucky Senate (1946-1948); commissioner of conservation (1948-1955); commissioner of highways (1960-1967); gubernatorial candidate (1967); born in New Hope and resides in Howey-in-the-Hills, Florida. George W. Robinson, ed., *The Public Papers of Governor Bert T. Combs* (Lexington, 1979), p. 188.

FALL CAMPAIGN OPENING
Shelbyville / October 4, 1951

ON May 29, 1951, I formally entered my name as a candidate for governor. At that time I announced that my platform was based on my record as a public official, on the program being carried out in the state government, and on additional progressive ideas I had in mind for the further advancement of Kentucky. After entering this race I made an active campaign throughout the state. I talked to thousands of fellow Kentuckians and discussed with them my ideas about the operation of state government.

On the first Saturday in August over 300,000 Democrats participated in our party's primary and selected me, with a record-breaking majority, as their nominee for governor.[1] Tonight, as we open our campaign for the election of the entire Democratic ticket in the November election, I would like to take this opportunity to publicly thank the many thousands of Kentuckians who expressed their confidence in me and the members of our ticket during the primary campaign, on primary day, and since we were nominated.

Since I was selected as the nominee of the Democratic party on the basis of my record and on the platform upon which I ran during the primary campaign, we intend to conduct the fall campaign in the same manner, on the same issues, and on the same program advocated then. When the members of a political party select their standard bearer in a free and open primary they have a right to expect that candidate to remain consistent to the program on which he was nominated. This I shall do.

As we open this campaign I would like to call to the attention of the voters of Kentucky and ask them to make a comparison of the ticket offered by the Democratic party and that offered by the opposing party. The background of our candidates, their training and experience, evidence their superior qualifications and personal fitness for the offices they seek.

Acree Austin is a businessman, and from his present post as Graves County circuit court clerk he is well suited to step into the position of clerk of the Court of Appeals. Herbert Tinsley, a distinguished minister of the Christian Church for many years, was a member of the Kentucky House of Representatives in the 1942, 1948, and 1950 sessions and served as Speaker and presiding officer of the House in 1948. Pearl Runyon served as deputy county court clerk of Pike County for thirteen years and as assistant secretary of state for two years. In 1949 Miss Runyon was appointed state treasurer and has acquired a working knowledge of the duties and responsibilities of this office. Ben Adams has long been a leader in agriculture and is recognized as one of Kentucky's outstanding farmers. He served as a member of the State Senate during the 1950 session and by appointment is the present commissioner of agriculture. Wendell Butler is a former Metcalfe County school superintendent and was a member of the State Senate in the 1948 and 1950 sessions. He understands the problems and needs of education on all levels. Jiggs Buckman, a prominent young lawyer, a former clerk of the Bullitt Circuit Court, a special circuit judge on numerous occasions, and a member of the House of Representatives in the 1950 session is well equipped to serve as attorney general. Charles O'Connell's experience in state government covers a period of twenty years. Having previously been secretary of state, Charlie will return to that office with an intimate knowledge of its operations. Emerson "Doc" Beauchamp, a farmer, started his career as a page in the House of Representatives, later serving as both assistant clerk and chief clerk of the Senate, Logan County court clerk, state tax commissioner, sheriff of Logan County, state director of personnel, and until recently rural highway commissioner. Few men in Kentucky history have had as varied and successful experience in public affairs as that enjoyed by Doc Beauchamp. He is admirably qualified by both training and temperament to make one of our great presiding officers of the Senate and an outstanding lieutenant governor.[2]

As you make the comparison you will see that ours is made up of men of experience, while on the other hand the ticket offered by the Republican party has little in the way of experience in government. . . .

During the regular session of 1950, I assumed an active role in securing the enactment of the new insurance code which combined in one law and into one department all of the regulatory provisions to which insurance companies operating in Kentucky must subscribe.[3] This law has given to the department the power so vitally necessary for the protection of policyholders and the regulation of rates.

A similar codification of all laws pertaining to motor transportation and common carrier activities was adopted.[4] This legislation allows the Motor Transportation Department to have hearings and fix rates in line with a fair return on the companies' investments so that utilities operating under this act cannot abuse the rights of the traveling public. . . .

Demands for additional services by the state government to its citizens are increasing. If we are to meet these demands, additional money must be provided. Who should determine what services are to be increased and how best to meet those needs? In my opinion the answer is the people. The people will answer these questions through their representatives on the Functions and Resources Committee and through their duly elected representatives and senators in the 1952 General Assembly. . . .[5]

Much of the material has been deleted here due to the fact that it is a restatement of the ideas found in the speech from July 24, 1951, in this section.

Shelbyville has been a traditional place to mark the opening of Democratic campaigns. In 1954 Alben Barkley began there his successful race for the United States Senate, while in 1955 Bert Combs began his unsuccessful race for governor. Governor Wetherby preferred it because the town had an ideal site for the rally, was situated between his native Jefferson County and the seat of state government in Franklin County, and could provide a good representation. Indeed, the governor's fifteen-minute speech was attended by bus-loads and motorcades of Democrats from all over central Kentucky. Also attending were two former governors—Albert B. Chandler and William J. Fields—two senators—Earle Clements and Tom Underwood—and several congressmen. Other party nominees spoke from the platform, including Emerson Beauchamp. Governor Wetherby was introduced by his campaign chairman, Judge Jesse Scott Lindsey of Carrollton. *Louisville Courier-Journal,* October 5, 1951.

1. Governor Wetherby won the Democratic primary by approximately 150, 000 votes. His opponent was Howell W. Vincent, an attorney and former deputy sheriff of Kenton County. *Louisville Courier-Journal,* August 5, 1951.

2. Acree Austin (1908-), Graves County, Kentucky Circuit Court Clerk (1946-1951); clerk of Court of Appeals (1951-1955); member, Young Men's Democratic Club of Graves County, born in Paducah. *Who's Who in Kentucky* (Hopkinsville, Ky., 1955), pp. 14-15.

Herbert D. Tinsley (1889-), member, Kentucky House of Representatives (1942, 1948, 1950), Speaker (1948); Kentucky state auditor (1951-1955); born in Buffalo, Missouri. Frank K. Kavanaugh, *Kentucky Directory* (Frankfort, 1952), p. 170.

Pearl Frances Runyon (1913-), chief deputy, county court clerk, Pikeville (1934-1947); assistant to secretary of state (1949-1950); Kentucky state treasurer (1949-1955); state chairman of Kentucky Women's Division, Adlai Stevenson campaign (1952); member, Democratic State Central Executive Committee; born in Belfry. *Who's Who in America, 1956-1957,* 29th ed. (Chicago, 1956), p. 2222.

Ben Adams (1914-), farm implement dealer (1938-1949); member, Kentucky Senate (1948, 1950); commissioner of agriculture (1951-1955); born in Hopkinsville. *Who's Who in Kentucky* (Hopkinsville, Ky., 1955), p. 2.

Wendell Pace Butler (1912-), member, Kentucky Senate (1948-1952); superintendent of public instruction (1952-1956, 1960-1964, 1968-1972); commissioner of agriculture (1964-1968, 1972-1976); born in Sulphur Wells and resides in Frankfort. *Who's Who in the South and Southwest, 1975-1976,* 14th ed. (Chicago, 1975), p. 99.

J. D. Buckman, Jr. (1911-), attorney; member, Kentucky House of Representatives (1950); attorney general (1952-1956); born and resides in Shepherdsville. Frank K. Kavanaugh, *Kentucky Directory* (Frankfort, 1952), p.170.

Charles O'Connell (1904-1957), deputy clerk, Kentucky Court of Appeals (1929-1932), clerk (1936-1944, 1948-1951, 1956-1957); secretary of state (1944-1948, 1952-1956); born in Frankfort. *Who's Who in the South and Southwest,* 1956, 5th ed. (Chicago, 1956), p. 665.

Emerson Beauchamp (1899-1971), assistant clerk, clerk of Kentucky Senate (1920-1924); county clerk, Logan County (1926-1932); member, State Tax Commission (1932-1935); sheriff, Logan County (1938-1941); chief clerk,

Kentucky Senate (1946); director, Department of Personnel (1947); rural highway commissioner (1948-1951); lieutenant governor of Kentucky (1951-1955); born in Logan County, Kentucky. Frank Kavanaugh, *Kentucky Directory* (Frankfort, 1952), p. 169.

3. *Acts of the General Assembly of the Commonwealth of Kentucky,* 1950, Chapter 21 (H.B. 116), pp. 52-312.

4. *Acts of the General Assembly of the Commonwealth of Kentucky,* 1950, Chapter 63 (H.B. 258), pp. 364-98.

5. Governor Wetherby's Republican opponent was Eugene R. Siler of Williamsburg. Siler had been elected to the Kentucky Court of Appeals in November 1945. Siler was a religious fundamentalist who emphasized morality in politics and the central role of the Bible in life. The fact that Governor Wetherby, a Methodist, was married to a Catholic, interjected a religious issue into the campaign. However, Siler's call for the enactment of the sales tax may have hurt him with the electorate. In the November election Wetherby received 346,345 votes to Siler's 288,014. The slate of Democratic candidates listed in this speech was elected as well. The relatively close vote may be due to the fact that Wetherby was associated with the city of Louisville, and that was considered a handicap in rural Kentucky, where suspicions and prejudices abounded against the state's largest city. Governor Wetherby was always quick to note that he was born in Middletown.

ALBEN W. BARKLEY NOMINATION FOR PRESIDENT
Typescript / July 1952

The candidate I propose for you tonight will clear the atmosphere of this convention, which is blessed with a wealth of willing and qualified aspirants to the Democratic nomination for President. The health of our party is dramatically shown by the several honorable public servants who want to lead our nation to greater and more comfortable heights. We are not beset with or dismayed by the clash of two irreconcilable factions such as battled here three weeks ago before a nation aghast by their slick factional tactics and the blunt news that money turned the trick.

The candidate I propose has been a central figure in national affairs since 1913, when he first served as a congressman in the long, hard, yet steady and successful fight for the security and prosperity our citizens so abundantly enjoy today.

While others may aspire to the presidency, our candidate is the only one who has genuinely earned the right to be the most important man in the government of this nation and the world. You know him as the man who served as Senate Majority Leader longer than any other individual in the history of our party and country. You know him as the chief legislative architect of the progressive and important social and economic programs that constitute the gibralter foundation upon which our party stands. In the last five Democratic conventions you recall him as permanent chairman and four times as keynote speaker. In 1948, at Philadelphia, you remember him as the fighting champion of Democratic principles. As a result of that oration you witnessed a change in party attitude—from despair to enthusiasm—from defeat to victory.

In his acceptance appearance on this platform he will again electrify the nation and will chisel in bold epitaph on the tombstone of the Republican Party its departing memory—"Died while running backwards." When nominated he will launch a vigorous, fiery campaign. He will make the Republicans sorry they ever seriously considered, no matter how ineptly or shabbily, to attempt to win the presidency.

The man we shall nominate here set aside his duties in Washington last year and came back to Kentucky, as he always has, to participate in our general election. Since 1923 he has made ten speeches on the day before the election, but last year he topped this performance by delivering twelve. A few days after the election he appeared in Korea befriending and encouraging our troops at the front lines. As a member of the team that carried us to victory in 1948, you shook hands with him on the West Coast. You loved his smile and applauded his humor on the East Coast. The great Midwest acclaimed him as a favorite son, and the South shared him as one of its own.

His box score as a candidate is the envy of every office holder. In Kentucky, he has made twelve major races—seven for Congress, four for the Senate, and one for vice president. The record shows that he won an average of seventy-two of each one hundred Kentucky voters in all these contests. With matchless skill and patience he has presided four years over the Senate. He is a legislator and parliamentarian without modern equal. The abilities and prestige he brought to the vice presidency have changed the heretofore impotent office into one of the most important policy-making posts in the federal government. Future vice presidents will become key men in government and individuals in history books because of the new vitality he has bestowed upon this office.

Enriched and ripened to full maturity by piloting the ship of state through the choppy waters of the past four years as second in command, he has a record of performance that supports the contention of his friends across the land that he will carry into the White House a genius for government and leadership unsurpassed in the annals of American history. Reflection on and consideration of this unparalleled record of service fortify me in the belief that our party, our country, and the free world cannot afford to deprive this generation of his wise counsel, strong leadership, and proven ability in civil government.

Government is not taxes for the military alone. Government is roads, schools, hospitals, public power projects, farm support, regulation where needed of working conditions and wages, social security, guaranteed bank deposits, guarding the growth of human rights, trade agreements, and the mandate to think about and enact programs for the betterment and welfare of the citizenry. The candidate I shall nominate understands all phases of government.

Aware of the solemnity of the times, with confidence bolstered by the indomitable will of our people and the strength and capacity of our free institutions, I believe I voice the feeling of the majority of the citizens when I say that they want and rightfully expect this convention to nominate a man whom they know, respect, and can support. The callous disregard the Republican Party has already shown for these basic considerations in the selection of a nominee, has created within its ranks a gulf across which a vast majority of their members cannot span and will not try. Let our standard bearer be one of the people. Nominate one whose great governmental principles and philosophies are known to every citizen of voting age. Select a candidate who is able and, most important of all, willing to tell the American people what his labors in the past have meant to them and what his program is for the future. Pick a man capable of drawing out of the reactionary and traditionally mum Republican candidate his real attitude and concrete position on the great domestic and world issues that personally affect every living American and the generations yet unborn. In my opinion these are some of the factors and questions with which our people are concerned.

The Democratic Party is so appropriately identified as the party of the people that I like to think of this great assemblage as a convention *of* the people. Therefore, let us give expression to their interests and aspirations.

Conscious of the unprecedented responsibilities reposed in you as delegates, I know you are going through a soul-searching experience endeavoring to find the right, the best candidate for president of the

United States. As a delegate and as a speaker before this great convention, I am doubly conscious of my responsibilities. Humble but proud, solemn yet enthusiastic, I say that you need no longer search your hearts or burden your mind for a great candidate, a winning candidate.

I offer in nomination the most illustrious gentleman in America, the "Veep," Vice President Alben W. Barkley.

Governor Wetherby led the Kentucky delegation to the Democratic National Convention at Chicago. He was personally committed to Barkley for the presidential nomination. This speech was not delivered to the convention because Barkley persuaded Wetherby not to give it, recognizing that he had no chance for the nomination. Barkley withdrew his name from contention on July 21, 1952, and accused labor union leaders of opposing his nomination. However, against his wishes, Senator Thomas C. Hennings, Jr. (1903-1960), of Missouri did place Barkley's name before the convention on July 24. Without preparations a ten-minute demonstration followed. Barkley received 67.5 delegate votes on the third ballot, including Wetherby's and the twenty-six Kentucky delegation votes. *Louisville Courier-Journal,* July 25-26, 1952.

TEARS FOR THE JEFFERSONIAN DEMOCRATS
Louisville / January 1953

THE new year is just under way. The current semester is reaching conclusion. Our classroom experience, I think, has been both interesting and informative and our teacher ever so helpful and understanding. Considered from the standpoint of "time" in reflection to both the year 1953 and as it applies to our educational journey, we should at once reflect with pleasure and peer into the future with confidence. This I am doing. No better proof could be offered than through a frank discussion of today's subject. While oratorical shortcomings and knowledge limitation prevent as full a treatment of this lofty and serious topic as it deserves, I do feel deeply about its importance.

"Tears for Jeffersonian Democrats" is a little phrase that has almost reached nationwide slogan proportions. It is now new, just better advertised through the miracles of radio and television. I deny that it has more meaning or validity than in past decades. Those who now profess alarm at this unfound thesis have simply fallen victim to the shrewd technique of mass propaganda.

For the sake of understanding let us pull this phrase from the context of history, politics, and philosophy and examine it under the more worldly light of purpose and effect. The first and most apparent feature of this demographic subject is that Americans generally and Democrats especially once had something great and governmentally wonderful, and as they watched this priceless heritage slipped right from under their noses. It is this idea to which I am vehemently opposed. It is the political capital that has been made by those opposed to the party Jefferson founded and this propaganda barrage against which I speak out.

Wishing to avoid the colorless web of crosscurrents that are commonly thought of in the fields of political theory and philosophy, I shall keep mainly at the task of laying bare the real reasons behind the incessant cry that the great ideals of Jefferson have been betrayed. Permit me however, if you will, and I trust that we are all in substantial agreement, to say that Thomas Jefferson represented the noblest ideals of the American Revolution and of the New Republic. The author of the Declaration of Independence, he was a profound scholar and prolific writer and thinker. His talents and accomplishments have few equals in recorded history. As governor of Virginia, secretary of state, and president of the United States, he stands out as one of our foremost political leaders. Stemming from his intellect and public-service experience Jefferson welded together his views and ideas into a systematized pattern that found expression through a political party. The cornerstone of Jefferson's philosophy and the basic platform of his party rested on individual liberty and unlimited respect for and confidence in the common man. His concern for the common welfare was sacred. It was as symbolic of Jefferson and his party as big business and monopolistic enterprise was of Mark Hanna[1] and William McKinley.

Much has been made of Jefferson's statement that the least government was the best government. Believing as he did that the rights of both individuals and property owners had to be protected and that democratic government was the only mechanism by which this could be done, who can doubt that he was thinking in relative terms? Measured in terms of wealth, population, and scope of responsibility, acknowledged even by Senator Taft[2] that only minor adjustments can be made both as to government spending and reduction of federal employees, only a doubting Thomas would hold that Jefferson would abhor the size of present government.

Recognizing the importance of farmers and farming to the nation, Jefferson contended that special means and effort had to be made to develop the soundest possible agriculture program. The economic security and well-being of those who labor in overalls received his sympathetic attention. Business and commerce were encouraged to flourish, with the resultant wealth benefiting all who helped in its creation.

This is only a partial and brief summary of Jefferson's pronouncements on matters of government and public policy. But they sufficiently represent a cross section to establish a trend of thought or a route to follow. And as the pages of history are turned, we find leaders of the Democratic Party guided and inspired by the sage of Monticello. We find the Democratic Party subscribing more and not less to the principles which he laid down. Who would have the effrontry, yea the gall, to exclude any one of these great Americans, great Democrats, and faithful followers, confirmed disciples of Jefferson—Andrew Jackson, Grover Cleveland, William Jennings Bryan, Woodrow Wilson, Al Smith, Franklin Roosevelt, Harry Truman, Adlai Stevenson.[3] Read in history the views and accomplishments of these earlier leaders and note how closely they parallel the teachings of Jefferson. Recall to mind how closely the footsteps of Jefferson have been followed by the immortal F. D. R., our courageous Harry Truman, and our brilliant Adlai Stevenson.

I say there is a continuity of thought and ideal, policy program, and record of performance as characteristic of the Democratic Party, and starting from Jefferson, as there is one of the Republican Party stretching from Hamilton to Bob Taft. The New Deal and Fair Deal, coping with problems of finance and agriculture, labor and race relations, war and peace, selfish interest as against the general welfare, have brought the practical and modern meaning to true Jeffersonian Democracy.

If these things be true, then, and I sincerely believe them to be, I say what manner of men echo this false and misleading doctrine? I assure you the only tears they shed are of the crocodile variety.

It is uncertain when this speech was delivered if, indeed, it ever was. Governor Wetherby believed that it was given at a Jefferson-Jackson Day dinner held at the Seelbach Hotel. However, the *Louisville Courier-Journal* does not mention the fact. It may be that the speech was written and then not delivered due to some need to cancel, such as inclement weather.

1. Marcus Alonzo Hanna (1837-1904), American industrialist and political leader. A follower of Senator John Sherman, he helped to elect William McKinley governor of Ohio in 1891 and president of the United States in 1896. Born in New Lisbon, Ohio, he went into the coal, iron, and shipping business on Lake

Erie. He served as a United States senator, 1897-1904. *Encyclopedia Americana* (Danbury, Conn., 1979), 13:772.

2. Robert Alphonso Taft (1889-1953), member, Ohio House of Representatives (1921-1926), majority leader (1925), Speaker (1926); member, Ohio State Senate (1931-1932); member, United States Senate (1946-1953); candidate for Republican presidential nomination (1940, 1948, 1952); born in Cincinnati, Ohio. *Encyclopedia Americana* (Danbury, Conn., 1979), 26:221.

3. William Jennings Bryan (1860-1925), United States House of Representatives (1890-1894); Democratic candidate for president of the United States (1896, 1900, 1908); secretary of state (1913-1915); born in Salem, Illinois. *Encyclopedia Americana* (Danbury, Conn., 1979), 4:662-63.

Alfred E. Smith (1873-1944), New York State assemblyman (1903-1915), Speaker of the Assembly (1913); New York County sheriff (1915-1917); president of New York City Board of Aldermen (1917-1918); governor of New York (1918-1928); Democratic candidate for president of the United States (1928); president of Empire State, Inc., a corporation that erected and operated the Empire State Building; born in New York City. *Encyclopedia Americana* (Danbury, Conn., 1979), 25:54-55.

Adlai E. Stevenson (1900-1965), delegate to United Nations (1946-1947); governor of Illinois (1948-1952); Democratic nominee for president of the United States (1952, 1956); ambassador to the United Nations (1961-1965); born in Los Angeles. *Encyclopedia Americana* (Danbury, Conn., 1979), 25:706-7.

UNITED MINE WORKERS LABOR DAY MEETING
Pikeville / September 6, 1954

It is something of a thrill to stand before this impressive throng on a day that means so much to organized labor and the working man. It is difficult to refrain from recalling that twenty or twenty-five years ago many of us would have had to draw upon an extra supply of courage to appear at a labor rally in public.

This assemblage and the dignitaries present are symbolic of the progress organized labor has achieved. Labor has come from bloodshed, tyranny, secrecy and setbacks into an accepted and vital part of American economic, industrial, and political society. Always in the vanguard of labor's long fight for respect and recognition have been the United

Mine Workers of America. You have not only brought about safer working conditions and reasonable wages; you have provided leadership in government and have helped Americans toward a plane of living that is the envy of almost all the world. True Americans are thankful for what organized labor has done directly and indirectly for all people.

I regret to say that within the past few years hard times have returned to eastern Kentucky. Your state government is seriously aroused about the plight of many people in the Big Sandy Valley. When part of Kentucky is lagging economically, our whole state feels the impact. Your problems are difficult to remedy through the facilities of state government. But the following facts must show that your state government is doing all it can to help you.

A high percentage of the public assistance funds distributed through agencies at Frankfort is sent into eastern Kentucky in the form of old-age pensions, aid to dependent children, and the needy blind. Many of your school districts receive substantial supplemental financial aid to keep your schools on a par with urban institutions. Your roads have posed problems that have baffled many state administrations, but roads are now better and more numerous than ever. Survey groups from the state Agricultural and Industrial Development Board have been in this area compiling data aimed at attracting new industry to eastern Kentucky. Congressional committees are continuously encouraged by the state to endorse canalization projects.

The state government does not desire to be complimented for this work. Democratic government is designed to help people who find it difficult, if not impossible, to help themselves. That is our duty and we have performed it with eagerness.

The federal government has been alerted again and again that economic conditions in eastern Kentucky are in serious sickness. This is the area the nation looks to for fuel and manpower in times of military crisis. But to date the federal government has shown little interest in bringing relief or new work into the Big Sandy. Perhaps this is because the present national administration seems primarily concerned with the welfare of millionaires.

The people have a peaceable recourse to bring about the things they want. It is a simple little event known as election day. Most of the time the people use this day with a wisdom that stuns smart politicians.

Just a few weeks ago, a Democratic primary was held here in the Seventh Congressional District. Democrat Carl Perkins[1] of Knott County has represented this district since 1948 with an energy and diligence that amazes his friends. Carl consistently votes for measures benefiting the welfare of miners. He is probably the best legislative friend organized labor has ever had. Carl has been tireless in his fight for the betterment of eastern Kentucky. His opponent in this primary contest chose to fight Carl by denouncing the state administration and me.[2] It was confusing at times to know whether Carl's opponent was running for an office in Frankfort or a Congressional seat in Washington. Carl won by a handsome majority. He carried every county in the district. It must be a genuine pleasure for the United Mine Workers to know that so many Democrats in this district supported him.

The state administration was attacked vigorously by Carl's opponent. The majority he received is rendered heartening to me and I am grateful that the Democrats of the Seventh District had that confidence in this administration. I have every confidence in the people of this district voting to return Carl to Congress in November.

I also have confidence in the outcome of another election—the race for the United States Senate in Kentucky this fall. The contest will be in the national political limelight. I vouch for this by the number of political writers and experts from all over the country who have been in my office for interviews and opinions. A Democratic victory in this election will be a great lift to Democrats in the United States and to all people yearning for freedom.

The Democratic candidate is here with us on the platform and in a few minutes you will have an opportunity to hear and see why Kentuckians should return this great American to a place of leadership in the legislative affairs of the nation. There are numerous reasons to be proud of him. His experience in the Congress has equipped him to apply skilled reasoning to the national and international problems confronting Washington. His record reflects many years of warm interest in the welfare of people. He is a fighter, a good candidate, and gives one a fresh feeling of patriotism in supporting him. He is as lovable and cheerful as ever.

Some Republicans cry that his age is a handicap. But when we send him back to his seat in the Senate, he will find himself among able colleagues who have seen more sunsets than he has. The Republicans are scraping through the bottom of the barrel if his birthdays are the only criticism they can level at him. Why the Republicans don't even believe themselves. His opponent will conduct a campaign fat with money, most of it from outside Kentucky. The Republicans have already announced they will ship into Kentucky a parade of backslappers and big business cheerleaders. They will be here in force to tell the voters of Kentucky how friendly and intimate the Republican candidate is with the president, how necessary the Republican candidate[3] is toward helping the "Team" carry out the "Program." What team? What program? The Republicans themselves seem to have carried the program out to the dressing room for burial.

Kentuckians have a grand chance this November to restore their national political standing to its rightful heights. This will be accomplished by returning the Veep to the Senate with a vote majority that will astonish the Republicans and gladden America.

I cherish the honor of presenting to you—Alben W. Barkley.

---

1. Carl Perkins (1912-), commonwealth attorney from the Thirty-first District (1939); member, Kentucky General Assembly (1940); Knott County attorney (1941-1948); member, United States House of Representatives (1948-). He resides in Hindman and Washington, D.C. Hambleton Tapp, ed., *Kentucky Lives: The Blue Grass State Who's Who* (Hopkinsville, Ky., 1966), pp. 189-90.

2. Carl Perkins defeated James Wine in the Democratic primary on August 7, 1954, by a margin of 3 to 1. Mr. Wine was a Pikeville attorney and former United States commissioner. *Louisville Courier-Journal,* August 8, 1954.

3. The Republican candidate for the United States Senate was incumbent Senator John Sherman Cooper.

POLITICAL ADDRESS
Radio / November 1, 1954

LADIES and gentlemen of the radio audience, I have never been more serious and sincere about anything in my life than I am tonight in making this appeal to you that you do everything in your power tomorrow to help elect Alben W. Barkley and the other nominees of the Democratic party.

It is my considered conviction that the state of Kentucky can never solve alone many of the complex problems which face it and its citizens. There are problems which extend beyond state boundary lines and the ability of the state to meet. They must receive the attention of the federal government if they are to be answered, and I know that it is important to have men like Mr. Barkley and the Democratic nominees for Congress in office at Washington to guarantee that those problems will receive the proper attention.

Unemployment is pressing heavily upon Kentucky now. We have our own jobless in the coal fields, in the railroad industry, and in many other fields, and on top of that we have countless thousands of Kentuckians back home now because they were laid off in the automobile and other plants of Michigan and other northern states. The unemployment problem has not been more serious in Kentucky since the days of the Hoover administration. Yet all we get from the present administration at Washington is a suggestion that the jobless be patient and the situation will iron itself out, or a proposal like that of Defense Secretary Wilson[1] that the jobless go out like bird dogs and scratch for their own food. It takes human warmth and understanding to cope with problems such as unemployment, and I am convinced that the Republican administration now entrenched at Washington lacks both such warmth and understanding.

It took the Democratic administration of Franklin D. Roosevelt to pull us out of the Hoover depression, and it will take another Democratic program at Washington to put us back on the road to economic stability and full employment now.

In the fields of education, flood control, major highway construction, and several other areas Kentucky needs the cooperation of the federal government if desirable objectives are to be achieved.

Every dime available to state government in Kentucky could be appropriated for education and we still would be below the national levels necessary for a sound educational program. Federal aid for education is the answer. The present Republican administration is against such aid. President Eisenhower has declared himself against it. His secretary of health, education, and welfare, Mrs. Oveta Hobby,[2] is opposed to federal aid. Senator Barkley stands firmly for federal assistance. In a strong statement made October 23, at Bowling Green, he declared: "If Kentucky is to keep pace with her sister states and the educational opportunities offered her children are to compare favorably with those of other states, assistance through federal aid to education is needed. The federal government ought to recognize a national obligation in this field and proceed forthwith to meet it."

Kentucky has more miles of navigable streams than any other state, and therefore it has great flood problems and yet great potential through the full development of its water resources. Democratic administrations of Roosevelt and Truman gave Kentucky an average of $18 million a year for these programs, but expenditures under Eisenhower have dropped to a third of that annually. Mr. Barkley took the lead for Kentucky when he was in the Senate and as vice president. Let us return him to help again in these fields.

Senator Barkley was one of the early pioneers in the movement for good roads, and supports strong federal aid for state programs.

Mr. Barkley today concluded a vigorous campaign. This will be the eleventh address he will have made today. He should win tomorrow, and he will win with your help.

I would like to present to you now a man with first-hand information as to why Senator Barkley is needed again at Washington. He is United States Senator Earle C. Clements.

---

1. Charles Erwin Wilson (1890-1961), vice president of General Motors concentrating on labor relations and production planning (1929-1939); president, General Motors (1941-1953); secretary of defense (1953-1957); born in Minerva, Ohio. *Encyclopedia Americana* (Danbury, Conn., 1979), 29:2.

2. Oveta Culp Hobby (1905-   ), parliamentarian, Texas House of Representatives (1926-1931); executive vice president and editor of the *Houston Post* (1938-1942); director, Women's Auxiliary Army Corps (1942-1945); secretary of health, education, and welfare (1953-1955); born in Killeen, Texas. She became chairman of the board of the *Houston Post* in 1965. *Encyclopedia Americana* (Danbury, Conn., 1979), 14:263.

CAMPAIGN ISSUES PRESENTED ON RADIO AND TELEVISION
Louisville / November 1, 1954

RADIO and television station WHAS[1] has kindly given the Democratic party this half hour to present the issues of this campaign, as was accorded the Republican party last Friday. On behalf of Senator Barkley, the Congressional nominees, and the entire Democratic party, I extend our appreciation.

The president, Vice President Nixon, Senator Dirksen,[2] Republican House Speaker Joe Martin,[3] and others equally acquainted with Kentucky, our people, and our problems have descended upon us for the purpose of telling us how to vote.

The other and brighter side of this contest centers around Kentuckians and Kentucky problems, apprehension, and hopes. I am a proud and loyal Kentuckian first and a political partisan second. As governor, my knowledge and interest in what is best for our state are founded on wide experience and detailed and intimate association with every county and community within our border. There is no segment of our society or phase of our economy foreign to my personal and official knowledge. This insight into our problems is gained by working for you and with you toward advancing Kentucky. It is not acquired by a hurried one to twenty-four hour plane trip. By what authority would I speak to the voters of Massachusetts, Illinois, or California other than to blindly urge them to lay aside the issues, forget their problems, ignore their best interests, and vote the party label. I have not, and I shall not, be guilty of such personal arrogance and ruthless partisanship. Yet these men dropping in from the sky have attempted to tell the people of Kentucky who is best suited to represent Kentucky in the United States Senate. Beware of their tidings, for they speak from a pedestal too high to comprehend our needs. They seek to lead blindly.

I am not before this radio and television audience as a stranger. You know of my role in the affairs of this state day by day and year by year. I feel my experience and tireless effort to push Kentucky forward equip me with a degree of knowledge of what is needed to continue advancing the welfare of our citizens and the improvement and development of our material resources. I feel competent to judge the character, ability, and capacity of individuals occupying high positions of leadership and responsibility if our people are to be best served.

To every citizen of our state, and with deep convictions and all sincerity, I proclaim Alben W. Barkley the greatest candidate for the Senate in this state or in any other. He is without a peer in all America. He is recognized in every city and state of this land as one of the half-dozen great international leaders of the twentieth century.

How did this acclaim, respect, and admiration attach to the name of Alben Barkley? Was it the nobleness of his heart? Was it the friendly humility of his smile? Was it his unimpeachable integrity? Was it the genius of his mind? He is blessed with all of these rich attributes in great abundance. But even more his towering name stands out as a symbol of service and performance for every man, woman, and child in America.

The record of Senator Barkley in the halls of the federal Congress is so monumental and far-reaching as to be without parallel comparison in American history. Only scholars of future decades can enumerate the massive impact and contribution he has made toward mankind's efforts for peace, freedom, prosperity, and security.

I remind the people of Kentucky that Senator Barkley is chiefly responsible, and we should give some credit to him even though his modesty abhors a claiming type campaign, for the great laws passed by Congress under President Franklin Roosevelt. Business and industry should not overlook what the Securities and Exchange Commission Act, Reciprocal Trade Act, and Federal Deposit Insurance Act have meant to your growth and prosperity. Farmers must not forget nor become apathetic toward the great program nurtured through Congress by Senator Barkley. I am convinced another Republican-controlled Congress will abolish, amend, repeal, and strangle the agricultural program, until farmers of this state and nation are again forced into bankruptcy and serfdom. The farsightedness and fighting spirit of a small group in Congress, numbered among which was Senator Barkley, initiated the great TVA development and the REA electrical system. I consider each of these important agencies to be in danger of dissolution if allowed to be directed by hostile hands. The lip service support offered these two programs so vital to Kentucky's welfare by Senator Cooper[4] is not enough. I say to the people in the TVA area and to the thousands of REA users the mighty voice of Alben Barkley is needed now.

No President, whether Republican or Democrat, would dare keep this fearless warrior cooling his heels in a White House anteroom while other Dixons and Yates[5] feast on the inside, devouring the wealth and resources of our state and nation.

The rights of labor have a champion in Senator Barkley. Who has contributed more to the security of the aged through Social Security? He has helped pass legislation to benefit all types of unfortunates among our citizens. Aged needy, dependent children, needy blind, and other groups of our people so long neglected were rescued from the brink of starvation by the wide range of social welfare legislation which he so magnificently steered through Congress.

Now contrast if you will some of the things he stands for, and will so forceably advocate upon the convening of the new Congress in January, with the claims of his opponents and of the national administration. Their technique of catchy phrases and platitudes, sometimes humorous, sometimes sad, but always dangerous, can best be summed up as a kind of government by advisory commissions that will hide out for months and then turn up with vague and empty-handed reports to be filed and forgotten. How illuminating his record will be compared to the fumbling, indecisive, foot-in-mouth kind of operation now being conducted in Washington.

Is it enough for those of you who are unemployed, and those of you who are certain to fall victim to this plague unless something is done, for the Republican administration to offer apologies, and sympathy, and distant hope? Conversation of this sort was all the Republicans offered the unemployed in the last depression. For the unemployed who cannot remember or have forgotten that era I ask, "Are you getting any more than that from the Republicans of 1954?" And with the Old Guard becoming stronger and more firmly entrenched in Washington with each passing day, I ask what kind of imagination it would take to assume that they are going to do more for you in the future than they have in the past?

Senator Barkley moved boldly and wisely in attacking this internal threat to our people and our economy, and as your representative in the United States Senate will speak out and act decisively again.

The farmers of this state who took President Eisenhower's word literally about agricultural parity and, placing full faith and credit in the Republican platform of 1952, voted for the Republican candidates for office, will have in Senator Barkley a spokesman who will cause the national administration to revise its farm program to meet your pressing needs or will assist his like-minded members of Congress in passing their own sound program—Secretary Benson, Senator Aiken notwithstanding.[6]

The Republican platform of 1952, in an effort to proselyte the labor vote from their normal Democratic voting habits, pledged to rewrite the labor laws so they would be fair to both labor and management. Not one act was passed in either session of the Republican-controlled Congress. Senator Barkley will work and fight for these needed revisions.

The concept of strength through weakness in providing for our Army, Navy, and Air Force will be called forcefully to the attention of the American people by Senator Barkley. During these times, when even the Republican isolationists of the country admit that an attack by Russia is as imminent as a handful of fanatics in the Kremlin may decide, I ask the people of Kentucky if reducing our armed strength isn't dangerous, foolhardy, and indefensible? Senator Barkley will strive to reverse this trend.

Senator Barkley and a Democratic Congress will vote to cancel the infamous Dixon-Yates contract. The Republican administration cannot silence his voice nor use a political caucus to lasso him into inaction on this vital issue as they will his opponent.

With Alben Barkley in the United States Senate, Kentucky and the nation will have one of the strongest advocates of a bipartisan foreign policy. The communist countries of the world do not distinguish in their dislike for Americans on the basis of whether they are Democrats or Republicans. There has not been a single responsible Democrat taken into the higher councils in our foreign policy development since the Republicans took office. The nation's unity of purpose at home and resoluteness in our diplomatic struggles abroad for freedom and peace cannot be geared to maximum effectiveness until the traditional plank in our foreign affairs that politics stops at the water's edge is again put into practical application. The record and attitude of Senator Barkley in this regard is brought into sharp focus when it is recalled that he recommended Senator Cooper as a member of this country's delegation to the United Nations.

In these few minutes I have mentioned only some of the many accomplishments, interests, and records of Kentucky's beloved Veep. His long life, boundless energy, and brilliant intellect have been dedicated to our needs and problems. I feel more secure, more confident, more enthusiastic about the future of myself and my children knowing that his firm, experienced hand will again be helping guide the destiny of our state and nation. I urge you to vote tomorrow. I also urge that you vote for Senator Barkley and a Democratic Congress.

---

1. Governor Wetherby was the first Kentucky chief executive to use extensively the new facility of television as a means to campaign and to inform.

2. Everett McKinley Dirksen (1896-1969), member, United States House of Representatives (1933-1948); member, United States Senate (1951-1969); born in Pekin, Illinois. *Encyclopedia Americana* (Danbury, Conn., 1979), 9:156.

3. Joseph William Martin, Jr. (1884-1968), member, Massachusetts House of Representatives (1911-1914); member, Massachusetts State Senate (1914-1917); member, United States House of Representatives (1925-1967), Speaker (1947-1949, 1953-1955), minority leader (1939-1947, 1949-1953, 1955-1959); born in North Attleboro, Massachusetts. Eleanor W. Schoenebaum, ed., *Political Profiles: The Eisenhower Years* (New York, 1977), pp. 414-15.

4. John Sherman Cooper (1901-), member, Kentucky General Assembly (1928-1930); judge, Pulaski County (1930-1938); circuit judge, 28th Judicial District of Kentucky (1946); member, United States Senate (1947-1948, 1952-1955, 1957-1973); U.S. Delegate to General Assembly of United Nations (1949-1951); ambassador to India (1955-1956) and to the German Democratic Republic (1974-1976); born in Somerset, resides there and in Washington, D.C. *Who's Who in America, 1982-1983*, 42nd ed. (Chicago, 1982), 1:667.

5. The Dixon and Yates issue arose from the public versus private power controversy. It began with the Eisenhower administration pondering a request from TVA for increased appropriations to build a power plant to serve the Memphis, Tennessee area. Eisenhower's advisors came up with a complex plan for two private utilities (headed by Messrs. Dixon and Yates) to supply power through a contract with the AEC. This led to a full-scale battle in the Congress which continued into the 1954 Congressional elections. The SEC approved the financing of the Dixon-Yates project, but the state of Tennessee opposed it. The conflict spread to several governmental agencies. It was suggested that Memphis build its own power plant; it did so and the government cancelled the Dixon-

Yates contract. A conflict of interest issue was raised in connection with the work which Adolphe Wenzell of the First Boston Corporation performed as a consultant for the Budget Bureau, and the government did not pay the cancellation costs. The Democrats considered this issue to be an attack upon TVA. Aaron Wildavsky, *Dixon-Yates: A Study in Power Politics* (New Haven, Conn., 1962), pp. vii-viii.

6. Ezra Taft Benson (1899-), with the University of Idaho's extension service in agriculture (1929-1938); executive secretary to the National Council of Farmer Cooperatives (1939-1944); member-chairman of the board of trustees of the American Institute of Cooperation (1952-1953); secretary of agriculture (1953-1961); born in Whitney, Idaho. Benson sought to reduce the federal role in agriculture and to modify existing price-support policies. His measures failed to stimulate farm prices and aroused bitter controversy. *Encyclopedia Americana* (Danbury, Conn., 1979), 3:557.

George David Aiken (1892-), member, Vermont House of Representatives (1933-1935), Speaker (1933-1935), lieutenant governor (1935-1937), governor (1937-1941); member, United States Senate (1941-1975); born in Dummerston, Vermont. *Encyclopedia Americana* (Danbury, Conn., 1979), 1:366.

PRIMARY CAMPAIGN SPEECH
Spring 1955

ALTHOUGH Chandler professes to have such a poor memory that he cannot remember Judge Combs' name, he should not delude himself that others are similarly afflicted. There are thousands of Kentucky voters today who are too young to remember the Chandler administration[1] of the thirties and consequently have nothing on which to base comparisons of the charges that Chandler is leveling at the present administration with accepted practices of his administration. He would have you believe that during that period state government was "sober," "graft-free," and all state employees were given complete freedom in political matters. However, there are thousands of others who do remember his regime very vividly—a fact which Chandler greatly deplores. In reviewing the statements of his campaign addresses, only one consistent policy is advanced by Chandler in all sections of the state: "Do as I say, not as I have done."

In his speech at Lexington on June 27, Chandler stated that he had been told that state employees in eastern Kentucky got two days off and two days pay for attending the Combs' opening in Shelbyville. The deliberate vagueness of that statement presents no basis on which it can be proved or denied. True, a number of interested state employees attended the Shelbyville opening, which was scheduled at 7:30 P.M. on June 2, the day before a legal Kentucky holiday on which all state, county and municipal offices, as well as banks, were closed. For the record, no state offices were closed and no work of any state agency was curtailed so that employees might attend that meeting; also, no state-owned automobiles were used for transportation.

Chandler would like you to believe that employees of the present administration are the first to attend political meetings scheduled for administration-supported candidates. Surely even a person with Chandler's memory can recall that cold winter afternoon in 1938 when his "loyal supporters" gathered in the rotunda of the Capitol to *urge* him to become a candidate for U.S. Senator against Alben W. Barkley. And who were the persons constituting 99-99/100 percent of that group? State employees who had been ordered from their jobs in all sections of Kentucky to come to Frankfort and stage that touching demonstration of the overwhelming demand of Kentuckians for Chandler to replace Barkley in the U.S. Senate. On that occasion all state offices in Frankfort were closed at 3:00 P.M., and the employees who were called in from eastern and western Kentucky not only got two days off and two days pay—they made the trip to Frankfort in state-owned cars and their other bills were submitted on state expense accounts.

After Chandler was "finally induced" to enter the senatorial campaign, his opening was scheduled at Hopkinsville in the First District on a Saturday in June. At that time state offices were open until noon on Saturdays. But not on the day of Chandler's opening. Again the orders went out to state employees and again the faithful gathered to pay tribute. Those to whom state-owned automobiles were available made the trip to Hopkinsville by car on the preceding Friday; for the benefit of the less fortunate, a special train was chartered. All state offices throughout Kentucky were ordered closed, and all employees in Frankfort were instructed to "be sure" to be on the train when it left at 5:00 A.M. No one who rode the "Happy Special" to Hopkinsville and back and tramped around the muddy fairgrounds there on that steamy June day has forgotten any part of that memorable occasion and well-remembered is the atmosphere at the Latham Hotel, which was headquarters for the leaders of Chandler's "sober" administration. It is easy to understand why Chandler would assume that circumstances are the same in the Wetherby administration.

Chandler can't seem to decide just what his policy is with reference to persons presently employed in state government, but on one point he does not waver—he has strong, conscientious objections to any employee contributing support of any type to the Combs' campaign. He alleges that state employees have been dismissed because they have not contributed campaign funds or because they support him, and strongly condemns such action as grossly unfair. Yet he frankly states that if elected he will fire all state employees who actively support Combs. Where lies the moral difference in discharging an employee for supporting the opposition before the election and in discharging an employee for supporting the opposition after the election?

The fact that employees of the present administration and the preceding one have not been assessed in any amount during any campaign does not prevent Chandler from repeating the charge in every address. The Chandler forces have given considerable publicity to the statute prohibiting state and federal employees being assessed from campaign funds and being coerced to support a specific candidate. To those not familiar with the events of those "Happy Days" in the thirties it would appear that at all times in the past Chandler adhered strictly to the provision of that law.

The law referred to was enacted at the 1936 regular session of the General Assembly, approved by Chandler as governor on February 25, 1936, and became effective on or before June 1, 1936.[2] Chandler strongly favored the enactment of that legislation because the financial assistance given his opponent in the recent gubernatorial campaign by state employees made a great impression on him. However, before the law was barely in effect Chandler began the first of his series of violations of it.

Soon after becoming governor, Chandler initiated his greatest construction project—the Trail of Broken Promises—by switching the support of his administration for U.S. Senator from John Y. Brown to the late J. C. W. Beckham. When the three-way primary campaign between Brown, Beckham, and the incumbent M. M. Logan got under way it became necessary for the Chandler administration to provide funds for Mr. Beckham.[3] Then, as now, Chandler's convenient memory came to the rescue and he "forgot" about the new statute he had so piously approved a few short weeks before. The state employees in 1936 were assessed a flat 2 percent of their yearly salaries before the August primary and another 2 percent in the November election. How much of the fund collected through the latter assessment was used to finance the campaign of the nominee, Logan, who defeated Chandler's candidate is not known. Although there was no state-wide campaign in 1937, the 2 percent assessment was levied twice that year. It is presumed that there was a specific reason for such action.

Then came the banner year of Chandler's administration, 1938. Chandler reluctantly accepted the will of the people and became a candidate for U.S. Senator. The tactics used in that campaign and the primary election concluding it do not honor Kentucky's political history; suffice it to say that before, during, and after Chandler's unsuccessful campaign against Barkley state employees paid a 2 percent assessment not once, but three times. The men who served as heads of the various state agencies were requested to give one month's salary. If anyone is of the opinion that the campaign fund collected from those state employees consisted of voluntary contributions, just let him ask the ones who paid, and paid, and paid. Not only did Chandler ignore this statute and assess state employees for funds to finance the campaigns of his candidates and himself, he also deemed it fitting and proper that his successor[4] should assess the employees of that administration the usual 2 percent before the primary and 2 percent before the November election, when he made his successful campaign for U.S. Senator following his appointment to the vacancy created by the death of Senator Logan.

It is repeated that no assessments have been made on state employees during the Clements and Wetherby administrations. During this period there have been eight primary elections, counting the one this year, and seven November elections. In this same period campaign contributions have been given by state employees only five times, and on a voluntary basis each time. No discrimination has been made between contributing and noncontributing employees at any time. Of course, the employees of the Chandler administration who failed to pay their assessments were not discriminated against after the election was over—they weren't there.

Chandler's viewpoint on the payment of campaign funds by state employees depends solely on whether he, or a man of his choice, is the administration's candidate or opponent at a given time.

This speech was given on several occasions in different locations throughout the state. Its attack upon Governor Chandler was in response to his tactic of deriding the Wetherby administration and its candidate, Bert T. Combs. It has been noted that Governor Chandler's primary campaign was run against the record of the Wetherby administration rather than against Judge Combs. The speech is an excellent example of the factionalism that then prevailed and characterized the Democratic party in Kentucky. In one of the most bitter primary battles in the state's history, Combs lost to Chandler.

1. Governor A. B. Chandler's first administration, 1935 to October 9, 1939.

2. This act made it a misdemeanor to obtain money by assessment, intimidation, or coercion from any state or federal employee, for any campaign or political purpose. For more information on this act, see *Acts of the General Assembly of the Commonwealth of Kentucky*, 1936, Chapter 49, pp. 140-42.

3. John Y. Brown, Sr. (1900-), member, Kentucky House of Representatives (1930-1932, 1946, 1954, 1962, 1966), Speaker (1932), floor leader (1966); member, United States House of Representatives (1933-1934); assistant to the United States attorney general (1935-1936); member, Criminal Code Commission (1958-1960); born in Union County and resides in Lexington. *Who's Who in American Politics, 1969-1970*, 2d. ed. (New York, 1969), p. 144.

J. Crepps Wickliffe Beckham (1869-1940), Speaker, Kentucky House of Representatives (1896-1898); lieutenant governor of Kentucky (1899-1900), governor (1900-1907); member, United States Senate (1915-1921); appointed chairman of the Commission for the Reorganization of Kentucky State Government and chairman of the Public Service Commission of Kentucky in December 1935; born in Bardstown, he made his home in Louisville. *Who Was Who in America, 1897-1942* (Chicago, 1968), 1:76.

Marvel Mills Logan (1875-1939), practiced law at Brownsville (1896-1912); Edmonson County attorney (1902-1903); first assistant attorney general (1912-1916); chairman, State Tax Commission (1917-1918); judge, Kentucky Court of Appeals (1926-1931), chief justice (1930-1931); member, United States Senate (1931-1939); born in Brownsville. George Lee Willis, Sr., *Kentucky Democracy* (Louisville, 1935), 2:14-20.

4. When Senator Logan died on October 3, 1939, Governor Chandler resigned his office and was appointed to the vacancy. His successor, Keen Johnson, assumed the office of governor on October 9, 1939, and was elected to a full term in November 1939.

DEMOCRATIC PARTY SUPPORT STATEMENT
Middletown / October 26, 1955

I AM delighted to be back in my home town, where I started my political activities so many years ago. I am here to speak in behalf of my good friend Bert VanArsdale[1] and the other members of the Jefferson County Democratic ticket.

There has been much discussion about the positions I have taken in this campaign. I thought I made myself perfectly clear on August 9 when I made the statement that I would support the Democratic party.[2] I have always supported the Democratic party. I have never been a bolter, a Dixiecrat, nor anything other than a Democrat, and I do not propose to change at this point. I have not changed my position in any way since August.

I felt then that we had a good administration in Frankfort. I am proud of the two administrations of which I have been a part during the past eight years. I have not changed my position in thinking that we have had a good road program for Kentucky, in thinking that we have had a good mental health program for Kentucky, a good welfare program for Kentucky, and, in general, a good progressive administration for Kentucky.

I believe that what we have done in the past eight years for Louisville and Jefferson County has been to the advantage of all Kentucky. I believed in August, and I believe now, that the toll road is good for Kentucky, that the new state Fairgrounds and Exposition Center are good, not only for Louisville and Jefferson County, but good for all Kentucky.

I have always been well aware of the great honor bestowed upon me by the people of Kentucky in electing me to the highest office in their power to give. I hold the office in great respect as one of dignity and honor. I will always defend the dignity of the governorship with the same vigor as I have and will defend my own personal integrity.

Working together, the state administration, the city of Louisville, and Jefferson County administrations have made much progress for Louisville and Jefferson County. I believe that the men on the ticket in Jefferson County today, by their election, can make additional progress for Jefferson County.

Governor Wetherby's attempt to clarify his earlier statements and to reaffirm his support for the Democratic party was due to the ticket's being headed by Albert B. Chandler. Wetherby had supported Bert T. Combs in the primary campaign against Chandler. Chandler ran against Wetherby's administrative record rather than against Combs in one of Kentucky's most tumultuous primary campaigns.

1. Bertram Calvin VanArsdale (1908-1979), attorney, secretary to Louisville Mayor Nevill Miller (1936-1937); secretary, Civil Service Board (1937-1942); probate commissioner of Jefferson County (1940-1943); Jefferson County judge (1954-1965); member, Board of Election Commission (1964-1979); born in Louisville. *Who's Who in Kentucky* (Hopkinsville, Ky., 1955), p. 345.

2. Governor Wetherby said: "Our great Democratic Party has chosen its nominees to represent it in the November election. I have always supported the nominees of my party, and I shall do that this November." *Louisville Courier-Journal,* August 10, 1955.

APPOINTMENT OF TOM UNDERWOOD TO THE SENATE

Letter / March 27, 1951

[To Mrs. E. H. Palmer, Lexington]

THANK you so much for writing me as you did on March 22 with reference to my appointing Tom Underwood to the United States Senate to fill the vacancy created by the untimely death of the Honorable Virgil Chapman.[1]

The realization that this position is especially fitted to his training, experience, ability, and background prompted his appointment, and I am fully confident that he can and will do an outstanding job in this capacity.

I am grateful for your kind and thoughtful expressions of commendation. With the help of interest and good will such as yours, I shall endeavor to push forward a program of advancement that will continue to merit the confidence of all our people.

---

1. Virgil Munday Chapman (1895-1951), editor-in-chief, *Kentucky Law Journal* (1917-1918); practiced law in Irvine (1918-1920); member of Franklin, Talbott, and Chapman lawfirm, Lexington (1920-1925); member, United States House of Representatives (1925-1929, 1931-1948); member, United States Senate (1948-1951). he was born in Simpson County. *Who's Who in America, 1950-1951,* 26th ed. (Chicago, 1950), p. 469.

Mrs. E. H. Palmer was secretary-treasurer, Kentucky Fraternal Congress.

GUBERNATORIAL RECORD AND PLATFORM

Letter / July 26, 1951

[To the Reverend James A. Shepherd, Louisville]

UPON announcing as a candidate for governor, I told the people of Kentucky that my record as a public official, which included a period of eight eventful months as governor, together with additional plans and ideas calculated to bring the greatest possible benefits and improvements to Kentucky and her people, would be my platform. While this record and general platform have been discussed by me in the many public appearances I have made during this primary campaign and have been treated rather fully in newspaper accounts, I should like to be recorded as advocating with special emphasis: 1) improvement of our state school system, 2) full development of our tourist industry, 3) better road system and continuation of the rural road program, 4) continuation of park development, 5) treatment program for our mental patients, 6) further industrial development for Kentucky, 7) a new registration and purgation law, and 8) full development of Kentucky agriculture, particularly dairy and beef cattle industry.

As to church connections, I should like to say that since my early youth I have been a member of the Middletown Methodist Church; I serve on its Board of Stewards and take a leading part in its affairs.

BARKLEY FOR PRESIDENT
Letter / July 14, 1952

[To David S. Sinaink, Philadelphia]

THE positive announcement of Vice President Barkely that he is a candidate for the Democratic nomination for president was greeted with solid acclaim by Kentuckians, as it was met by our friends in Philadelphia.

The Kentucky delegation and the Veep will be at the LaSalle Hotel in Chicago during the convention in need of all the help we can get. I personally have sent letters to delegates in all the states urging them to be for Senator Barkely in his earned right to the nomination.

We well appreciate your enthusiasm over the Barkley announcement and are aware too that you were a pioneer outside of Kentucky in this effort to maintain our party on the victorious side.

David S. Sinaink was chairman of the Young Democrats for Barkley in Philadelphia.

DEFEAT OF ADLAI STEVENSON
Letter / November 14, 1952

[To Governor Adlai E. Stevenson, Springfield, Illinois]

My shoulders sag every time I realize we Democrats, and particulary you, were defeated in the election. It calls for stern restraint to keep from becoming appalled at the mandate of the American public. I feel they have accidentally wronged themselves.

Your campaign—its pleasant vigor, its aggressive clarity, its charm and enlightenment—will never be forgotten by those associated with you in the cause of peace and prosperity. My wife said yesterday, "I am sorry the campaign has ended. I enjoyed Adlai's explanations and observations so much." Surely destiny has an important notch for you.

The counters have completed their dismal arithmetic. But I trust we have not lost you or your incisive and colorful leadership. The setback in no way lessens the pride I feel in having been ardently for you.

Governor Wetherby at first supported Vice President Alben Barkley for the Democratic nomination for the presidency. However, when Adlai Stevenson received the bid, Governor Wetherby switched his support. The men were governors of adjoining states, had served together on committees, and were well acquainted by 1952. Governor Wetherby admired Stevenson's executive abilities and intellectual prowess, although he advised him during the campaign to speak to the level of the general populace. The two men continued to corrrespond until Stevenson's death. For more information on Wetherby's support of Stevenson in 1956 see letter from June 17, 1955, in this section.

DENOUNCEMENT OF SENATOR JOSEPH McCARTHY
Letter / May 13, 1953

[To Mayme Wills, Taylorsville]

There is no arguing with your statement that communism is our greatest danger and that to be a good American is more important than being a Democrat or a Republican, although being a member of either party is a mark of good Americanism.

I have studied books on the life of Senator McCarthy[1] and followed his activities closely in the press and magazines. I believe his methods are brutal and detrimental to the stability of government. I believe he uses his methods to remain in the headlines, perhaps for the purpose of some day seeking a higher office.

The great amount of communications we have received concerning my unwillingness to be photographed with him is in strong support of my reaction. Only one of the many letters from Wisconsin was critical.

I hope I did not make a mistake, but I do thank you for sending your views.

The letter refers to an incident that occurred at the Kentucky Derby in Louisville on May 2, 1953. When Governor Wetherby refused to meet there with Senator Joseph McCarthy, his statement of condemnation was quoted extensively by the news media. Wetherby received many letters both supportive and derogative of his public rebuff of a visitor to the Derby.

1. Joseph Raymond McCarthy (1908-1957), elected circuit judge in 1939; served as a Marine in World War II, rising from the rank of private to captain; member, United States Senate (1946-1957). On February 9, 1950, he claimed to possess a list of names of card-carrying communists in the State Department. On December 2, 1954, the United States Senate censured him by a vote of 67 to 22. Born in Grand Chute, Wisconsin. *Encyclopedia Americana* (Danbury, Conn., 1979), 18:21-22.

SUPPORT FOR BERT COMBS
Letter / June 14, 1955

[To W. S. Brogdon, Bowling Green]

LAST Thursday I was through Bowling Green and heard about the very fine and effective contribution you are making to the campaign of Judge Combs. While I didn't have the pleasure of seeing you, I want to acknowledge the support you are giving this outstanding young man and to lend my approval and encouragement to your continued efforts.

As I am often asked why I am supporting Judge Combs and assume you are likewise called upon for an explanation of your poisition and attitude in this regard, I am submitting a brief outline of my reply. There are many specific reasons, but this is a general outline of my feelings.

Bert will make an honest, dedicated, and progressive governor. He will get behind and push the educational, economic, and industrial levels of the state. I know we have made some progress in all these fields in the past few years, but we had so far to come that the crest of the hill is yet to be topped. It is essential, in my judgment, that the next governor strain every muscle in Kentucky's body, both physical and psychological, if we are to build for our people the kind of life to which they are entitled and which the citizens of many states already enjoy.

On the other hand, I am convinced that Chandler is a reactionary in his thinking and extremely biased and selfish in his actions. I feel he would set Kentucky back rather than push it forward. Frankly, he is not the kind of man Kentucky needs as governor.

SUPPORT FOR ADLAI STEVENSON
Letter / June 17, 1955

[To Henry Belk, Goldsboro, North Carolina]

At the present time it seems to me Adlai Stevenson is the most desirable Democrat for election as President in 1956. Governor Harriman and Governor Williams are formidable statesmen and politicians, too.[1]

One of the healthiest aspects of the Democratic party is the fact that we have a strong field of potentials, showing that our party is by no means weak or must run one particular candidate next year. Our most recent ex-President is far from a slouch in this game.[2]

I believe Stevenson's patriotism, his intimate awareness of the needs of America and of our role in the free and peaceful world, qualify him to receive the support of the majority of our citizens. If given a chance at the presidency again next year, Stevenson will provide millions of Americans an opportunity to erase the mistake they made in 1952.

---

1. W. Averell Harriman (1891-), vice president of the Union Pacific Railroad (1915-1920); member, W. A. Harriman & Co. banking firm (1920-1931); chairman of the board, Union Pacific Railroad (1932-1946); administrator, National Recovery Administration (1934-1935); associated with the United States Department of Commerce's Banking Advisory Council (1933-1940); ambassador to the USSR (1943-1946); secretary of commerce (1946-1948); director, Mutual Security Administration (1951-1953); governor of New York (1954-1958); served in various diplomatic positions (1961-1969); born in New York. *Encyclopedia Americana* (Danbury, Conn., 1979), 13:811-12.

Gerhard Mennen ("Soapy") Williams (1911-), attorney, Social Security Board (1936-1937); assistant attorney general of Michigan (1937-1939); governor of Michigan (1948-1960). He was an avowed New Deal Democrat. In 1961 he became assistant secretary of state for African affairs. He was born in Detroit. *Encyclopedia Americana* (Danbury, Conn., 1979), 28: 788-89.

2. Harry S. Truman.

Henry Belk (1898-1972), newspaper editor and civic leader; editor, managing editor, *Goldsboro News* and *Goldsboro News-Argus* (1929-1955); president, Eastern North Carolina Press Association (1944), North Carolina Press Association (1950-51), Associated Press News Council (1953); born in Monroe, North Carolina and resided in Goldsboro. William S. Powell, ed. *Dictionary of North Carolina Biography,* vol. 1 A-C (Chapel Hill, n. d.), pp. 128-29.

ADMINISTRATION ACCOMPLISHMENTS AND SUPPORT FOR BERT COMBS

Letter / July 26, 1955

[To Oscar Clifford Bentley, Greenup]

I AM cognizant of your interest and support and of the assistance being rendered by you in behalf of Judge Combs, and am most appreciative. I should like to discuss the Greenup County situation with you; however, it is impossible for me to be in Frankfort between now and primary day because of the schedule of speaking engagements which has been made for me in various sections of the state. All possible effort is being expended in that direction.

In connection with the thoughts expressed in your letter of July 22, I am enclosing some information bearing on the subject which may be helpful, and you may feel free to include any or all of the statements in your letter. Also enclosed are reports from the Highway Department setting out in detail all road improvements made in your county during the past seven and one-half years as contrasted against improvements made during the time Chandler was governor. This record speaks for itself.

keep plugging for Judge Combs and we shall do everything possible to award him the impressive majority he deserves.

[The following was enclosed in the letter.]

As I am often asked why I am supporting Judge Bert Combs for governor, I am submitting a brief outline of my reply. There are many specific reasons, but this is a general outline of my feelings.

In connection with interest in the school people of Kentucky, the present administration supported in every manner possible the adoption of the amendment to the constitution affecting schools in the 1953 general election. This amendment was passed and as a result we now have a minimum foundation program for schools in Kentucky. This administration has increased appropriations to the common school fund alone more than $10 million per year. The teacher retirement system has been adequately financed as evidenced by a recent appropriation of $400,000 from the governor's emergency fund. The governor also recently appropriated from this fund $450,000 for a new building at the University of Kentucky, and $1 million to be spent on buildings at the four state colleges.

During the last seven and one-half years, 239.563 miles of road have been built and improved in Greenup County, as well as bridge painting and repairs, costing a total of $2,873,780.02 as contrasted with $671, 619.31 for 52.939 miles in Greenup County during the four years Chandler was governor.

We can support Judge Combs with the firm knowledge that he will continue these programs and be for the things that are worthwhile for Kentucky. Judge Combs will make an honest, dedicated and progressive governor. He will get behind and push the educational, economic, and industrial levels of the state.

Recently, through the cooperation of citizens in the Greenup County area and the Fish and Wildlife Resources Commission, funds were raised to construct Greenbo Lake, which will be turned over to the Department of Conservation for the development of a state park. Under the leadership of Judge Combs as governor, this project will be completed. It will be a superb boating, fishing, and swimming spot in eastern Kentucky.

TRANSPORTATION & PUBLIC SAFETY

LOUISVILLE AUTOMOBILE ASSOCIATION
Louisville / April 16, 1951

It is a pleasure to be here with you and a privilege to speak before an organization which has a history of distinguished achievement in a field of vital importance to Kentuckians.

When the automobile became a part of our civilization a half-century ago a man did not often say that he was a Kentuckian. More often, he styled himself as being from western, central, or eastern Kentucky. Our people were region conscious and did not generally feel a strong kinship for residents of each part of our state, as do Kentuckians of today. I do not think it amiss to give a great part of the credit for eliminating sectionalism in Kentucky, as well as in the entire nation, to the automobile.

The automobile has been a means to economic development, to improvement of our schools, to the strengthening of our churches, and to the increased availability of medical care for our citizens. The cause of education has been served both through a broadening of interests on the part of those who have gained the new associations and experiences that come with travel and through the consolidation of schools with expanded education facilities.

The effective role of our churches in community life has been enhanced through the improved transportation of modern cars and roads. Automobiles and service roads carrying year-round travel have made life tolerable for the country doctor. I know, because my father[1] was a country doctor, and they have made possible the establishment of health units on a county basis.

So completely has the automobile become identified with our present-day way of life that it is nearly impossible to conceive life in modern America without the conveniences and benefits of auto travel. The fields it has opened up and its contribution to our economy are such accustomed parts of day-to-day living that it is needless even to mention them. The manufacturing and servicing of cars, trucks, and buses is an integral part of our economic life, and the actions of the automotive industry have a major role in establishing our economic pattern.

In the span of less than a lifetime we have witnessed man's greatest travel change since the dawn of time. This highest achievement of man's genius for development has required far-reaching social and economic development. Organizations such as this one have been a vital force in securing those adjustments. The Louisville Automobile Association was among the first to undertake the work of arousing the public interest in securing necessary action by the federal Congress and state legislatures to provide highways, traffic laws, and safety regulations to accommodate the nation's travel.

Today, the Louisville Automobile Association covers half of our state and includes 24,000 members. The service interests of your organization have kept pace with this increase in membership. Your club wrote and sponsored early motor vehicle legislation establishing maximum speed laws, penalizing automobile theft, and equalizing tax and license fees. The members of your organization have made an untold contribution to the development of one of the mainstays of Kentucky's income—the tourist industry.

In the field of safety alone the work of the Louisville Automobile Club has been of incalculable worth. Necessity for your maximum contribution in this field has never been greater than it is today.

There have been indications at times that a right approach to the solution of America's traffic accident problem was being made. That the answer has not yet been found, however, is evident from the latest traffic statistics in Kentucky and across the nation. Some of you may have seen the Associated Press report in yesterday's paper which states that America's traffic fatalities in 1950 were greater than at any time since 1946. This article made the dramatic statement that, according to the present trend, a traffic accident some time this fall will cause the death of the millionth American since 1900. It pointed out that the total of United States citizens killed in the three wars in this century is less than half the number of deaths on American highways over the same period of time.

Kentucky bore its share of the loss, destruction, and grief that are mirrored in the cold statistics of the year's accident reports. There were

656 Kentuckians killed on our highways; 23,000 were injured, and economic losses exceeded $42 million. Thus far in 1951 Kentucky has had 151 traffic fatalities. It is clear that death on our roads is keeping pace with the awful record set last year.

The time is now to stop viewing this situation with a "Let George do it" attitude. I believe the people of Kentucky are anxious to support a traffic safety program conducted as a relentless fight against an enemy twice as destructive as any enemy which has ever engaged America in war. I have confidence that an undertaking I have in mind will prompt the hearty approval and full cooperation of every Kentucky family which has experienced, or which stands to suffer in the future, a loss through a traffic accident. It is not the law of nature for man to be visited with problems which he can never surmount. We can defeat the traffic problem. We must do so if the benefits of the automobile are not always to be marred by the shameful tragedies which have thus far accompanied its use.

As with any other problem in a democracy, solution of this one depends upon the will of the people in concerted action. A determined public can do more than all the law enforcement officers state and local governments can provide or all the experts in highway safety engineering. The law officer and the engineer can be successful only as far as the people of Kentucky extend their success.

In the final analysis, the one which counts, the matter hangs in balance with the motorist. Nowhere is the adage more true than with those privileged to drive on the highway, that responsibility must accompany privilege. And Andrew H. Brown[2] never stumbled nearer the truth than when he said a man can't drive safely with his car in gear and his mind in neutral.

A safety rally at a conference table does not decrease our traffic tolls unless the resolutions made there are translated into safe driving practices on the open road. To carry the important facts concerning highway safety from the conference room to the consciousness of the motoring public, I am shortly going to call a statewide highway safety meeting in which all Kentuckians will be encouraged to participate.[3]

I am asking you as citizens and as members of the Louisville Automobile Club to help us in this meeting. Your history of progress in all phases of improved highway travel insures that you will be valuable members of the meeting. Let the leaders have your ideas and be generous with the cumulative knowledge of your organization. Already several of your club's officers have agreed to serve on committees at the conference, and their understanding of the situation will be a big help. Your president, Frederick Thompson,[4] will be a member of the engineering committee at the conference and your secretary, Eugene Stuart,[5] has agreed to serve as chairman of the conference's enforcement committee. I hope that the rest of you will decide to participate when the conference is called, for your help is vital if we are to be successful in carrying this program to the motoring public.

We have the resources and the required leadership to combat the menace on our highways. It is my conviction that the people of Kentucky will show their interest by active participation in this safety conference. With the help of you and other organizations, and the determination of the people to make safe driving a habit in 1951, we can reduce the role of the automobile as a killer and let it fulfill its purpose as a nondestructive servant of the American people.

The Louisville Automobile Club was organized in 1903. It is one of the earliest clubs of its type in the country and is only one year younger than the American Automobile Association. It is a civic-service organization providing assistance to the motorist. From an early date the club worked for improvements of arterial streets in the city and for good roads throughout the state. *Kentucky Tour Book* (Louisville, 1928), p. 5.

1. Samuel Davis Wetherby (1869-1926), physician, born at Middletown.

2. A reference to a famous radio character portrayed on the program "Amos and Andy."

3. For Governor Wetherby's address to the delegates of the highway safety conference see speech from May 18, 1951, pp. 122-25.

4. Frederick Sallada Thompson (1890–1978), high school teacher in California (1914-1917); with General Electric Company (1917-1928); general manager, vice president, president, chairman of board of Corhart Refractories Company, Louisville (1928-1958); born in Wapakoneta, Ohio. Information supplied by Joan Steel Knight, administrative assistant, Louisville Automobile Club.

5. Eugene Stuart (1885-1960), secretary-manager of Louisville Automobile Club (1914-1959); helped to establish Otter Creek Park in Meade County; born in Fleming County. Information supplied by Joan Steel Knight, administrative assistant, Louisville Automobile Club.

KENTUCKY DAM BRIDGE DEDICATION
Gilbertsville / May 12, 1951

It is a pleasure to be here today and join with the officials of the Tennessee Valley Authority in the dedication of the Kentucky Dam bridge. With many of you this occasion symbolizes the completion of a vision which through your efforts is now the vital link of an important east-west highway. With U.S. 62 routed across this bridge it will increase further the tremendous volume of traffic and number of visitors to Kentucky Dam.

This is a bridge that began at home. As early as ten years ago the Kentucky Lake Development Association was formed and led in the fight for the development of the entire lake area. The construction of this bridge was one of its main projects, and I know that this is a great day for Ed Paxton, Jr.,[1] and other officials of the association.

Working closely with the people in all fifteen counties of the Kentucky Lake Association were the Chamber of Commerce groups in this area. In 1945 the Paducah Association of Commerce, of which George Katterjohn[2] was president, became convinced that a bridge could be secured across Kentucky Dam and never thereafter relented their efforts until steel and concrete began taking form.

With the federal government in the dam-building business and the state in the road-building business difficult legal questions involving responsibility of each in providing funds for the cost of the bridge soon arose. After full exploration the operating areas of each became clear and undisputed, and with the federal government agreeing to bear the cost of construction of the bridge and the state joining in building of the approaches, the path was cleared for action. With construction beginning in December 1948, this $1.2 million structure was pushed to completion in two years.

The state Highway Department within recent days has advertised for bids for surfacing of the road it has constructed from Kuttawa to Kentucky Dam, and the survey is now being completed for a new highway to lead from the dam to Paducah. The other great water barrier on this route is well on the way to being spanned through the bridge that is being constructed across the Cumberland River with matching funds contributed by state and federal governments.

On U.S. Highway 62 alone, the road leading into the dam and state park area from both east and west, a total of $1,940,278.12 of federal and state money is now being spent. Considered from the standpoint of the state's overall Kentucky Lake Development program, however, this represents only one portion of the capital expenditures made since Kentucky gained title to the Kentucky Dam village and park area.

Americans have long marveled at the transaction that gained for colonial settlers the ownership of all Manhattan Island in return for a few trinkets valued at twenty-four dollars. Presumably that purchase is unique in all of history. It has never been equalled, but it does have a parallel. Within our view is the land and improvements that make up Kentucky Dam Village State Park. In 1948, at a cost of only thirty-one thousand dollars, Henry Ward and our park officials negotiated this purchase for the state from the Tennessee Valley Authority. Included in the array of assets gained in that purchase are 1,000 acres of land with choice shoreline, thirty-nine vacation cottages, picnic area and shelter, and an entire village containing asphalt road network, all necessary utility installations, and buildings you now recognize as the restaurant and dining room, auditorium, administration building, and one of the lodges.

Your state government, recognizing the opportunities of Kentucky Lake as one of its greatest tourist attractions and vacation spots, began at once a renovation and expansion program that has helped make Kentucky Lake the favorite fishing and recreation place of this part of the nation. Improvements made by the state include complete renovation of all buildings, construction of ten new cottages, making a total of forty-five cottage rental units which are further supplemented by forty-four lodge rooms, construction of a $100,000 bath house and swimming beach, and the addition of an airport with building facilities. A nine hole golf course is under construction. We have acquired a camping and trailer area from the Tennessee Valley Authority and impressive improvements will be made on the two boat docks in the Kentucky Dam Village State Park.

Up the lake a few miles is another rapidly developing state park[3] that is assuming a more important role each day in the state's tourist development program. This season a new sixty-two room lodge is scheduled to be completed. Among other improvements there will be a new site for the boat dock with every service that the fisherman might desire, even including a fish cleaning building and facilities for quick-freezing the catch.

These parks afford the vacationists many hours of restful leisure and offer to the sportsman unlimited outdoor recreation. In addition to the enjoyment opportunities offered Kentuckians at home, the same appeal reaches beyond our borders and increases by many millions the tourist dollars spent annually in Kentucky. Last year, gasoline taxes alone collected from out-of-state motorists in Kentucky amounted to more than $6 million.

Accompanying the new industry in western Kentucky has been unprecedented industrial growth already exceeding the fondest imagination of those who began a decade ago to promote the development of the Kentucky Lake area. We are glad to have here today officials of the Atomic Energy Commission and representatives of the private industry that forms the already substantial nucleus of the vast industrial growth that is foreseen for this area. We invite the industries that have located here to join with Kentucky in its promotion and to publicize this vacation area through their trade magazines.

This bridge stands as a symbol of service to the commercial user and pleasure traveler alike. It is an impressive monument to the American people and testimony that their public servants on local, state, and national levels have worked together in the public interest.

I know that all who have had a part in this great achievement are proud of its magnificence and join with me in its dedication for the benefit of all our citizens.

---

1. Edwin J. Paxton, Jr. (1912-), reporter, *Paducah Sun Democrat* (1933-1942), associate editor (1945-1961), editor (1961-1977); manager, radio station WKYB, Paducah (1946-1957); manager of WPSD-TV, Paducah (1957-1961); president, Kentucky Lake Association (1948-1954); member of committee on Public Education of Kentucky (1960-1963); trustee, Tenn-Tombigbee Waterway Authority (1963-1979); born in Paducah and resides in Cocoa Beach, Florida. Letter, December 12, 1980.

2. George W. Katterjohn (1899-), manufacturer of concrete products, president of Paducah Association of Commerce (1943-1945); born and resides in Paducah. Letter, December 10, 1980.

Mr. Katterjohn writes, "During the time I was president of the Association of Commerce, as it was then called, and two years after, I made many trips to Washington, D.C., seeking funds to build a vehicular bridge over Kentucky Dam. There were no funds in the original construction project for this bridge, TVA had no funds, U.S. Engineers had no funds, both the state and Federal Highway departments had no funds. It finally wound up that I had Congressman Noble Gregory and Vice President Alben W. Barkley to attach an $8 million ammendment to the omnibus bill. . . . The bill passed, our funds were available, and the vehicular bridge over Kentucky Dam was built according to this procedure."

3. Kenlake State Park.

BURKESVILLE BRIDGE DEDICATION
Burkesville / May 16, 1951

TODAY is a day hoped for since this area was settled in the latter years of the eighteenth century. We are dedicating and placing in service the first span across the Cumberland River between Burnside and the Tennessee border. Nowhere along the river's course could a bridge be better located to serve both its immediate environs and at the same time fit into the state's overall transportation network.

The richness of the bottom land in this area so impressed its settlers that they likened the valley to the "marrow of a bone." Their appraisal was justified, for the first and second bottom lands along the Cumberland produced a combination of corn, hogs, and cattle that resulted in prosperous farmers and thriving communities. From its timbered slopes came choice hardwoods measured in millions of board feet. The waters of the Cumberland deposited the rich alluvial soil. Its swift currents carried rafts of logs and lumber to the southern markets, and up and down its stretches between Nashville and the river landings farther upstream plied the colorful and economically important steamboats.

But while the river served in all these ways, the swiftness of its currents, the destruction and turbulence of its flood stages have made it the enemy of man's progress. It has been a barrier separating those living on one side from their neighbors on the other bank.

In early days, the people of the Cumberland Valley were less dependent on outside sources for the material requirements of daily living. The handy canoes and dependable river-swimming horses and mules permitted those crossings which were absolutely necessary. The coming of the stage coach greatly increased overland travel, but the Cumberland River remained a formidable barrier. To meet the growing demand for improved transportation ferries began operating at various points. The histories of Burkesville, Rowena, and Greasy Creek ferries are steeped in legend. The disappearance of the ferry marks the passing of an age. With it go many fond memories and delightful river-crossing tales. The inconveniences and tragic misfortunes, however, that mar the history of the Burkesville Ferry make it a pleasure, I am sure, to relegate the old waterhorse to the past. The new bridge will soon acquire its own tradition, affording less adventure but more service. The danger has been eliminated. Motorists traveling Highway 90 no longer need allow for the time-consuming ferry crossing.

With the dedication of this $800,000 structure another great link in Kentucky's highway improvement program is placed in service. This is one of the five bridges across the Cumberland River recently completed or under construction.

This bridge, and the area it will serve, are ideally located within the very heartland of Kentucky's fast-developing tourist attractions. New and expanded facilities at Cumberland Falls have made it one of our most important and delightful state parks. Its appeal is universal among tourists and vacation travelers. Mighty Wolf Creek Dam, 101 mile Cumberland Lake, and the new state park have a great future in Kentucky's tourist program.

You have already experienced at firsthand the effect of tourist trade and travel. The steady weekend streams of fishermen pouring through Burkesville on their way to Dale Hollow have left many dollars with your merchants, filling station operators, motels, hotels, and other service type enterprises. From 1947 through 1950 Kentuckians had a tourist income of $867 million. Every sale of gasoline by a Kentucky dealer adds to the funds earmarked for construction and maintenance of roads and bridges.[1] The part of Kentucky's tourist income which found its way to the Highway Department has helped bear the cost of the most extensive road-building and improvement program in the state's history.

Road funds have not been channeled into the building and upkeep of crosscountry thoroughfares exclusively or for bridge structures as expensive and imposing as this one. Important rural road projects have been included in the road work in Cumberland county and every county of the state during the past three years, with the miles of road built or improved each year topping the prior year's record. The same emphasis on the state's rural road program is being continued and more miles of farm-to-market roads are planned for 1951 than have been built in any previous year. Every state agency and group is participating in Kentucky's highway network. The state Chamber of Commerce has centered the sixth tour of state parks and tourist attractions around this dedication.

You have been fine hosts, and I know I speak for every member of the tour group in expressing appreciation for your hospitality and for the occasion of pleasure which you have afforded.

---

1. In 1948 the Kentucky General Assembly enacted a bill that appropriated two-sevenths of a gasoline excise tax for rural and secondary road work. For more information see speech from July 24, 1951, in the Democratic Party Leadership section.

KENTUCKY HIGHWAY SAFETY CONFERENCE
Lexington / May 18, 1951

THE history of mankind is a narration of his reaction to challenge. The will for self-preservation has carried him past threatened destruction in every age.

Recognizing the threat of warfare to his existence, man's moral, spiritual, and intellectual genius time and again has been poured into the effort to end war.

Dreaded plagues, which once wiped away large areas of the world's population, are no longer a menace because man recognized and successfully grappled with the challenge.

The ancient visitations of flood and famine have stimulated man to take steps necessary to preserve himself and assure the survival of his posterity.

Through the ages humanity has escaped the forces of destruction by invoking the will to live.

This program today is in recognition of a modern threat which, in violence and scope of destruction, is as great a challenge to us in 1951 as have been the classic challenges of other ages.

This problem is highway traffic safety. It must be thought of, talked about, and measured in numbers of people killed and injured and with the realization that any one of us may become a traffic accident statistic.

If today all 700 people of my hometown of Anchorage were instantly killed through sudden tragedy, I feel sure we would adjourn this meeting in deepest mourning for the victims, their families, and loved ones. Such an incident would be headlined in every newspaper in America. If we received at this moment news that sudden disaster had bodily crippled the 23,000 men, women, and children of Frankfort and Middlesboro, we would be thrown into a state of emergency. Every available man from the State Police and National Guard would be rushed to the disaster scene. Facilities of every department of our state government would be brought to bear to relieve the condition. Citizens across the country would join in making available relief and help to meet the emergency and, like the Texas City explosion of 1947, the Middlesboro and Frankfort catastrophes would be remembered for generations. Under such circumstances the entire state of Kentucky would be emotionally shocked, and we would go to any length in determining the cause and preventing the recurrence of such horror.

Unbelievable as it sounds, however, the people of this state have for years tolerated, without audible protest, the mass slaughter of as many Kentuckians as live in Anchorage and the injury of the same number of our citizens as live in Frankfort and Middlesboro.

Because, in traffic accidents one, two, and three at a time are killed or injured in western Kentucky on Route 41, in central Kentucky on Route 25, and in eastern Kentucky on Route 15, the fact that in a year 700 die and 23,000 are hurt lacks the dramatic impact of a sudden catastrophe.

As a result the human waste of automobile accidents is brought home only to those directly involved, and interest is localized within the family and community in which an accident occurs. We lose sight of the urgency of the problem which condemns on an average one out of every three of our children and our neighbor's children to be victims of automobile accidents.

Motivated by this dark reality, I have asked you citizens of every section of Kentucky to assemble here in Lexington to launch the most concerted safety campaign in the history of our state.

I regret that Kentucky has been no pioneer in highway safety. Other states which have waged a scientific, well-planned, and coordinated safety campaign over a period of years have materially reduced accident tolls. By example they have shown what can be done through the cooperative efforts of state and local governments, safety organizations, and private citizens.

Over a period of thirty years 15,087 deaths on Kentucky highways have been recorded. If Kentucky had equaled each year the record of the state doing the best safety job there would have been less than 5,000 fatalities.

The state of Rhode Island has been a leader in highway safety. In 1937, Rhode Island's death rate was 8.2 per 100 million miles traveled. Kentucky's was 24.9.

There were some who entertained doubt then, and there may be those who are doubtful now, that a safety program can really be made into a life-saving undertaking. But about the same year we began to hear a little about highway safety, and by 1944 Kentucky's rate had dropped from 24.9 to 15.6. Since that time, our accident rate has been a year by year barometer of the activity of government, safety organizations, and individual citizens in promoting highway safety.

You have accepted an invitation to a "working" conference for the purposes of developing a workable, long-range Highway Safety Action Program and the means to execute that program on a continuing basis.

In the weeks since the committees of this conference were appointed, they have devoted much thought and work to a program for saving lives in Kentucky. The program they will suggest to you today is based on the most extensive information and best safety procedures known in America. It takes into account detailed analysis of what government agencies have done and what they need to do. It reflects the best thinking of your public officials concerning the problem and, most important of all, the program that will be laid before you is based on successful accident prevention experience throughout the nation. Theory and guesswork have at last been superseded with knowledge and experience.

I want to thank those who have accepted the responsibility of committee assignments for their willingness to devote to the problem the time and study necessary to prepare the recommendations and information which will be brought before this assembly. To the committee and to each of you who has taken time from your own busy schedule to participate in this meeting, I want to express my thanks. The reward for a job done, a mission accomplished, will earn for you the lasting gratitude of a state made safer by your efforts.

The degree of highway safety that will exist in Kentucky tomorrow and next year rests largely with you and the follow-up use you make of the information and guidance furnished at this conference.

Regardless of your occupation or role in your community, there is a definite job for each of you. When you are behind the wheel it is careful driving. When a pedestrian it is to follow safe and sensible walking practices. As a citizen it is to support your traffic and law enforcement officers and to stand behind your court as it fulfills its duty. As a parent or as a teacher it is to see that our children receive sufficient instruction to drive an automobile with competence and safety. At all times, it is to advocate the application of sane and common-sense driving with common courtesy and respect for the rights of other highway users.

I know this project we are launching today will arouse within many of you a personal zealousness. It may be with you, as with myself, that a discussion of traffic accidents refreshes again the memory of tragic family loss.[1] Until highway safety is a national habit you more fortunate have no assurance that you will not someday have a similar experience. Let us all put our hearts and our minds to this compelling task and devote the time and energy required to meet the challenge. Let's make Kentucky safe.[2]

The conference was the second to be held, and it met on the campus of the University of Kentucky. The principal speaker was Colonel Franklin M. Kremi, director of Northwestern University's Traffic Institute. Police Commissioner Guthrie F. Crowe attended the conference. Various committees suggested recommendations to him and to others in order to improve highway safety in Kentucky. Statistics indicated that the number of highway deaths was increasing rapidly during the early 1950s. *Lexington Herald,* May 19, 1951.

1. Governor Wetherby was recalling the death of his father, Samuel Davis Wetherby, in an automobile accident at Anchorage, on September 23, 1926. Later, his brother, George Schenck Wetherby, Jefferson County judge, was killed in an accident on U.S. 60 near the Jefferson-Shelby county line on March 19, 1954. Judge Wetherby was on his way to Frankfort to address legislation pending before the Kentucky General Assembly. This personal loss was a factor that explained Governor Wetherby's strong support for highway safety and improvements.

2. The conference recommended that every driver be required to pass an examination at least once every five years. Approximately 1,000 persons attended the conference. *Louisville Courier-Journal,* May 19, 1951.

MARY INGLES HIGHWAY ASSOCIATION
Augusta / May 21, 1951

IT is always good to come to northern Kentucky. You never fail in extending a hearty welcome. There is nothing unusual in this because Kentuckians are noted for their warm and friendly hospitality, and you folks have indeed demonstrated your ability to uphold this proud tradition. I want you to know that I am enjoying my visit with you.

It is a real privilege to talk to a group who are interesting themselves in a vital function of our state government. A system of good roads is one of the most important responsibilities your state government has to fulfill. As a public official it is encouraging to know there are civic groups such as yours working for a greater community and a greater state. Kentucky stretches some four hundred miles from east to west and is traversed by several natural barriers that have made travel difficult. Only with the era of good roads have Kentuckians in one section been able to acquaint themselves with those in other parts of the state.

Last week, I was in western Kentucky. I was several hundred miles from where we stand today but was yet close to the Ohio River. In earlier days the Ohio was the only link between that part of the state and the northern Kentucky area. Then it would have taken days of river travel for a citizen of Bracken County to reach far western Kentucky. Today you are linked with all parts of the Commonwealth by a system of highways that makes statewide travel easy and fast.

Highways have been a big factor in enabling Kentucky to develop from the wilderness that existed in pioneer days. Buffalo and Indian trails were the only roads by which our first citizens were guided. It was over such a crude system of trails that Mary Ingles[1] made her escape from the Indians in 1756.

It is this brave pioneer woman, said to be the first white woman in Kentucky, whom your organization honors. The highway you support follows her escape route as she made her way east toward civilization. The noble contribution made by our early settlers has afforded a substantial part of our state's greatness, and I am happy that you have such an awareness of early Kentucky history.

While conscious of your rich heritage, you are also looking toward the future. Your association is working for improved highways that will lead to greater prosperity and happiness. The future will show increased highway building in this section and the continuance of a program announced three years ago to construct a new segment of the Mary Ingles Highway each year. The highway already stretches eastward to the Campbell-Pendleton county line. The section from Mentor, Campbell County, to the Pendleton-Bracken county line is now under construction and soon to be completed.

This stretch was started last year and is being built under 1950 contracts. It is nearly four and one-half miles long and will cost around $237,000. The 1951 contracts of the Mary Ingles Highway improvement program are soon to be let. Next in line for construction is about four and one-half miles from the Pendleton-Bracken county line to Willow Grove. The estimated cost of this new stretch is $305,000.

Your Department of Highways intends to continue the Mary Ingles Route and to make it an integral part of the state-federal highway system. This administration is making every possible effort to provide the people of Kentucky with an adequate system of highways. The task is one that requires vision and the industry of many persons if our highway network is to meet the needs of our rapidly expanding tourist traffic, industrial expansion, and agricultural development.

A builder of roads must be a philosopher. If he sees in his task only the gathering and putting together of materials he is missing the point of his job. The men who design and construct our highways are philosophers in the field of service, for they see every road as an instrument of benefit and a symbol of progress. Our great rural road program stemmed from this theory of service and recognition of pressing need.

Important rural road projects have been included in the road work of Bracken County and every county of the state during the past three years, with the miles of road built or improved each year topping the prior year's record. The same emphasis on the state's rural road program is being continued, and more miles of farm-to-market roads are planned for 1951 than have been built in any previous year.

As impressive as our road-building accomplishments have been during the past three years and as extensive as are our plans for the future, I would be less than frank if I did not tell you that we are confronted with difficult problems. The curtailment of steel production for civilian use is today affecting our road and bridge-building program. National defense needs may well cut so deeply into road-building supplies that current construction will be greatly retarded and future projects seriously affected.

The problem of maintenance, always a substantial and costly one, is especially critical this year. The unusual severity of the past winter has left Kentucky highways in a bad state of repair. Eight million dollars that had been counted on for new construction or for routine maintenance will have to be diverted to meet the present emergency. Despite these difficulties, however, we plan to forge ahead. We intend to go ahead with our plans on the Mary Ingles Highway.

Before relinquishing the speaker's stand I want to call your attention to another important matter. It is more vital to you and me individually than building new roads, making money, or reaching the pinnacle of success in our chosen fields of endeavor. It is saving human life through safety on our highways. At the statewide safety conference last week, a program was outlined designed to save lives that will be lost through traffic accidents unless vigorous steps are taken.[2]

I ask your undivided support of this endeavor. With your help we can make the Mary Ingles Highway, and all Kentucky highways, the safest in America.

---

1. Mary Ingles, the wife of William Ingles, was taken captive, along with two sons and a daughter, by Indians at Drapers Meadows on the headwaters of the Roanoke River near the upper reaches of the New River in Virginia in 1755. They were taken west to the Shawnee town near the mouth of the Sioto River. There Mary became a domestic slave and earned the Indians' respect for her diligent work. While on a visit to Big Bone Lick, she made her escape along the south side of the Ohio River, a route that is followed by state highway 8.

Eventually, she reached the safety of the New River region and was returned to her people after five and a half months among the Indians. She died in 1815 at the age of 83. Henry P. Scalf, *Kentucky's Last Frontier* (Pikeville, Ky., 1972), pp. 38-41.

2. See speech from May 18, 1951, pp. 122-25.

HIGHWAY 80 BREAKS CELEBRATION
Breaks of Sandy / June 10, 1951

KENTUCKIANS are proud to meet with officials and citizens of our mother state in celebrating an important link which joins our states still more closely together.

It was largely through the effort of courageous and pioneering Virginians that Kentucky's wilderness was explored and tamed. Numerous Kentucky families still retain close kinship connections with descendants of those who remained in Virginia during the settlement of the Bluegrass country. Virginia furnished the pattern of Kentucky's state government, and from the Virginia Assembly Kentucky's early legislators gained the experience that equipped them to be the architects of the new Commonwealth. Our courts, in interpreting the common law, turn today to the jurisprudence of Virginia which links Kentucky's legal system to the great English code of law.

It is fitting that we representatives of these two great commonwealths assemble here to give joint attention to a mutual undertaking. Frequently, representatives of our states have met in this same spectacular Breaks area to plan for mutual defense against the Indians, to establish boundary markers, or, in more recent time, to discuss the need and feasibility of constructing the highway linking Kentucky and Virginia at this junction. For countless reasons—kinship, commerce, and mutual helpfulness—Kentuckians and Virginians have maintained contact, and even during the bygone feuding era they continued to seek each other out.

We meet here today to observe the completion of a long-dreamed-of project, one keenly anticipated by the people of this area. Each state has realized that a road built to the line without a continuing outlet would be little better than a dead-end street, and it was apparent that a cooperative undertaking between the two states was required.

Both in Richmond and in Frankfort the Breaks road has received the finest joint attention any interstate undertaking ever enjoyed. For three years highway officials and engineers of both states have worked in close harmony. They have demonstrated unity that might well serve as a pattern in meeting common problems extending beyond state borders and, like you people of Pike, Dickenson, and Buchanan counties, they have proven that accomplishment is the natural product of cooperation.

Route 80 will now carry commercial and tourist travel from Meadow View and Haysi, in the Old Dominion State, across the magnificent Breaks of the Cumberland Range and the Big Sandy and westward through Kentucky's mountain Pennyrile and Purchase sections to the extreme western tip of Kentucky and the mighty Mississippi.

Along its 500 mile path, this road links more natural scenic and historic attractions than any other highway in America.

Gifts of nature and genius of man have combined to furnish a series of matchless vacation spots and travel attractions. For natural splendor the forest-covered mountains of this area are without challenge. The Breaks are said by many to be the most beautiful view in the eastern half of our nation. Dewey Lake, Cumberland Falls, Cumberland National Forest, Wolf Creek Lake, Zollicoffer Memorial Park, Mammoth Cave, Jefferson Davis Monument, Kentucky Lake, Columbus-Belmont Park—these are but a part of the guideposts along Highway 80.

No road has more to offer the tourist who seeks both quantity and grandeur of attractions. It is one of the vital arteries of Kentucky's tourist industry. In recent years Kentucky has made determined effort to develop our vast tourist and vacation resources. In doing so, we have realized one of our most important dollar/volume industries.

The completion of Highway 80 facilitates travel from Kentucky to the eastern seaboard. It likewise permits westbound travel through the heart of Kentucky, with connections to every section of the nation.

We are living in a travel-conscious age with modern transportation allowing the folks in one state to spend a weekend in another and return in time for the following week's work. You who live in Virginia are invited to join your friends who are enjoying the fishing, vacation, and recreation facilities that abound throughout Kentucky.

Governor Battle,[1] you didn't invite me over here today to drum up trade, but I do promise you Virginia folks that if you leave your own beautiful state long enough to come over to our side of the line you will find a warm-hearted welcome and a memorable vacation.

This road, which we officially open today, is an investment by each state in the development of its own resources. In years past, descriptions of this majestic gorge have been carried throughout the country by the adventurous few who could penetrate the rugged and forested terrain that curtained the Breaks from the outside world. With this new accessibility, traveling America will come here to see this masterwork of nature. In my judgment this area affords unlimited opportunity for park development, and its popularity with sightseers will justify careful consideration of the federal Congress and the National Park Service. It is my hope that this will be the site of the next addition to the chain of national parks for the benefit and pleasure of our citizens.[2]

Governor Battle, it is a pleasure for us to join with you today in celebrating completion of this addition to the Breaks-Lakes-Park Road, and to extend the hand of friendship as we place in use the connecting link of Kentucky-Virginia State Route 80.

---

1. John Stewart Battle (1890-1972), member, House of Delegates of the Virginia General Assembly (1929-1934); member, Virginia State Senate (1934-1949); governor of Virginia (1950-1954); born in New Bern, North Carolina. *Who's Who in America, 1954-1955,* 28th ed. (Chicago, 1954), p. 163.
2. In 1954 the state of Kentucky joined with Virginia to develop an interstate park at the Breaks of the Big Sandy River. See an Act relating to a Compact between the Commonwealth of Kentucky and the Commonwealth of Virginia providing for the creation, development and operation of an interstate park to be known as The Breaks Interstate Park, *Acts of the General Assembly of the Commonwealth of Kentucky,* 1954, Chapter 82 (H.B. 25), pp. 247-51.

OUR ROAD CRISIS
Lexington / September 1, 1954

THE inadequacy of our system of streets and highways is one of the greatest problems facing the nation. We have more than 3 million miles of rural roads and over 300,000 miles of streets. We have over 50 million motor vehicles, or almost one vehicle for every three persons in America. We would all ride if we had roads. We have the cars. Paradoxically, all but an insignificant portion of this tremendous fleet of swift vehicles must travel over roads built to the standards and motor vehicle performance of twenty-five years ago or longer.

A great deal of concern is expressed, and rightfully, for the casualties of war, the Korean War, for instance. According to the latest available figures, the total casualties in Korea have amounted to about 125,000, of which about 20,000 have been killed in action and about 15,000 are listed as missing. There are no figures readily available as to how much this war has cost in dollars. During the Korean trouble there have been more than 4 million people injured and nearly 100,000 killed in automobile accidents in the United States of America. The economic loss has amounted to nearly $10 billion. This is one measure of the inadequacy and urgency of doing something about the outmoded highways, streets, and roads in our country.

Our American automobiles are one of the outstanding engineering achievements of all time. It is superfluous to point out that automobile transportation is now one of the most vital phases of our whole social and economic system and that its importance is increasing at an accelerated rate. With all their adjuncts and accessories, these have been constantly improved since the development of mass production in America a few decades ago. The obvious result is that today automobile transportation has far outstripped the capacity of the road system and this is piling up an economic and social loss that staggers the imagination. It is estimated that the traffic volume will be doubled by 1970. Belatedly, the seriousness of the problem is being recognized. Something is now beginning to be done, but that Kentucky is lagging behind other states must be obvious to anyone who goes beyond its borders. This alarming situation and the possibilities of action about it invite careful and objective scrutiny.

Kentucky, in 1924, decided to "pay as you go" when it rejected a $50 million road bond issue. This was the estimated cost at that time of completing the primary highway system. While physically this system is now, thirty years later, substantially complete, it has been at the expense of greatly inferior roads and many compromises that had to be made in the early days when it was a responsibility of the county government to obtain the right-of-way and to raise a substantial portion of the construction funds. As we can now see, to our regretful dismay, "pay as you go" meant that we didn't go very far, or far enough anyway.

What can we do about the result of this choice, or more directly, what can be done about this increasingly imperative problem, now approaching the emergency state? Quite a bit; but before suggesting remedies, it may be well to take brief stock of the resources that are applicable to the task.

Human resources are the most important factor of all and we are exceptionally fortunate. Kentucky has an excellent Highway Department. In fact, it is generally recognized in the engineering profession as one of the best anywhere. This agency is staffed with highly skilled engineers of wide experience, many of whom have spent their entire professional lives there. They attend their work with a sincerity and devotion that can only be understood or appreciated by long and intimate contact with them. Their services and experiences will never be duplicated. We also have in Kentucky several private consultants with experienced and capably staffed organizations that are available to the Highway Department. The University of Kentucky can handle many important phases of the task. Except, perhaps, for specialized problems of the most unusual character, it is doubtful if the available human resources are drawn on, that it will be necessary to go beyond the borders of Kentucky for any engineering personnel to originate, design, and see through to completion any program of highway construction that Kentucky may find it necessary to undertake. However, one critical fact may as well be faced by Kentucky and the Highway Department. The present staff of engineers, many of whom are long past retirement age, can never be replaced by the department. Younger men are not filling the depleted ranks, so that increasing dependence must be placed on the use of engineering talent outside the department, if the road problem in Kentucky is to be met within any reasonable time.

The construction industry in Kentucky is well organized and adequately financed, equipped, and staffed to undertake any road construction program in Kentucky. So far, therefore, as the most important element of all is involved, human skill and resources, the situation in Kentucky is a favorable one.

The Highway Department currently estimates that it will cost about $164 million to bring the approximately 2,400 miles of our primary road system to adequate modern standards. This figure is probably far too low. In any case, income now available, or anticipated, will not provide this money and funds for maintenance of the existing system. There is no apparent solution under existing laws and through present income sources. It is estimated that by 1960 the demands for maintenance alone will be so great that there will be little money left for new construction or reconstruction of our inadequate facilities. While we may be able to raise modest amounts of money by capitalization of some of our present income for work on important improvements and routes, for instance, the simplest and most practical means of financing our primary routes and important secondary routes appears to be by way of toll charges for use of the new roads and the sale of obligations in the form of revenue bonds, pledged against the collections of the tolls on them.

It seems economically obvious that the road users should, and must in the end, pay for the cost of them, regardless of how they are built, and that if toll charges for usage are made, these must be sound economically in that they represent a saving to the traveling public. Additional taxation, other than as a direct and optional charge for service and usage imposed on an economy already taxed to a dangerous degree, does not appear to be a sound source of money to rebuild the highway system of America. The time factor alone is an important consideration. Simply or restated, then, this means that if our road system is to be reconstructed in any reasonable time the users must pay a charge for travel over it and this means a "toll road" or "turnpikes." Far from being new, this method of financing, road building, and operation is an old one with a successful record extending into the misty realm of antiquity.

As the future is involved, two important advantages are gained by resorting to toll highways. Heavy and commercial traffic can be directed to the self-supporting and liquidating faster trunk routes where it can be better controlled, and more income from existing sources will be left available for extension and upkeep of the feeder system.

The revenue bond method has been widely used throughout Kentucky and elsewhere for many years in the financing of school buildings and other public improvements and in general is nothing new. Its use, in the case of the Highway Department, accomplishes several desirable purposes. In addition to speed, sufficiency, and simplicity, an important one of these, if not the most important, is that it will in effect and in a large sense allow the collective will of the people to be expressed very quickly. The legislature, representing the people, has enacted or could enact, if they don't exist, as the future unfolds, laws enabling the Highway Department to transfer the nominal and legal title to the roads to a "Turnpike Authority." This agency in turn enters into a contract, lease, and option with the Highway Department. It issues bonds against revenues from tolls and uses the proceeds of the sale of these bonds for the construction of roads. These roads are in turn to be leased to the Highway Department for operation, maintenance, and the collection of tolls for debt service. When sufficient funds have been collected for the retirement of the bonds, and interest, title to the roads reverts to the Highway Department. Such bonds are almost equal to an obligation against taxation and find a ready sale. The demands for such obligations have probably never been so great. The great pools of liquid wealth, for example, such as are held by large insurance companies and philanthropies, have never been so pressed for investment sources. In addition to normal requirements, the need of funds for pensions, annuities, and other such demands will probably increase in future years, and this is a way to put this money to work on a sound basis.

Here, then, is a ready source of money for the reconstruction of our major highways without an increase in taxes or subsidy from the federal government. Better routes and roadways that will permit full use of the efficiency of modern motor vehicles will result in savings to the traveling public, beyond ability to estimate, that will much more than offset the toll charges, so that the traveling public can realize a profit on the improvement, as it properly should.

Commencing with the Pennsylvania Turnpike, built several years ago, the economic soundness and popularity of the toll road is now being accepted, revived, and applied on a large scale by the current construction of toll-paying, "expressway" type highways in various sections of the country, of which the Kentucky Turnpike now in the engineering stages, is typical. However, these great thoroughfares, elaborate to a high degree, are expensive and can be economically justified only where a high traffic volume can be anticipated, and they are of relatively limited application. Where adaptable, the solution is apparently satisfactory, financially and physically, but because of the foregoing restriction these roads do not resolve the traffic problem on the important secondary routes where it is most acute and which comprise so large a portion of the highway system.

There appear to be two practical ways by which this situation may be relieved. Some improvement may be obtained by rebuilding, straightening, and improving the visibility on some, a few, of the existing roads. The other and most promising is by construction of new and often more direct routes, to higher standards of alignment and visibility but on a less elaborate scale than the spectacular "expressways" and "superhighways," and to operate them as toll roads. The immediate, direct, visible saving, in addition to added convenience and safety, will be the most compelling inducement to general acceptance and usage.

Many of the roads now in use, and which were constructed in the early days of instrumentally controlled highway construction, were located with the idea of serving the greatest number of people and without much concern for alignment, visibility, or directness of route, which means low capacity for traffic. It has been observed that these resulted in many diversions and "political curves," but since these were the result of popular demand for roads, the final effect was, in fact, the extension of roads to a large number of people. Modern vehicle speeds and traffic volumes were not foreseen, of course. It is this particular circumstance that now opens definite possibilities for great improvement, and if the traffic problem of the country is to be met in any responsible time it can, nay, must be done with the capitalized revenue from tolls on such routes in rural areas with a current traffic flow of 750 to 1,000 vehicles per day.

Obviously, then, such a road need not and could not economically be built to the standards of the current "superhighways," with their elaborate interchanges, grade separations, rest havens, and other expensive appurtenances. Limited access, Class A single roadways, with narrow roadway separation on "blind" curves, "off center" passing lanes at intervals, provision for future traffic increases, simple functional interchanges, drainage and toll collection facilities, without excessive architectural adornment are all that is needed. Such a road will permit a sustained speed of seventy miles per hour and will have a safe capacity of over 3,000 vehicles per day. With equipment now available, such a road can be built, even in the mountainous regions of eastern Kentucky, for less than $200,000 per mile and in more favorable terrain, such as exists over much of Kentucky, for considerably less. This contrasts quite visibly with $1 million or so per mile for the "expressways," "turnpikes," "superhighways," and "thruways."

Much careful engineering study will obviously have to be given to this problem and especially to the search for shorter and better routes. The Topographic Mapping Program, carried out by the A & I D Board[1], is about completed and the data that has been accumulated will greatly simplify this problem. Active attention should be given to this very important matter at once.

A convincing example of the existence of a shorter and better route, such as is here proposed, exists on Kentucky 15, in the mountainous southeastern part of the state. This route is sometimes known as the Trail of the Lonesome Pine, after the novel of that name by John Fox, Jr., which had its setting in this romantic part of Kentucky. This section lies between Campton in Wolfe County and Quicksand, a short distance south of Jackson in Breathitt County, although Kentucky 15 in entirety can be greatly improved. Constructed prior to 1930, the portion running via Stillwater, Landsaw, Van Cleve, Keck, and Jackson is a winding circuitous one, very tiresome to drive, over thirty miles long. For several miles north of Jackson the present route follows the grade of a former logging railroad, crossing a large mountain with numerous hairpin curves and switchbacks. The proposed alternate route is from Campton via Holly Creek and Van Cleve to the outskirts of Jackson thence to Quicksand and is slightly over nineteen miles long in all. The travel distance is shortened by 12 3/10 miles, or more than a third. For a Class A roadway, there will be no necessity for any curve greater than six degrees and no grade in excess of 5 percent, and as already indicated such a road will permit high speeds with safety. . . .[2]

From a usage standpoint the expressways, operated as toll roads, are often a matter of choice with the motorist, against a free route. Roads such as here proposed are much less so because of the greater relative and apparent saving and the absence of competitive free routes of comparable convenience.

Physically, the route suggested as an alternate for Kentucky 15 is an exceptionally favorable one for construction and for low cost right-of-way. Only two small streams are crossed and, with the exception of one section of about four miles, with fairly heavy earthwork, other construction is quite moderate. An estimate showing the various cost items is appended.

In keeping with and in support of this general idea as applied to Kentucky 15, the distance south between Quicksand or Jackson and Hazard can be shortened about 12 1/2 miles over the presently used route of forty-four miles of Kentucky 15. This is by way of Duane and Lost Creek. A portion of this location has already been built and the remainder is in the final engineering stages. This situation, with respect to such roads, can be duplicated many times in Kentucky and elsewhere.

The Kentucky 15 Association, a civic group organized to promote the construction of better roads and to encourage tourist traffic into the depressed coal-producing region in Kentucky River Valley, is advocating a "Midwest to Miami," federally designated road of which the section considered is a portion. The tourist trade is now considered a big industry in Kentucky and one that will increase with improved roads, especially in the mountainous areas. The route that the Kentucky 15 Association proposes is the most direct one available from the Middle West to the Southeast and the east coast of Florida, but many of the existing roads are poor, particularly those crossing Kentucky. The subject improvement would probably give impetus to this proposal.

Speed of construction, under the direction of outside engineers which has by-passed the bureaucratic inertia, formalities, and rigidity of some of the state and federal agencies, has been one of the outstanding developments in connection with the recently built turnpikes. Use of newly developed engineering techniques has also been an important factor. There is no apparent reason why the undertaking here described could not be completed within twelve to fifteen months, depending somewhat upon the season in which active work commences and if authority is adequately delegated and procedures used elsewhere with notable success are followed.

1. Agricultural and Industrial Development Board. For more information see letter from July 18, 1951, in this section.

2. Governor Wetherby interjected here a detailed analysis of the economic aspects of the relocation of Kentucky 15. Terming them impressive, the governor estimated that it would save the traveling public $314,200 per year. The overall construction cost of $3,264,000, or $164,800 per mile, would be repaid over thirty years at an interest computed at 3.5 percent. The traffic flow of 750 vehicles per day would more than justify the construction costs, providing an annual excess of $48,450. Lower interest rates and higher traffic volume would increase the economic base. The new road would also mean increased safety and accident reduction and time saving. These advantages were difficult to reduce to figures or measurable terms of general welfare and social benefit.

HIGHWAY SAFETY PROGRAM
Letter / January 11, 1951

[To Mrs. Ike Miller, Jackson]

THE heads of the Highway, State Police, and several other Kentucky departments are outstanding in their willingness to cooperate and coordinate their efforts toward accident prevention and highway safety. It is felt that this holds great promise for the reduction of traffic accidents in our state.

Kentucky has initiated a broad Highway Safety Program and is working in conjunction with the President's Highway Safety Conference in meeting individual and collective responsibilities on our highways. State and local officials are working together with increased harmony and effectiveness to help make our streets and highways safer.

So that those on the Governor's Coordinating Highway Safety Committee may be appraised of the expression of interest of the Jackson Woman's Club in this important matter, we have asked Mr. Guthrie Crowe,[1] Chairman of the Committee and Commissioner of State Police, to contact you further in this regard to the end that working and cooperating arrangements might be effected between the safety committee and your club.

1. Guthrie Ferguson Crowe (1910-), attorney, practiced law in La Grange (1933-1942, 1946-1952); judge at La Grange (1938-1942); state representative (1942); commissioner of Kentucky State Police (1948-1952); United States district judge in Canal Zone (1952-1977); born in La Grange and resides in Fort Lauderdale, Florida. *Who's Who in America, 1978-1979,* 40th ed. (Chicago, 1978), 1:730.

Mrs. Ike Miller was a member of the Jackson Woman's Club.

MILITARY DEFENSE TRANSPORTATION
Letter / March 27, 1951

[To Earle C. Clements, Washington, D.C.]

DURING the past few weeks as motor transport activity has increased as a result of the accelerated pace of defense production, attention has been more acutely focused on load limit restrictions and truck license requirements imposed by the state. The overall importance of this matter is substantiated further by an increasing number of communications received both here in the office and in the Highway Department, from other governors, highway department officials of other states, various federal agencies and officials, and Council of State Governments.

The purpose of my writing you is to call your attention to the nature of the problems we are facing and to advise you of the type of difficulties we are encountering. I do not know that you are in position to be of assistance in helping us overcome those problems now, but felt that you should be acquainted with our situation so that your specific assistance could be more effectively used in the event we have to appeal to the top officials in the defense establishment or the national production authority.

To facilitate the movement of motor vehicle carriers loaded with defense material operating in Kentucky, I named on December 15, 1950, M. F. Johnson, director of the Division of Maintenance, Department of Highways, and A. R. Steele, director of the Law Enforcement Division, Department of Motor Transportation, as liaison officials to cooperate with the Military Traffic Service. This step was taken pursuant to a letter received from E. G. Plowman, director, office of the Secretary of Defense, Military Traffic Service. This committee began serving at once in a liaison capacity between the state, the American Association of Motor Vehicle Administrators, and the Department of the Army, and is functioning generally in accord with the directive sent out with Mr. Plowman's letter. Since that time, however, the Defense Transport Administration, with James K. Knudson as administrator, has stepped into the picture, causing considerable doubt and confusion as to just what the policy of the federal government is in the transport field.[1]

The above-mentioned state committee may grant special size, weight, and license dispensations. This may be accomplished, however, only upon the application of authorized representatives of the military departments with prior committee authorization granted before movement of the load over Kentucky highways. Thus far there has been apparently no concerted effort by the military authorities to effect approval by the committee on these overloaded trucks in the state prior to their movement over Kentucky highways. As a result there is an increasing number of excessively loaded trucks doing further damage to our already battered highways.

This brings us to the critical point which I am anxious for you to understand. That is, while the Highway Department is deeply interested in facilitating the flow of legitimate military transport, this lack of prior approval by the official state committee permits chiseling that could be avoided through more uniform federal policy. There are already instances where sealed trucks are moving across our highways with strong reasons for believing that the nature of the load is alien by any standard of measure to the war mobilization effort. The Highway Department is keeping in close touch with surrounding states and entertains the hope that, through a sensible and conciliatory approach to the problem by both state officials and federal authorities, an acceptable policy on the part of all concerned can be adopted and adhered to without leaving loopholes for flagrant violations by the trucking industry and irreparable damage to our highways.

With the foregoing outline at hand I believe you will be in a position to better handle future problems similar to those involving overloaded trucks held in various towns and about which you called last week. It may also be helpful in the event the situation grows worse and we are forced into lodging a bill of complaints with the Defense Department and seek your guidance and help in channeling it to the proper sources.

This letter was written in light of the emergency situation created by the Korean War.

1. M. F. Johnson (1902-), joined the Kentucky Department of Highways in 1922; paving engineer, United States Air Force, Langley Field, Virginia (1947); route planning engineer with Kentucky Department of Highways (1957); born in Virgie and resides in Frankfort. *Who's Who in the South and Southwest, 1959-1960,* 6th ed. (Chicago, 1959), p. 420.

A.R. Steele, no vita available.

Edward Grosvenor Plowman (1899-), director of Bureau of Business and Social Research and dean of Extension Division, University of Denver (1930-1935); executive assistant to Board of Water Commissioners, Denver (1933-1936); traffic manager, Colorado Fuel and Iron Corporation (1937-1943); director, Military Traffic Service, Department of Defense (1950-1951); vice president in charge of traffic, United States Steel Corporation (1944-1962); chairman, Maine Transportation Commission (1965-1968); president and chairman, Transportation Research Foundation (1968-1973); born in Brookline, Massachusetts. *Who's Who in America, 1978-1979,* 40th ed. (Chicago, 1978), 2:2587.

James K. Knudson (1906-1963), attorney; reporter, copy desk writer, editor of numerous school, church, national publications (1924-1951); president of Knudson-Skidmore Fruit and Produce Company, Brigham City, Utah (1928-1930); attorney, United States Department of Agriculture (1935-1940); became owner of Hotel Brigham Properties (1945); administrator of Defense Transportation Administration (1950-1958); born in Brigham City, Utah. *Who's Who in America, 1954-1955,* 28th ed. (Chicago, 1954), pp. 1493-94.

KENTUCKY RIVER TRANSPORTATION
Letter / July 18, 1951

[To Major General Lewis A. Pick, Washington, D.C.]

SINCE the announcement that the U. S. Corps of Engineers had decided to abandon locks 8 through 14 on the Kentucky River as of August 1, 1951, I have had occasion to discuss this move with many people in the area directly concerned. In the course of these discussions it has been brought to my attention that while no use of the transportation facilities of the upper river is being made at this time, definite plans are under way to barge several thousand tons of coal down the river annually. It is my understanding that these plans have reached the stage where contracts are being negotiated between coal producers of the Hazard Field and such customers as Eastern Kentucky R. E. A. for coal to be delivered to their authorized generating plant at Ford, Kentucky, and the Kentucky Utilities Company for coal to be delivered to their plant at Tyrone, Kentucky.

The state of Kentucky is making every effort to bring industries within her borders in order to furnish employment locally and thus lessen or stop the migration of workers from Kentucky to other areas. In negotiating with industrial prospects, the State Agricultural and Industrial Development Board[1] finds the area in which a majority of those prospects are interested to be those counties along the Kentucky River between Winchester in Clark County and the mouth of the river. This can be explained in part by the excellent rail and highway transportation facilities available in the area, but consideration is also given to the possibility of bringing fuel for operation and heating down the Kentucky River and to the possibility of bringing such heavy raw materials as steel and iron to, or near, the industrial sites by water from the Pittsburgh and Youngstown areas.

As governor of the Commonwealth of Kentucky, I feel that the savings in transportation costs to the consumers of Kentucky coal and to those industries receiving raw material by barge will be many times greater than the cost involved in the continued operation of locks 8 through 14.

For the above reasons I therefore request that the Corps of Engineers reconsider its decision to close locks 8 through 14 on the Kentucky River.

---

1. The board was created in 1948 by an act of the General Assembly. It was directed to develop and maintain an inventory of Kentucky's natural and human resources. The results were made available to business and other groups, both governmental and private, for the purpose of attracting their attention to the industrial, commercial, and agricultural potentialities of the Commonwealth. It was directed by a board composed of no more than nine members, appointed by the governor, who designated a chairman. In 1952 this chairman was Earl R. Muier of Louisville. The members were chosen for their experience and served without compensation, except expenses. The board employed a hired director who served as executive officer. *Acts of the General Assembly of the Commonwealth of Kentucky,* 1948, Chapter 48 (H.B. 199), pp. 98-101.

Lewis Andrew Pick (1890-1956), civil engineer with the Southern Railroad (1914-1916); United States district engineer, New Orleans (1925-1928); instructor, Command and General Staff School (1934-1938); executive officer to divisional engineer, Ohio River Division, Cincinnati (1939-1941); chief of engineers, Department of the Army (1949-1953); vice-chairman, Georgia-Pacific

Plywood Company (1953-1956). Pick was born in Brookneal, Virginia, and promoted to the rank of lieutenant general in 1951. *Who's Who in America, 1954-1955,* 28th ed. (Chicago, 1954), p. 2121.

RURAL ROAD IMPROVEMENTS
Letter / September 11, 1951

[To Wallace Coomer, Edmonton]

THIS acknowledges your letter in the interest of Prices Creek Road in your county.

We are glad to pass the information contained in your communication along to the Rural Highway Department for consideration. In doing so, permit me to point out that more miles of rural roads have been built and improved in every county in Kentucky during the past three years than ever before in the history of our state. While the distance that must be covered is such that it has not been possible for all of the rural roads of every county to be improved during that period, every citizen for the first time may now look forward with a degree of hope never before enjoyed that "their" particular road can be placed on a year-round travel basis within a reasonable time.

The Highway Department has been requested to inform you if available funds will permit early improvement to the road in which you are interested.

HIGHWAY IMPROVEMENTS REVENUE
Letter / December 28, 1951

[To Herman Schmeing, Louisville]

THE note enclosed with your much appreciated Christmas greeting brought to mind an event that has been clouded by time but one which I now recall. If my memory is not too hazy, the bad mud road which we encountered, at least for the moment, served a good purpose. The new direction which we were forced to take carried us into good bird hunting country, and I believe our day was right successful.

However, do not conclude from this episode that mud roads lend any gratification to those who must travel them, even the most casual user, for I have long felt that one of the most stifling effects on the progress of our state has been the lack of year-round usable rural roads. It was this very deep convinction that prompted my concerted effort in the 1948 General Assembly towards the passage of the so-called two cent gasoline tax measure.[1] During the three years this additional revenue has been spent on Kentucky rural roads, an almost magic change has been accomplished in wintertime travel in our rural counties.

While I am familiar with the disappointment of many individuals in many counties who have not thus far been successful in bringing a good rock-surface road by their property or through their neighborhood, these same people now, for the first time, have a real chance to witness such an improvement during their lifetime. I trust this covers your situation in Russell County and that before too long the stretch of road in which you are interested can be placed on a year-round travelable basis.

---

1. *Acts of the General Assembly of the Commonwealth of Kentucky,* 1948, Chapter 45 (H.B. 195) and Chapter 46 (H.B. 196), pp. 92–95.

Herman Schmeing was Louisville assistant postmaster.

SUPER TOLL ROADS
Letter / August 13, 1953

[To Mrs. John Mathias, Louisville]

THE question and answer news item regarding both merits and objections to toll roads attached to your August 11 letter has been read with interest. As all sides to an issue or a program that is controversial and is yet in the embryonic stage are essential if the right solution is to be reached, I particularly am interested in the negative views of the *American Motel Magazine.* I shall likewise try to review the *Coronet* article.

The proposed meeting of state governors and officials who would appropriately be concerned with the idea of a Chicago-to-Florida superhighway will be purely exploratory, with emphasis placed on the feasibility of such a joint undertaking.

While I personally am not ready to express an opinion on a subject as broad and complex as that of super toll roads, I am sufficiently informed and deeply enough concerned with highway accidents and general traffic congestion on many of our main thoroughfares to say that some drastic changes must be made in highway facilities if the American traveling public is to continue the accelerated use of the automobiles now being manufactured. It is up to the road building engineers, traffic and safety technicians, and public officials in a position to give expression to the desires and wishes of the majority of our citizens to take corrective measures in meeting this steadily mounting problem.

I assure you whatever moves Kentucky may make along this line will be done only after exhaustive study and consideration are devoted to the subject and with the best interests of the state and her people in mind.

LAKES-GULF HIGHWAY
Letter / December 7, 1953

[To Frank Smothers, Chicago, Illinois]

In talking with Herb Wiltsee[1] some time ago, I did not intend to give the impression that there were extensive details embracing both the purpose and progress of the so-called Lakes-Gulf Highway as to constitute a formal article in the very fine Council of State Governments publication *State Government.* However, as an indication of what has thus far transpired in this area of interstate interest and cooperation, I recite the following.

On September 27 and 28 a meeting was held at the Kenlake Hotel, Kentucky Lake State Park, with representatives present from Indiana, Kentucky, Tennessee, Georgia, and Florida. It was agreed immediately that the meeting was not called for the purpose of discussing and planning for the construction of toll roads as such. Rather, the interest of the five participating states centered around the increasing problem of highway traffic and the growing need for improving and expediting north-south traffic accommodations. It was declared that the matter of financing and constructing improved north-south roads in each of the states involved was the proper and exclusive concern of those states. The interest of each state represented was simply to develop through coordinated plans a north-south highway or highways that would take care of the traffic flow through each of the states.

Indiana, Kentucky, and Florida all were frank in appraising their respective problems and their inability to take care of the ever-increasing traffic by freeway or conventional road systems. All three states are turning immediately to at least one toll, limited-access road. The proposed road of each is north-south. In view of this, it seems only practical that close coordination be maintained so that a feasible link-up at state boundaries might be effected. To achieve this, a committee was composed of the highway commissioners or chief highway officials of each of the five states participating, with the option that Alabama and Mississippi would be permitted to become affiliated if they so desire. The title of the organization is the Governors' Lakes-Gulf Highway Planning Commission. They were instructed to meet at the earliest possible date.

The question of a Lakes to Gulf superhighway was answered eventually with the enactment on June 29, 1956, of the Federal Aid to Highway Act. Section 108 declared that it was essential to the national interest to complete the "National System of Interstate Highways" that was begun in 1944. A period of thirteen years was provided for their completion. Governor Wetherby encouraged President Dwight Eisenhower to support the construction of the interstate highway system. See *U.S. Statutes at Large*, 1956, Vol. 70, Public Law 627, Chapter 462 (H.R. 10660), pp. 374–87.

Kentucky built a toll road between Louisville and Elizabethtown prior to the enactment of the federal act. Later, this section of the road was incorporated into the interstate system, becoming a segment of Interstate 65. The bonds providing for its construction were retired in 1976, more than twenty years early.

The construction of the Kentucky Turnpike initiated an extensive toll-road system that eventually touched every section of the state. The road was not without its opponents, however. In the Democratic primary race in 1955, gubernatorial candidate Albert B. Chandler called it a road that began nowhere and ended nowhere. The statement did nothing to ingratiate him to the people of Louisville or Elizabethtown. For more information see letter from January 8, 1954, in this section.

1. Herb Wiltsee was with the Council of State Governments under Governor Wetherby and in charge of operations of the Southern Governors Conference when Wetherby was chairman in 1955.

Frank Albert Smothers (1901-), United Press Association (1924-1925); *Chicago Daily News* (1925-1942); editor, *Chicago Sun* (1942-1946); born in Rossville, Illinois, and resides in Chicago. *Who's Who in the Midwest*, 1949, 2d ed. (Chicago, 1949), p. 1163.

KENTUCKY TURNPIKE CONSTRUCTION
Letter / January 8, 1954

[To Burtis R. Kessler, Miami, Florida]

THE 1950 session of the Kentucky General Assembly passed an enabling act permitting the Highway Department to provide for the construction of toll, limited-access roads.[1] Engineering and preliminary survey work on the financial feasibility has been under way for more than a year. Recently the report was completed. A route was designated between Louisville and Elizabethtown, Kentucky, a distance of about forty miles, which was described as being capable of drawing a volume of traffic required to make the revenue bonds attractive to investors.

As soon as this was established, a test suit was filed to determine the constitutionality of the act. A decision by the state's highest court upholding the toll-road act in all respects was handed down a few weeks ago.[2] With this green light, plans are being vigorously pushed toward the letting of the contract so that actual construction can be started at an early date. This will be Kentucky's first link in the proposed Great Lakes to Gulf Expressway.

In September a meeting was held in Kentucky with representatives from Indiana, Kentucky, Tennessee, Georgia, and Florida present for the purpose of effecting cooperation among the states in the development of this promising interstate expressway.[3]

---

1. The decision to construct toll roads began under the administration of Governor Earle Clements. In 1950 the General Assembly enacted legislation in order to provide for the construction of "modern express highways or superhighways." Its purpose was to facilitate vehicular traffic, remove many of the handicaps and hazards on congested highways, and promote the agricultural and industrial development of the Commonwealth. The Department of Highways was authorized to issue revenue bonds, payable solely from revenues, to

finance the projects. The department was responsible for constructing, maintaining, repairing, and operating the turnpike projects. See *Acts of the General Assembly of the Commonwealth of Kentucky,* 1950, Chapter 157 (S.B. 109), pp. 618-33.

2. The constitutionality of the toll-road construction act was questioned since state road funds were used to survey and maintain toll roads. The Kentucky Court of Appeals ruled on December 18, 1953, that the act did not violate the constitution's prohibiting expenditure from the state road fund on any but public highways since a toll road, being owned by the state and open to public travel, constituted a "public highway." *Guthrie* v. *Curlin,* Ky. 263 S.W. 2d 240. See *Kentucky Decisions* 262 S.W. 2d–265 S.W. 2d (St. Paul, Minn., 1954).

3. For more information see letter dated December 7, 1953, in this section.

TRUCK WEIGHT LIMITS
Letter / January 15, 1954

[To George R. St. Clair, Brandenburg]

THERE is evidence of increasing interest in the important, yet controversial, subject of truck weight limits. However, there is nothing unusual about this situation, as differences of views and opinions have existed since the trucking industry became a factor in the state's transportation network.

While I have no fixed convictions on the subject, I am deeply interested in the proper use and maintenance of our public highways. At this time, I am glad to report that the Kentucky Highway Department has participated in a lengthy series of tests and experiments held in Maryland, the purpose of which has been to determine the effect that trucks with varying load weight and axle accommodations have on different kinds of highway surfaces and road beds.

My own views and recommendations to the General Assembly, if offered on this subject, will be based exclusively upon the advice of the Highway Department engineers.

The issue of truck weight limits led to a struggle between the trucking and railroad interests within the state. Governor Wetherby personally intervened and called representatives of both sides to meet with him. While an agreement was reached that seemed to satisfy both interests, no legislation concerning truck weight limits was enacted by the General Assembly in 1954.

This letter, written by Governor Wetherby to Judge George R. St. Clair, was in response to a resolution adopted by the Meade County Fiscal Court on February 9, 1954, protesting any increase in truck weight limits.

George R. St. Clair (1899-), magistrate of Meade County (1933); county judge protem (1933-1937); county judge (1949-1965); born in Breckenridge County and resides in Irvington. Letter, December 12, 1980.

TOURISM

RENFRO VALLEY
Mt. Vernon / January 7, 1951

KENTUCKY, rich in scenic grandeur and with a wealth of historical landmarks, enjoys the privilege of playing host each year to millions of the American traveling public. Our Commonwealth, through the cooperation and efforts of various agencies of state government and the Kentucky Chamber of Commerce, began about three years ago to make her bid to increase her tourist industry.

During this period tourist trade in our state almost doubled. Long before this program was initiated, however, John Lair[1] of Renfro Valley was a self-appointed one-man Chamber of Commerce for the Blue Grass State. By use of the air waves for several years, one of his primary duties has been publicizing Kentucky through his renowned Renfro Valley radio shows. His enthusiastic endeavors in radiating happiness and friendliness are reflected in the hearts of thousands and do not go unheralded. It is a pleasure indeed to recognize his contribution to Kentucky by commissioning him as a Kentucky Colonel. Colonel Lair is a tried and true ambassador of good will, good fellowship, and good fun—the ingredients of wholesome living.

The people of Kentucky, although dynamic and energetic in modern and progressive planning, have still retained down through the years the art of leisurely living, the type of living that prompted Stephen Collins Foster to write his immortal and imperishable song "My Old Kentucky Home," and the type of living that has made Renfro Valley a homespun community where neighborliness and everyday living have become traditional.

To all of our out-of-state radio listeners of Renfro Valley we extend a cordial invitation to visit the land of the Blue Grass, where a friendly welcome awaits you. We urge you to partake of the hospitality of the folks here at Renfro Valley, hospitality that is symbolic of the entire Commonwealth.

We have fun in Kentucky and especially do we have fun here at Renfro Valley, but along with our gay entertainment we feel a deep sense of world responsibility. We eagerly face the future with the confidence that the people of Kentucky will join the citizens of other states throughout the land in exerting whatever effort or sacrifice may be required in the pursuit of peace. Our first contribution is to the cause of world peace, and as we go about our daily tasks it is my prayer that through our efforts and with the divine guidance of mankind's Guardian the rays of freedom soon will shine again throughout the world.

Renfro Valley is located in Rockcastle County, Kentucky. The area lay astride the Wilderness Road and was settled in 1791. On November 4, 1939, a country music program originating there was first broadcast over the radio and was called the Renfro Valley Barn Dance. In the beginning the program was carried by station WLW in Cincinnati, later by WHAS in Louisville, and eventually seven days a week over the CBS radio network. In 1956 a series of television films was made there. John Lair, *Renfro Valley Then and Now* (Renfro Valley Enterprise, 1957).

1. John Lair (1894-) formed a country music group and first broadcast over station WLS in Chicago. He came to Renfro Valley, built a barn, and began to broadcast his show in 1939. Born in Livingston. John Lair, *Renfro Valley Then and Now* (Renfro Valley Enterprise, 1957).

BRIDGE DEDICATION
Burnside / March 31, 1951

MR. TAYLOR,[1] honored guests, and friends: It is an honor and a privilege to be with you today. Kentuckians everywhere will join with me in extending sincere greetings and best wishes.

We are all proud of this great development and the four beautiful and serviceable highway bridges to be dedicated. We are proud of this great north-south highway and of two fine east-west travel routes. We are proud of the work you Pulaski countians are doing to develop another great tourist objective here in the gateway foothills of the Cumberland Mountains.

In the late 1800s and the early 1900s Burnside was noted as a river port and a beehive of shipping industry, the largest between Cincinnati and Chattanooga. It was also noted as a resort. Fine hotels catered to pleasure-seekers who found the clear waters of the Cumberland River and the green mountains surrounding the town picturesque and restful. The old Seven Gables Hotel, mecca for thousands of tourists, was surrounded by well-tended lawns and statuesque and luxury carriages.

A splendid macadam toll road was reached by a ferry over the Cumberland's South Fork and several excellent river steamers, the Rowena, the Celina, and others, afforded luxury river transportation. Travel between Burnside and Monticello was provided by two stagecoach lines. The high-wheeled coaches drawn by four white horses over the river and through Bronston and Mill Springs, always with a capacity load, presented an impressive picture. The original stage was probably the oldest in operation in our state when the automobile bus took over.

Bright pages from the history of a thriving industrial Burnside dulled somewhat when the river traffic ceased and the great lumber mills moved away. The town settled down to a comfortable size and joined the ranks of other solid Kentucky villages.

The red-letter day arrived when the great Wolf Creek Reservoir was no longer a rumor but became a venture under construction. It was moving day for the old town, and move it did. The results are in evidence everywhere. You planned your new town to fit the pattern of the new future. It is easy to predict a bright new future for Burnside and for this whole Cumberland development.

In the process of this development we have been privileged to extend every possible cooperation. The future, not only of Burnside and of this area but of all Kentucky, is brightened immeasurably by the prospects offered here. The addition of this great tourist objective will mean many more tourist dollars for Kentucky.

This great industry, the tourist business in Kentucky, which has had its first development and greatest growth under the present administration, has multiplied with breath-taking rapidity. Only a few years ago our state's tourist business was valued at $71 million. In 1950, out-of-state visitors spent $293 million in Kentucky, more than three times the earlier figure. They traveled one and one-third billion miles on Kentucky highways. They paid $7 million into the state's road fund. Last year more than 1.7 million people visited our state parks. The splendid new state park you are to have in this section will add its share to the total attractions and will bring rich benefits to a wide area.[2]

Time was when it was thought that the tourist trade benefited only garages, service stations, restaurants, and hotels. We have come to realize that tourist money flows into every business channel in the community. And that every community in the state benefits from the tourist business in every other community. You are joining as partners in the expansion of one of the state's biggest sources of income. More and more of the right kind of facilities to take care of the increasing tourist trade will be needed and provided. This section will join in the great expansion program now characterizing the state. In the past two years Kentucky added more than a hundred new motor courts, motels, and hotels. Food establishments, services of all kinds are experiencing the same growth.

You in the area have been richly endowed. The lure of your magnificent natural scenery has been enchanced by developments affording wonderful recreational facilities. And the initiative and interest of your people, as evidenced here today, will translate your opportunities into achievements.

Your state administration is fully convinced that a greater Kentucky will result from this new and growing industry. Tourists have a way of going back again and again to places they like. They like Kentucky. Vacation visits may well lead to settling here, investing money, contributing to the economic life of the community and state. The ultimate potential of Kentucky's tourist program is limited only by our imagination and our energy.

Since January 1, 1948, 7,146 miles of new roads have been completed or placed under contract in Kentucky. These raods, as Commissioner Curlin mentioned, are new, smooth surfaces which will contribute their part in this overall tourist program. Roads and bridges cost a lot of money today. We have spent, or contracted to spend, in the past three years almost $90 million in this, Kentucky's greatest and most comprehensive road-building program.

As we dedicate these fine bridges that constitute so substantial a part in this great development, let us rededicate ourselves to a continued program of building for the future of Kentucky.

On April 1, 1951, Governor Weatherby dedicated four bridges in Pulaski County. The bridges were made necessary with the creation of Cumberland Lake. Their total cost exceeded $4 million. The dedication ceremonies were arranged by the Greater Burnside Chamber of Commerce with the assistance of the Somerset Chamber of Commerce. Governor Wetherby was accompanied to Burnside by a large number of government officials, including Emerson Beauchamp, Rural Highway Commissioner. Senator John Sherman Cooper also attended. *The Commonwealth,* Somerset, April 4, 1951.

1. Norman I. Taylor was retiring president of the Burnside Chamber of Commerce and master of ceremonies at the bridge dedication. Later that day he presided at a luncheon in honor of the governor and his party at the Lake View Restaurant.

2. General Burnside State Park.

MOUNTAIN LAUREL FESTIVAL
Pineville / May 25, 1951

EACH year the Mountain Laurel Festival takes its place among the annals of Kentucky's most beautiful pageants. To all of you from within and without our borders I bid you welcome. After you have witnessed this inspiring coronation ceremony I am confident you will be glad you came.

In the chord of pomp and parade that is characteristic of this pageant may also be heard a note of solemnity and sacredness. This occasion tells a story that the pen cannot adequately describe nor the artist sufficiently portray with color.

Few states are blessed with a diversity of mountains, forests, streams, and lakes that have long attracted visitors to Kentucky; here and in Laurel Cove is a rich example of the fascinating beauty with which nature has so kindly endowed our beloved Commonwealth.

There is no more typical Kentucky event that gives more effective advertisement to the attractions that eastern and southeastern Kentucky offer to tourists and to residents of other sections of the state than the Mountain Laurel Festival. The mountains of eastern and southeastern Kentucky present a majestic panorama of timber-covered slopes broken by picturesque streams and valleys. The word Cumberland is of special significance, for in Kentucky a great river, a mighty falls, a spectacular gap, and an imposing mountain range proudly bear this name.

As we recall the purpose of the Mountain Laurel Festival, to develop an appreciation of the beauty of our land, to lead people to understand and appreciate the majesty of our mountains, the loveliness of our flora, the marvelous scenery of our highlands, and the kindliness and generosity of our people, I am confident that you who have witnessed and participated in this year's festival will agree with me that each successive Kentucky Mountain Laurel Festival has accomplished the purpose for which it was designed.

We boast not only of the beauty of Kentucky's scenic wonders, but also of the charms and grace of her young womanhood. Look at these lovely ladies, each the pride of her school, each a queen.

All of you look forward to the crowning of the Laurel Queen who will be chosen to reign over this festival, but none of you looks forward to it more than I do.[1]

---

1. The Mountain Laurel Queen for 1951 was Betty Lyen a native of Harrodsburg, who represented Transylvania College. *Louisville Courier-Journal,* May 26, 1951.

HISTORIC PRESERVATION
Letter / April 3, 1951

[To J. Winston Coleman, Lexington]

THERE are throughout the state many historical buildings, with intriguing architectural designs, already serving as an important link in our tourist attraction program or capable of being renovated for that purpose. It is clear that in many instances the importance of these old buildings is not fully appreciated from the historical and architectural side and there has been little consideration over the years devoted to their maintenance and rehabilitation; nor has there been attention paid to the general responsibility by civic groups, local or state governments toward providing for their preservation and upkeep.

Looking toward the establishment of a constructive policy and approach, I am giving consideration to the naming of a state committee composed of individuals who have a special interest in such matters and who might be willing to devote time and study toward ascertaining just what assets the state might have worthy of special interest. The purpose of this communication is to determine whether you would be willing to accept appointment on such a committee.

John Winston Coleman, Jr. (1898-), tobacco planter and author. Engaged in engineering work in New York, Kentucky, and other states (1920-1923); organizer and president of Coleman and Davis, Inc., general contractors, engineers and builders; owner and operator of Winburn Farm; author of many books and articles pertinent to the history and culture of the Bluegrass area of Kentucky; born and resides in Lexington. *Who's Who In America, 1952-1953,* 27th ed. (Chicago, 1952), p. 485.

ECONOMIC & INDUSTRIAL DEVELOPMENT

SOMERSET CHAMBER OF COMMERCE BANQUET
Somerset / March 31, 1951

IN attending this year's Somerset Chamber of Commerce annual meeting I realize that I follow a series of distinguished speakers, and I appreciate the honor which this occasion bestows. Through the years, this meeting has become a highlight among community gatherings both in Somerset and throughout southeastern Kentucky.

You have kindly granted me wide latitude in choice of speaking subject, but, to my way of thinking, the ties and sentiments of home overshadow all else in importance and there is no need to wander far afield.

I believe the advancement of this community and our state are primary interests of the Chamber of Commerce and the friends and guests attending this program, and I think you, like myself, are deeply interested in the economic growth, industrial development, and agricultural progress being made in Kentucky.

The will that prevails in the entire state to move forward is shown in the enthusiasm of this gathering tonight. One can hardly find a community where this march of progress is better typified than in Pulaski County and the surrounding area.

Broadly speaking, your state government and its activity in any field is but an example of the combined will of the citizens of the state. I believe the people of Kentucky want and are entitled to the best services which government can properly provide.

I am certain that it is our responsibility to furnish the best educational program the state can maintain. I believe the same interest of Kentucky citizens is centered in the proper care and treatment of patients and inmates in our welfare institutions. Old age and child welfare fund recipients deserve the maximum support which can be provided. The action taken by the special session of the state legislature in support of these programs is proof of the concern of the general public for further advancement in these fields.[1]

In agricultural services, conservation, and park development the public demands and the government is obliged to furnish the best it can provide in technical skills and progressive leadership.

It has long been apparent that the people of the state generally recognize the need for an upgrading in both industry and agriculture to reach an economic balance between the two. Since 1947, I have taken part in your state government's most vigorous and best-planned effort to strike an equitable balance between agriculture and industry. During these three years remarkable strides have been made in changing our state's predominantly agricultural economy to an economy that can depend upon both agriculture and industry for its prosperity. We must continue in strong pursuit of the balance that we are working toward—we are nearer today than ever before to being able to face and defeat the economic difficulties that invariably follow a drought year in agriculture or a depression year in industry.

New industrial payrolls pouring into the channels of trade and commerce have raised the volume of retail sales and the purchase of agricultural, dairying, and industrial products to unprecedented heights. In 1950, Kentucky acquired sixteen new major industries having tangible assets estimated at over $50 million.

As examples of the movement of industry from the North and East toward the South I cite three major plants that have taken up residence in Kentucky within the past ninety days: one is the Corning Glass Company at Danville. Another is the Baxter Laboratories at Greenville, and just yesterday National Carbide and Chemical Corporation announced construction of a $10 million manufacturing plant at Calvert City near Kentucky Dam. These, of course, are in addition to the giant Atomic Energy Commission Plant at Paducah. This, in my opinion, is the most far-reaching industrial asset that has yet come into our state. Transcending its immediate importance in the war emergency will be its future contribution to our present peacetime economy. Atomic engineers are working with confidence toward the day—and it is within the forseeable future—when the miracle of this released energy will be safely harnessed and geared to civilian production and benefit.

The economic progress that is bringing to the outskirts of many peaceful Kentucky cities the hum of busy machinery, manned by skilled and well-paid workers, is being accomplished only through the combined efforts and vision of leaders in industry, business, and government. Your state government, through the Agricultural and Industrial Development Board and its other agencies, the State Chamber of Commerce, local chamber affiliates, community development organizations, all these are working as partners for the advancement of this area and the whole state.

The city of Somerset is far from lacking in industry and, proud as you are of those industries which are situated here, I know you seek additional industrial development. You enjoy an enviable location with respect to many vital and determining factors that enter into plant site location. The area has abundant manpower, and within close proximity are rich natural resources of coal, timber, and unlimited water for industrial uses.

A discussion of Kentucky's economic growth or of this new area would be incomplete without mentioning a recently accelerated but highly important industry—Kentucky tourist travel. Tourist money does not reach the garages, service stations, restaurants, and hotels and stop there. It flows into every business channel in the community and adds to the wealth of the entire state. I am tourist minded. I am conscious of unlimited possibilities that can be more fully developed. The tourist business is already paying undreamed dividends, and if continued emphasis is placed on its promotion it will amount to a paid-up insurance policy, guaranteeing a steady flow of outside dollars for our state. Kentucky lies in the cross-roads of the national tourist pattern, and last year tourists left in Kentucky the staggering sum of $293 million.

In all of Kentucky I know of no town which is better located than Somerset to share in the tourist business. The distance between Somerset and Cumberland Falls is only a few minutes' travel. With the improvements that have been and are now being made at this nationally known tourist center, attractive accomodations for tourists and visitors are available. Mighty Cumberland Lake reaches within a stone's throw of your doorstep. The new state park, with initial work already under way, is little more than an hour's drive from here.

As the state expands its commercialized operations in each of our state parks, more of the right kind of privately owned facilities will be needed for the increasing tourist trade. Each will be the complement of the other. In this lake area and in nearly every section of Kentucky, an increased building program is already under way. In the past two years Kentucky added more than a hundred new motor courts, motels, and hotels—with a similar increase in the number of food establishments and service type businesses.

Kentucky has lost the feeling of sectionalism that at one time pitted one geographical region against the other. Improved communication and transportation make it inevitable that the state rise or fall as a unit. Progress in one locality reflects favorably throughout the state and benefits in one way or another every section of the Commonwealth. For example, last year the state Department of Agriculture added Somerset to the list of six other Kentucky communities where annual dairy shows are held. While primarily intended to give residents of this locality the opportunity to exhibit and view high-quality dairy entries, the success of that show has been instrumental in expansion of the dairy industry in this territory. There have since been around 120 registered dairy heifers brought into southeastern Kentucky for herd improvment purposes. The state Department of Agriculture furnished an expert on dairy cattle to accompany individual and group buyers and assist them in selection of highest-quality breeders. Through the normal sales of the Registered Dairy Cattle Associations these heifers and their offspring will, in due time, be found among countless dairy herds throughout the state, where they will continue the chain of improvement that began here in Somerset.

A sportsman knows you won't catch any fish without dipping into the pool. Kentucky's reservoirs of undeveloped wealth, especially the tourist and raw material processing industries, have waited many years for a state administration that would team with community effort and local enterprise to use our vast resources for the benefit of Kentucky and her people.

As long as I share in the responsibility and can influence the course Kentucky follows, I want to champion the cause of a greater Kentucky. Many of you feel as I do. The same fibre of ambition for community and state development has woven the business people of Somerset and this area into an active and enthusiastic Chamber of Commerce capable of turning out as you have tonight. This gathering demonstrates that you know the value of community effort.

Unity of will and singleness of purpose are the first ingredients of progress, whether that program be sought for community, state, or nation.

---

1. Governor Wetherby was alluding to the extraordinary session of the General Assembly that met in March 1951. For more information on the session see speeches from February 21, 1951 and March 6, 1951, in the Legislative Messages and Statements section.

WOLF CREEK DAM DEDICATION
Jamestown / September 1, 1951

IT is a pleasure for me to be back in this part of Kentucky today. The people of southern Kentucky have graciously given me invitations to speak before them several times within the last few months, and it has always been a privilege to accept.

It is a special privilege and one which I have long awaited to be here at the dedication of Wolf Creek Dam. This dam will be one of the most important structures in our entire Commonwealth, and this occasion symbolizes the completion of an effort that will mean greater things not only for the people in the Wolf Creek area, but for all Kentuckians.

The flood control provided by the dam will benefit a large portion of our state where both agriculture and industry need protection from flood waters. The electric power produced here will make it possible for south-central Kentucky to receive industries that never could have come in otherwise. The recreational facilities which will accrue will mean that all central and southern Kentucky will have a new playground. It will be a playground that will attract not only the citizens of Kentucky but those of surrounding states, and Kentucky will thus receive additional financial benefits from the tourist dollars attracted here.

Wolf Creek Dam is a project that has long been planned. The fact that it is today a reality is a tribute to the Corps of Engineers, the construction companies that worked on it, and to the citizens of this area who promoted it and gave unselfishly of their time and substance to make it possible.

I give my congratulations to all groups who aided in the building of this magnificent structure, and on behalf of the people of the Commonwealth of Kentucky I thank them for their part in adding so greatly to our state's resources.

The dedication of Wolf Creek Dam is a proud time for all who have had a part in its construction, but the dedication of the dam is only a starting point of responsibility for seeing that its potentialities are fully realized. Just as it took the efforts of the people of the Wolf Creek area to help bring the dam to reality, it will also take their efforts to make it serve them to the greatest extent.

We all want new industry in this area. With increased electric power available, we have a good talking point for industries, but we will have to work for them. We will also have to work if we make this section live up to its recreational possibilities. We now have a large lake whose beauty is unsurpassed in any part of the Commonwealth,[1] but it will have to be sold as a vacation spot, just as we will have to sell this section as a site for industry.

Your state government is well aware of the development that is needed here and of the part the state will have to play. Already the state Agricultural and Industrial Development Board and the state Department of Conservation have made studies to see where they can help, and they are planning development along industrial and recreational lines. It is my hope that you citizens of the Wolf Creek area will make the most of your opportunity here, and I pledge the cooperation of all state agencies in helping you.

It is my great privilege to present to you one of the best-loved men and one of the most-successful statesmen in America today. He is a native of Kentucky and as a Kentuckian shares with us the pride that we have in this new dam.

He has long been in public life and has held office on the national level during most of the time that water development projects such as this have been considered vital by our national government. He has consistently been an advocate of conservation measures and has used his influence so that such structures as this dam could come into existence to serve the people. Because of his position as the number two man in our national government and because he is loved by his fellow Kentuckians, he has been invited to dedicate this dam that will mean so much to Kentucky.

We know that he is happy to be back in his native state for this occasion, and as governor I am happy to welcome him back. I present to you the vice president of the United States, our own Alben Barkley.

---

1. Lake Cumberland.

EASTERN KENTUCKY TOWN HALL MEETING
Ashland / November 20, 1952

IT is appropriate that we hold this meeting here in Ashland, one of Kentucky's important industrial workshops. One of the earliest centers of Kentucky's iron industry, it is today the home of Kentucky's largest steel mill. In a very few years a great oil industry has developed here from small beginnings to make the name of Ashland a familiar roadside sign. I mention, also, your foundries and other metalworking shops and your other plants working with products of coal, wood, leather, and textiles.

There are few sections of Kentucky more blessed with natural resources than the thirteen counties represented here. You have many of the mines that put Kentucky third among the states in national coal production. Kentucky's great gas field is in the Big Sandy counties, and you supply not only many of your own demands but industrial areas to the north and east with fuel. Over in Carter and Rowan you have the clay industry which supplies fire brick to the steel mills and supplies all-purpose tile to a large section of the country. Throughout this area are brines, clays, oil, limestones, moulding, and glass sands which can be exploited far beyond their present uses to make a prosperous eastern Kentucky. There is probably no area in the country more fitted by its mineral resources for the establishment of chemical plants.

All of your communities need diversified industry to furnish employment for all and to build a well-rounded economy. You have other resources which provide the raw materials for smaller industries. Eastern Kentucky has some of the finest hardwood forests in the country. We have long furnished lumber to the nation. It is time that we ought to start making more highly finished wood products—furniture, plywood, charcoal, and wood distillates come immediately to mind. There is a field here for local enterprise and local capital to develop a new wood-using industry.

Contrary to general opinion, this is by no means the poorest section of Kentucky agriculturally. Five percent of Kentucky's farms was in these thirteen counties, and it is significant that their value doubled in the five years from 1945 to 1950, according to the U.S. Census. Our own Department of Agriculture figures show an increase of cattle, hogs, and other livestock in these counties in the last few years. There is every reason to think this area will become a tree-farming and an orchard region in the future.

It is significant that the cities of Ashland, Paintsville, Pikeville, Prestonsburg, West Liberty, Morehead, Grayson, and Greenup showed substantial gains in population at a time when many towns throughout Kentucky were standing still or showing losses. It is evident that eastern Kentucky has alert citizens who are working to build up this area. What is regrettable, of course, is that nine of the thirteen counties showed losses rather than gains and that there is substantial unemployment throughout the entire area. We know that in the ten-year census period some 400,000 of Kentucky's finest citizens of working age, many of them from eastern Kentucky, left their homes to seek employment in northern industrial communities. That is why we are here today—to do something about the situation and to develop new job opportunities for Kentucky citizens, particularly in the Big Sandy.

What is your state government doing to help in the development of eastern Kentucky? For one thing, Kentucky's Agricultrual and Industrial Development Board is set up to do the job of assisting Kentucky communities in finding out what their resources are and in helping them to bring them to the attention of industrial investors. The board is made up of nine Kentucky citizens who devote their time and effort without charge to the Commonwealth in the development of more prosperous Kentucky. The board includes two members from this part of the state, Harry LaViers of Paintsville and Martin Bowne[1] at Morehead.

The board, and other agencies of the state government and the university, have already devoted a great deal of effort to pushing the advantages of eastern Kentucky for greater industrial development. One that I am sure you have heard much about recently was the attempt to secure a new atomic energy plant in this area. The board marshaled figures on the population and labor force, on the available power and coal resources, and the excellent community facilities in the area near the proposed Greenup County site. They pointed out that in this tri-state area there is a network of cities and smaller communities equal to a much larger metropolitan area for the purposes of the Atomic Energy Commission. We were able to sell AEC on the advantages of this location but unfortunately could not provide the necessary level acreage, and the commission located its plant just across the river. I believe we will have many advantages in trade and employment in this area even with the Portsmouth location of the AEC plant; and I am sure that we will be able to obtain some of the satellite industries that will grow up in the neighborhood of the plant.

The Development Board has made detailed industrial surveys of most of your cities, among them Ashland, Louisa, Paintsville, Pikeville, and Morehead. Other surveys are in process for Prestonsburg, Grayson,

Olive Hill, and West Liberty. We have found these to be the best possible tools for presenting the advantages of Kentucky, as elsewhere. We have made a start but we have not yet done enough to bring more industry to this area.

I have, therefore, today instructed the members and staff of the Development Board to devote their time to making a complete economic base survey of eastern Kentucky. This includes the mineral and water resources, the agricultural and timber products, wholesale and retail trade, your communities and their labor supply. I have asked the board to secure the aid of the United States Department of Commerce, the Bureau of Mines, and other federal as well as state agencies to work out a plan for bringing the industrial potential of this area to the attention of chemical and woodworking industries, and to provide information for those interested in developing new industries in this area with local capital. You can be assured that you will have the entire cooperation of every agency of the state government in this undertaking.

So far we have been talking about new industry for east Kentucky and saying very little about the important existing industry. We have kept our coal associations informed of Marshall Plan and NATO coal purchases. We have repeatedly made AEC and other government agencies aware of our coal production and are working at the present time with TVA to see what can be done about getting more eastern Kentucky coal to steam plants. We have set up a Contract Information Center of the Governor's Small Business Commission in Louisville. The center has the job of letting every government procurement officer and every government prime contractor know what services are available to him from Kentucky manufacturers. I have called the attention of the Small Business Commission to the need for more contracts in eastern Kentucky, and can assure you that any eastern Kentucky businessman will have close cooperation in any efforts he may be making to secure defense work.

Thus far, I have talked about what your state government has done and will do to work with you here in eastern Kentucky. I am sure every person here knows, of course, that the answer to eastern Kentucky's need for more development will come, not from Frankfort or from Washington, but from you people who live here. It is up to Kentucky's communities to decide how strong they want to be, what industry and agriculture they need to support their people, and what steps they will take to develop their human and physical resources. We are proud of eastern Kentucky and of her people. We want to work with you for a greater Kentucky.

Governor Wetherby was interested in the economic diversification of Kentucky and believed that a healthy economy depended upon it. Although a majority of Kentucky's people subsisted on the basis of agriculture, he believed that more industry was needed, and he sought to induce out-of-state businesses to locate their plants and factories here. Eastern Kentucky was characterized by a depressed coal industry and high unemployment, and the governor hoped to attract industry there in order to stop the mass exodus of its residents. While his efforts in that region were not greatly successful, he did induce industry to other sections of the state. For a description of new industry in Kentucky see speech from March 31, 1951, in this section. For a description of business conditions in the state in 1953 see letter from October 30, 1953, in this section. For a discussion of the AEC decision see letter of August 28, 1952, in the Energy and the Environment section.

1. Harry LaViers (1900-1978), director of Big Sandy Elkhorn Coal Operators (1955); chairman, South East Coal Company of Irvine; member, Kentucky Agriculture and Industrial Development Board and the Kentucky Regional Planning Council; born in Wellston, Ohio. *Louisville Courier-Journal,* July 22, 1978.

Martin Starr Bowne (1889-), American Sewer Pipe Company (1912-1917); Robertson Clay Products Company (1920-1925); Lee Clay Products Company (1926-); member, Kentucky Agriculture and Industrial Development Board; born in Elmira, New York. Hambleton Tapp, ed., *Kentucky Lives: The Blue Grass State Who's Who* (Hopkinsville, Ky., 1966), p. 49.

TWO MILLION BARREL CELEBRATION AT THE BLANTON DISTILLERY
Frankfort / June 23, 1953

SINCE the repeal of prohibition in 1933, the whiskey business has been an extremely important factor in the economic life of the Commonwealth of Kentucky. As one of our leading industries, the manufacture of distilled spirits means much to the Commonwealth tax-wise. I note, for example, from some statistics prepared for this occasion we celebrate tonight, that the Albert B. Blanton Distillery alone has paid out over $7.5 million in taxes to our state during the twenty-year period of its two million barrel production. Over $5 million of that has been in the form of production taxes, and almost $2.5 million of it in other types of state taxes. It has been pointed out that this total would operate our state government for fourteen days, based on the 1951-1952 fiscal year budget. For that same fiscal year, it represents about 6 percent of the total tax income for our Commonwealth.

The Blanton Distillery is but one of the many large distilleries which operate within our state, all of which also contribute materially to the economic well-being of our local communities and of the Commonwealth itself. This industry not only has paid millions of dollars to the state, counties, and other taxing districts but has also afforded a livelihood to many thousands of our citizens, and has contributed much in the field of industry.

In speaking of industrial accomplishments in this Commonwealth, I would certainly like to toss a bouquet to the Kentucky Chamber, which is sponsoring this program tonight. Through its capable directors and staff, this organization has done an outstanding job over the past several years in inducing new industry here and in working in close cooperation with existing businesses. This recognition dinner tonight is a good example, I believe, of their fine efforts in the latter field. As our great state grows industrially, so shall we prosper. That's why it is so important to promote the development of new industry and to recognize the advances of existing ones. As long as the state, its industries and such excellent organizations as the Chamber of Commerce continue to work together harmoniously as a team, we will all benefit in turn.

On this occasion I cannot overlook paying a personal tribute to my friend and yours, Colonel Albert B. Blanton,[1] dean of America's distillers and the one man more than any other responsible for the two million barrels of Kentucky bourbon being celebrated tonight. Mr. Blanton for fifty-five years has been associated with the distillery now named in his honor. Now that he's retired, though still a consultant, the distillery has suffered a great loss of his services. But if I know Colonel Blanton, I'm sure that he'll always be close by to lend a helping hand, just as in the past. For this the Blanton distillery and Schenley can be thankful. And for his friendship to so many of us over the years, we all can be most grateful. Let us hope, Colonel Blanton, that we shall continue to enjoy your consul and your warm friendship for many more years to come.

To mark this occasion, Governor Wetherby dedicated a small one-barrel warehouse that still stands at the Blanton Distillery in Frankfort.

1. Albert Bacon Blanton (1881-1959), with Stagg Distillery, Frankfort (1897-1952); he rose from office boy to regional manager and vice president of Schenley Industries, Inc.; in his honor the Stagg Distillery was renamed the Albert B. Blanton Distillery. *Louisville Courier-Journal,* May 22, 1959.

NATURAL GAS NEEDS IN CENTRAL KENTUCKY
Letter / April 16, 1951

[To Louis Elvove, Paris, Kentucky]

SINCE becoming governor in November I have continued to place emphasis on the need of expanding and developing Kentucky's industrial production and made strenuous effort to continue the program along this line which was initiated at the beginning of the administration. As an indication of the aggressiveness and foresight which is going into this undertaking, I sent a wire seeking an appointment with the president of the Columbia Gas System[1] for Kentucky representatives to meet and discuss with him matters of urgent and vital concern to this area regarding the inability of the Central Kentucky Natural Gas Company to supply gas for industrial purposes.

Arrangements have been made to meet with the representatives within the next few days and you may be sure every effort will be exerted and every point made which might tend to impress the officials of the parent organization of the Central Kentucky Natural Gas Company with the pressing need for additional gas volume in this area to meet current and future industrial requirements and domestic uses.

---

1. Stuart Miller Crocker (1898-1956), assistant to chairman of board of General Electric Company (1922-1927); vice president, treasurer of United Electric Securities Company (1928-1929); vice president international of General Electric Company (1930-1943); president, director, chairman executive committee of the Columbia Gas System (1943-1951); chairman, chief executive officer, chairman executive committee of the Columbia Gas System, director of Central Kentucky Natural Gas (1951-1956); born in Cambridge, Massachusetts. *Who's Who in America, 1954-1955,* 28th ed. (Chicago, 1954), p. 594.

Louis Elvove (1911-), deputy city clerk of Paris (1938-1950); city clerk (1950-); secretary, treasurer, director Paris Chamber of Commerce (1939-1953); born and resides in Paris. Letter, December 8, 1980.

SMALL BUSINESS PROBLEMS
Letter / May 7, 1951

[To Senator John Sparkman, Washington, D.C.]

THE opportunity you extend Kentucky in your April 25 letter to bring to the attention of your Small Business Committee matters pertaining to the place of small business in the nation's mobilization program is appreciated. In this connection, for your information and for the general consideration of the committee, I should like to mention the following as general problems which are having a current and definite bearing on Kentucky's small businesses.

1. Small- and medium-sized plants, many of which had important prime contracts in World War II, are finding that they are not receiving an allotment of scarce materials sufficient to enable them to keep in business, nor have they been able to secure government contracts or subcontracts.

2. As a result of the above difficulties, irreplaceable skilled labor will have to be laid off, with the certainty that it will be impossible to gather together a competent force if they are requested to do defense work in the future.

3. Prime contractors in some cases report lack of information as to where they can find available and competent subcontractors.

4. Now that government procurement agencies have entered on a policy of handling more than ninety percent of their procurement by negotiations rather than by open bid, it is almost impossible for the plant located outside of the few leading industrial areas to get a chance to bid.

So that more concerted attention can be devoted to the problems which small businessmen of the state are encountering, I recently named a state-wide Small Business Committee. This group is now in the process of compiling rather detailed information on this subject and is working in close liaison with Kentucky's two United States Senators.[1] It is the intention of the committee to transmit soon all available data bearing on the subject to Senator Tom Underwood for presentation to your committee.

---

1. Earle Clements and Tom Underwood.

John Jackson Sparkman (1899-), attorney, practiced law at Huntsville, Alabama (1925-1936); member, United States House of Representatives

(1937-1946), majority whip, (1946); member, United States Senate (1946-1978); Democratic nominee for vice president (1952); born near Hartselle, Alabama. *Who's Who in America, 1978-1979,* 40th ed. (Chicago, 1978), 2:3066.

NATURAL GAS NEEDS STATEWIDE
Letter / February 13, 1952

[To Senator Earle C. Clements, Washington, D.C.]

As you will recall, on a recent visit home we discussed and even set up a meeting for the purpose of determining ways and means to increase the volume of natural gas available for both existing and prospective industrial use in Kentucky. For some time now it has been apparent that additional gas supply is essential if we are to avoid a solid stone wall in our promotion of future industrialization.

Last week the meeting which was first scheduled at the time you were here was held in my office and, in addition to those who were originally invited to attend, we had with us Mr. Stuart Crocker, chairman of the Columbia Gas System. While it was felt and agreed that the problem with which we are confronted is indeed a difficult one and does not lend itself to an early and complete solution, the consensus of thinking developed at the conference held hope for a start toward the goal of sufficient gas volume to meet our state's growing need.

The purpose of this letter is to acquaint you with the problem and the initial work that is being done on this level and to formally solicit the assistance and cooperation of both you and Senator Underwood, to whom I am sending a copy of this letter.

In the way of a start, the Texas Gas Transmission Corporation has an expansion program application now pending before the Federal Power Commission (Docket No. 01847). It is very important that every effort be made to secure expedition of this certificate hearing. Any assistance you might be able to render in this cause will be both helpful and appreciated by all those interested in working for a greater Kentucky.

ECONOMIC RESOURCES OF SOUTHEASTERN KENTUCKY
Letter / December 10, 1952

[To Maurice K. Henry, Middlesboro]

THE economic condition and the potentialities of eastern and southeastern Kentucky are within the ken of the state government, and I am always glad to receive encouragement on this subject from leaders in that area, such as you.

Of course, I had nothing to do with what the *Wall Street Journal* published about Kentucky. I talked with a reporter one afternoon, but I understand the newspaper had several men in the state working various angles. I regret they did not see their way clear to do a piece on southeastern Kentucky, as it would have been extremely helpful to that area.

During the past few weeks I have received several communications from people in your section of the state, and all of them have raised disaster signals. Early next year the state government will undertake an economic and resources study of eastern Kentucky, so when new industry contemplates locating here we shall be in position, with facts and figures, to urge them to set up in your part of the state.

I am in complete agreement with your description of eastern and southeastern Kentucky as our number one development problem. We are going to try to bring you some relief in the form of new industry and a revitalized economy. Kentucky will never be as she should be until all areas are prosperous and active.

Suggestions and conscientious cooperation are primely needed, and I trust and pray that your section of our Commonwealth will start moving foward soon.

Maurice Kent Henry (1916-   ), teacher-principal in the Virginia schools (1936-1942); general manager and stockholder of the *Middlesboro Daily News* and radio station WMIK; director of Citizens News Company and Cumberland Gap Broadcasting Company; became president of Tri-State Poster Advertising (1959); born in Daleville, Virginia. Hambleton Tapp, ed., *Kentucky Lives: The Blue Grass State Who's Who* (Hopkinsville, Ky., 1966), pp. 243-44.

CANALIZATION OF THE BIG SANDY RIVER

Letter / April 23, 1953

[To Senator Earle C. Clements, Washington, D.C.]

IT is indeed heartening to know that the Senate Public Works Committee has renewed its interest in the canalization of the Big Sandy River in eastern Kentucky.

This long-overdue project is one of the most serious denials or oversights that Kentucky has endured. Economists, industrial experts, and practical citizens have advocated the canalization for many years. The economy of eastern Kentucky has caused widespread unrest, outright fear, and the departure of thousands of young mountain people Kentucky should not lose. The canalization would revitalize eastern Kentucky, particularly with respect to the coal industry, which has slumped to an alarming degree.

Canalization of the Big Sandy would bring eastern Kentucky to a point that would elude the possibility of the area becoming a territory almost totally dependent on federal and state financial assitance.

The mail received in this office from eastern Kentucky reflects the growing awareness of intelligent citizens who realize the demolition being caused by the lack of help to bring this potentially great area to its rightful position among the prosperous, self-sustaining sections of the nation.

Your support of this project will be deeply embedded in the memory of the people of the Big Sandy country, and whatever weight this communication might provide goes with heartfelt strength and urgency.

BUSINESS CONDITIONS IN KENTUCKY

Letter / October 30, 1953

[To Tom McLaughlin, Colorado Springs]

IN reply to your October 27 inquiry regarding business conditions in Kentucky, I am glad to submit the following:

1. The year 1953, business-wise, has added up to our expectations for it. With some softening in rural areas, retail sales have held up remarkably well on a state-wide basis and have shown substantial gains over 1952 in some of our cities. Indexes show retail prices on the whole continue to rise, although more slowly than in years past. Generally speaking, wholesale prices have shown more of a leveling off, especially since midsummer.

Kentucky still feels the impact of continued industrial growth. For one thing, it has meant through 1953 a continued very high level of construction activity. Notable categories in the industrial field include electric utilities, chemical plants, and electrical appliance expansion. Most striking is a new $300 million plant under construction by General Electric in Louisville, scheduled to employ 16,000 workers. Since January, twenty-three new plants or expansions, representing investments of $97 million and with scheduled annual payrolls of $23 million have been announced. In terms of manufacturing employment, during 1953 Kentucky began to feel the full impact of new plants and plant expansions completed in 1952, particularly in steel, chemicals, and automotive components.

The "soft" spot in the Kentucky picture for 1953 was farm income. The years's tobacco crop has yet to go to market, but no great problem is involved there. However, Kentucky farmers have suffered severe losses in connection with the sharp decline in beef cattle prices and lower milk prices. All of this has been greatly aggravated by acute drought conditions which have forced marketing of cattle and destroyed pasture and grain seedings.

2. While predictions are risky, the major development during 1954, for which tangible evidence can be found, will be a continuance of new industrial growth in Kentucky. Since summer, industrial development officials have received a noticeably larger number of inquiries from out-of-state manufacturers studying expansion possibilities and plant location in Kentucky, compared to the first six months of this year. Unless business conditions nationally induce these firms to revise or postpone their expansion plans, during 1954 Kentucky may well welcome a larger number of new industries than during 1953.

3. Kentucky's business and industrial economy is so closely geared to the national economy that activity for 1954 in terms of employment, income, and wholesale and retail sales will more than likely move in whatever way the economy as a whole moves.

Agriculturally, the present production control and price support program for tobacco means that Kentucky growers expect 1954 to be as good a year as 1953, provided the market nationally shows stability.

The outlook for the livestock industry and dairying is less certain and will be determined in important part by the type of farm program the new national administration and the Congress develop.

In 1953 the economic prospects of Kentucky were clouded by the end of the Korean War and a severe drought. The previous year had brought disastrous forest fires to large sections of the Commonwealth. During the war industrial production contributed to higher state revenues. However, the state's income decreased during 1953, forcing the governor to cut budget appropriations made by the 1952 General Assembly. By 1954 the General Assembly had a more difficult time allocating its diminished resources. The governor's State of the Commonwealth address is testimony to this fact. For the text of the governor's address see speech from January 12, 1954, in the Legislative Messages and Statements section.

Tom McLaughlin was editor of "The Gasser," a publication by the Colorado Interstate Gas Company.

PLIGHT OF SOUTHEASTERN KENTUCKY COAL MINERS

Letter / November 23, 1953

[To Payton Wolford, Majestic]

NO one is aware more than I am of the critical economic conditions among the coal miners of Pike County and all of southeastern Kentucky.

It is difficult to find a solution to your situation but we are trying. For instance, the state Agricultural and Industrial Development Board has undertaken a survey to determine whether or not that section of Kentucky has resources in addition to coal and her people. I have written letters to Washington outlining the plight of southeastern Kentucky. Congressman Carl Perkins has succeeded in having the federal government declare several counties in that area as surplus labor counties, an inducement to the government and private industries there.

The situation is deplorable and the worst feature about it is that so many of our youths are leaving southeastern Kentucky with the thought of striking out for areas where jobs are available. Progress in your section of the state seems impossible if our young people are leaving us.

Again let me say we are cognizant of the bad luck that has befallen the coal counties and we are attempting to dig out an answer.

Payton Wolford was president of United Mine Workers of American Local Union Number 6095.

DEVELOPMENT OF STATE AIRPORTS
Letter / December 1, 1953

[To Charles H. Gartrell, Frankfort]

DURING the last few years the Commonwealth of Kentucky has experienced a general awakening evidenced by improvements in agriculture, rapid industrial development, and in many other fields of endeavor.

Of prime importance to the state's progress is the development of a network of modern airports. Aviation is destined to play an increasingly important role in any expanding economy. We feel that we are building not only for the present, but for the future good of Kentucky.

During the years of the Wetherby administration the railroads, particularly the Louisville and Nashville, remained a powerful economic and political force. Nevertheless, Governor Wetherby supported the development of local airports, and during the years 1950-1955 Kentucky expanded greatly this service to communities, pushing the state to the forefront of like services in the nation.

Charles H. Gartrell (1914-), alderman of city of Ashland (1940); deputy commissioner of aeronautics (1940-1943); lieutenant commander, United States Navy (1943-1945); director of aeronautics commission (1945-1947); Democratic candidate for lieutenant governor (1947); first commissioner, Department of Aeronautics (1948-1956); member, Kentucky Airport Advisory Board (1960-1963); mayor, Ashland (1968-1972); administrative supervisor, Kentucky Department of Human Resources (1975-1982), born in Boyd County and resides in Louisville. Phone interview, December 3, 1980.

ECONOMIC DEVELOPMENT OF EASTERN KENTUCKY

Letter / January 18, 1954

[To Sinclair Weeks, Washington, D.C.]

REPRESENTATIVES of your department have been in touch with the staff of our Kentucky Agricultural and Industrial Development Board regarding a survey of industrial facilities and opportunities in eastern Kentucky, where reduced coal-mining acitivity has resulted in extensive and severe unemployment.

I am writing to assure you of the full cooperation of the Development Board and other state agencies in the proposed survey.

As you undoubtedly know, the eastern Kentucky area has relatively few manufacturing plants, especially of the type in position to take advantage of the preferential treatment in defense procurement bidding now available to manufacturers in areas of substantial labor surplus. On the other hand, coal operators and miners would benefit greatly from vigorous application of that policy in connection with federal purchases of coal for military and other purposes.

The area does have an abundant labor supply and forest and other resources adequate to support sizable manufacturing growth. It is excellently situated with respect to the country's major industrial and consumer markets. However, the opportunity to develop these resources is seriously restricted by reason of limited industrial water supplies. In that connection, the area's heavy rainfall means that projects designed to impound water for industrial and other purposes offer realistic possibilities.

These and other water resources projects, particularly canalization of the Big Sandy and improvement of locks and dams on the Kentucky River, are, of course, measures which require federal assistance. They are vital to the area's economic future and, if inaugurated, would enhance its attractiveness to manufacturers interested in taking advantage of the added tax amortization benefits now available to firms building defense industrial facilities in labor surplus areas.

For more information on the economic conditions in eastern Kentucky see speech from November 20, 1952, in this section.

Sinclair Weeks (1893-1972), American industrialist and public official; member, United States Senate (February-December 1944); national finance committee chairman of the Republican party (1949-1952); secretary of commerce (1953-1958); born in West Newton, Massachusetts. *Encyclopedia Americana* (Danbury, Conn., 1979), 28:571.

KENTUCKY RIGHT-TO-WORK BILL
Letter / February 8, 1954

[To Louisa Walker Grant, Owensboro]

IT is unusual to the point of being almost unheard of for me to tell anyone that they do not have the basic understanding of the subject matter about which they may write or discuss with me. However, in view of the severe intensity of the remarks contained in your February 10 letter, I cannot help but feel that you are grossly uninformed on what the federal and state law is regarding the right of employees to organize and the substance that those laws then give to the labor union organization.

As part of my platform on which I was elected governor and as a basic matter of public policy that I have endeavored to follow since becoming governor, I have publicly proclaimed my opposition to all legislation introduced in the 1952 General Assembly and that which has thus far been introduced during the current session to all measures considered by me to be antilabor. My decision regarding each individual bill is made after studying and analyzing each measure. I consider the various charges embraced in your communication to be ridiculous and unworthy of a specific reply to each.

For your information, the right-to-work bill, which was sponsored by the Associated Industries of Kentucky, was reported unfavorably, with my blessing, by the committee by a sixteen-to-one vote. This in effect killed the bill for this session of the General Assembly.

Governor Wetherby was an advocate of organized labor and publicly made known this fact. This commitment stemmed from his early support for the New Deal labor policies of Franklin D. Roosevelt and from his formative years spent in proximity to an urban center.

ENERGY & THE ENVIRONMENT

DIVISION OF SOIL AND WATER RESOURCES
May 11, 1954

SOIL conservation retains its place among the most vexing, important and challenging problems confronting the Commonwealth. By nationwide reputation we are considered a rich state agriculturally but here at home, as far as soil is concerned, we know that only a part of our state is rich.

Nature endowed the Commonwealth with mountains, rolling plains, and vast stretches of flatlands. The first settlers found the earth of Kentucky fortified against the ravages of erosion, the number one enemy of the soil. Under the brunt of heavy rains, trees and brush held the topsoil to the hillsides and mountainsides. Grass and brush locked the fertile covering to the subsurface in the more level areas. As long as nature was taking care of herself the land was well preserved.

Man needed food and food means farming. Decade after decade man planted and brought forth food, first for himself and then for hundreds of others. In his eagerness to produce food he mistreated nature, and nature has made him pay for it. He felled the trees on the mountain slope and slashed away the brush. When the rains tumbled from the skies the rich topsoil loosened and caught by the pressure of the downflow rolled to the water level of some stream or river lost forever.

On the rolling terrain and on the tablelike plains man planted the same crops year after year. Corn, for instance, needs certain chemical elements in the earth. A succession of this crop in the same area soon divested the earth of the elements needed by corn. When the elements were depleted corn could grow no more on that land, nor could other crops. The generosity of nature had been violated.

These are sharp examples of a situation in Kentucky once generally true. Many men have the fortunate faculty of recognizing their own mistakes. Man became aware of the fact that in destroying the land he was destroying himself. If he could not save himself he could seek help from others.

Grim factors such as these led to the development of the great scientific field of soil conservation, the fight to rectify the wrongs that man had imposed upon the soil. The federal and state governments plowed financial assistance into studies leading toward practices to rehabilitate the soil. The research has been vast, the results of incredible effectiveness. The government and universities operate laboratories, direct field experiments, work the trial-and-error method, and try new theories with all the zeal that goes into medical and surgical techniques. Provided there are ample willing hands to carry out instructions, it is almost possible today to run a farm out of a textbook, and not a bad farm at that. The farmer who utilizes soil conservation principles will be in business longer and more substantially than the farmer who chooses to go it alone.

State law provides for soil conservation districts which are established locally by a vote of the farmers. Each district receives considerable technical and mechanical assistance from the state. Once a farmer becomes a member of the local district, he is entitled to scientific guidance for the improvement of his farm. In a way, he joins a group pledged to conserve and nourish the land. The leaders of a soil conservation district have all the know-how about the prevention of erosion, flood control, the importance of maintaining dams and reservoirs, the navigability of rivers, the preservation of wildlife, and the promotion of the general welfare. They can also advise a farmer as to how to protect his tax base.

As the industrial potential of Kentucky attracts more and more factories and commercial enterprise, the role of agriculture must keep pace. Our economy must be maintained in balance. Manufacturing will pull ahead unless every farmer in Kentucky avails himself of conservation skills, the ground rules of better agriculture, and the land management techniques man has forced himself to adopt.

This speech was made as a recording. It cannot be determined exactly where or when it was used, but there is a good possibility that it was broadcast over the radio.

STATEMENT BEFORE THE TASK FORCE ON WATER RESOURCES AND POWER
Chattanooga, Tennessee / June 1, 1954

THE Tennessee Valley Authority is a monument to man's right and his ability to serve himself. This awesome project has rescued the Tennessee Valley states from the economic doldrums, and has been a tremendous factor in the prosecution of national defense efforts. It is a symbol of progress and ingenuity. It must not be a target of partisanship for political reasons alone.

Kentucky has achieved vast strides of agricultural and commercial development through the work and planning of the TVA. Our people are confounded by threats and designs to curtail or impede the benefits the TVA has brought to this section of the nation. The byword for the TVA should be expansion; not the reduction of the services of this man-made, benevolent giant.

There may be areas in the federal government vulnerable to reorganization and shrinkage, but the TVA must not fall in this category. It has cooperated with state and local governments to the satisfaction of all. Its records in the fields of flood control, the harnessing of electrical power, and the generally beneficial ideas and plans it has brought to the valley have the esteem and respect of all the citizens who glow in the enormity of its programs.

All forward-thinking Americans are courageous supporters of the TVA and it ill behooves any government to attempt to frustrate the advance of an agency that is reaching its purposes to the credit of mankind. Any reduction in the scope of the TVA program will cause unrest in the valley.

The benefits with which the TVA has endowed the valley are such that they should be cherished and protected. A government of completely good conscience would in no way force fear upon the people of the valley or in any way lead the people to believe that they should not have the utmost confidence in a project of this nature.

I urge the commission to proceed with the most cautious wisdom, for the citizens of the valley will never understand how such a magnificent venture in government should be subjected to the political erosion of groups who contend private business can perform such work in a manner superior to that of responsible government. The Tennessee Valley belongs to the people and they enjoy this stewardship. The TVA has brought them new industry, recreational facilities, and a new sense of self-respect that a philosophy of change-for-the-sake-of-change should not destroy.

With this statement, I am including two studies showing the impact the TVA has made upon industrial and agricultural development in Kentucky. The task force will readily observe that these phases are not to be regarded dispassionately.

Governor Wetherby, a New Deal Democrat, was committed to TVA and to the concept of government sale of electricity. This speech was delivered at a time when it appeared that private interests were attempting to encroach upon the TVA scene. Some people thought that the Eisenhower administration might use the Dixon-Yates request to eventually turn all of TVA over to private utilities. For an explanation of the Dixon-Yates controversy see speech from November 1, 1954, in the Democratic Party Leadership section.

GREEN RIVER WATERSHED SOIL AND WATER CONSERVATION

Letter / January 15, 1951

[To Frederick J. Lawton, Washington, D.C.]

ON November 6, 1950, the U.S. Department of Agriculture submitted to the Bureau of the Budget a program for runoff and water flow retardation and soil erosion prevention for the Green River watershed in Kentucky and Tennessee. This program, in a survey report form, has been reviewed and endorsed by the states of Kentucky and Tennessee and all federal and state agencies that would in any way be affected. In simple terms, this plan calls for an "on the land" flood control program. It has become increasingly apparent that floods cannot be controlled by the building of dams and levees alone. The water must be held where it falls on the land through reforestation, development of cover crops, terraces, and other soil conservation methods.

I sincerely trust that the Bureau of the Budget has been favorably impressed with this report, as the measures recommend for soil and water conservation are very badly needed by our Kentucky farmers. Uncontrolled waters have carried tons of topsoil into our streams, so restricting channels as to cause adjacent bottom lands to be flooded by progressively less amounts of rainfall. These bottom lands, often the most fertile on the farm, are rendered practically useless, as frequent floods are destroying more crops each year.

Soil and water conservation are becoming more necessary each year, particularly in Kentucky. Erosion is destroying thousands of acres of tillable land, and thousands more acres are ruined because of improper drainage.

This program is designed to correct these situations by providing our farmers with technical and monetary assistance in establishing, where needed, subwatershed waterways, farm waterways, terraces, diversion ditches, gully stabilization, sediment control, erosion control along roads and railways, perennial vegetation, pasture development, farm ponds, wildlife area development, forest planting, adequate fire control, land acquisition, tributary channel improvement, stream bank stabilization, and other soil and water conservation practices to complete a basic system of soil and water conservation in accordance with the needs and capabilities of the lands of the watershed. We also consider this program desirable as a companion program to complement the development of the larger streams by the U.S. Army engineers.

Our farmers have just gone through a period of intensive cultivation which seriously depleted the fertility of their soil and in all probability will be called on for the next few years to again produce in maximum quantities. This program, therefore, becomes increasingly important, as its application will obviously save much land from being further depleted, if not utterly destroyed, during this period of high productivity.

I join the farmers of Kentucky in urging you to expedite the introduction of this program to the Congress for its authorization at the earliest possible moment, and to provide funds for its initiation as expeditiously as possible.

Frederick Joseph Lawton (1900-1975), began federal government service with the Treasury Department (1921); executive assistant and acting assistant director of Bureau of Budget (1935-1948); administrative advisor to the president of the United States (1948-1949); assistant director of Bureau of Budget (1949-1950); member, Civil Service Commission (1950-1953); born in Washington, D.C. *Who Was Who in America, 1974-1976* (Chicago, 1976), 6:241.

FLOOD CONTROL PROGRAMS
Letter / February 21, 1951

[To Knox T. Hutchinson, Washington, D.C.]

UNUSUALLY heavy damages to crop lands caused by severe flooding of our Kentucky streams during the past year have brought to my office many inquiries as to the possibility of getting flood control programs for each of our Kentucky watersheds similar to the U.S. Department of Agriculture program for Green River.

The most recent of these severe floods occurred in January of this year on the Upper Cumberland River. This watershed needs a soil and water conservation and flood control program very badly, but I understand the U.S. Forest Service has not yet made a survey. The Forest Service is now making a survey of Salt River, and we feel that they should start the Cumberland River survey immediately after submitting to the secretary their report on Salt River.

We also understand that the Soil Conservation Service is making surveys of the Kentucky and Licking rivers. In order that we may correctly inform the people in these watersheds, would you please advise me on the present status and approximate date of completion of each of the surveys now under way and when we might expect surveys to be started on the Cumberland and lower Ohio rivers.

Fearful that someone, not realizing the vital need for and the tremendous potential benefits of these watershed programs, might advocate their suspension, I respectfully suggest that the Department of Agriculture keep these programs moving on an uninterrupted schedule.

Knox Thomas Hutchinson (1894-1957), teacher in high schools, Nashville, Tennessee (1919-1927); director, agriculture education, State Teachers College, Murfreesboro, Tennessee (1927-1936); president, Middle Tennessee Electric Membership Coop (1935-1949); member, Tennessee State Senate (1939-1940); assistant secretary of agriculture (1949-1953); born in Fayetteville, Tennessee. *Who Was Who in America, 1951-1960* (Chicago, 1960), 3:434.

GREEN RIVER SOIL CONSERVATION

Letter / January 23, 1952

[To Joe B. Bates, Washington, D.C.]

THE United States Department of Agriculture has submitted to Congress its survey report for run-off and water flow retardation and soil erosion prevention for Green River, Kentucky, known as H. D. #261, 82nd Congress, 1st Session—Green River Watershed Kentucky and Tennessee.

The program it proposes is very badly needed in the watershed and will result in tremendous benefits to the agricultural interests, as well as greatly reduce the enormous damages suffered each year from flood waters.

While the estimated total cost of the program is, in rounded figures, $86 million over a twenty-year period, contributions by landowners will amount to $30 million if the federal government will spend $56 million.

Another favorable feature of the report is that the entire program is to be carried out in cooperation with the Soil Conservation District boards of supervisors in each county who are elected by the people who will be affected, and each step, as the program develops, will have the approval of the Flood Control Division of our Kentucky Department of Conservation.

As this program was especially designed to eliminate a large portion of the damages caused by uncontrolled waters in the watershed, as local interests are ready for and have asked for the program, as it will result in lasting benefits to a large portion of our Kentucky people, and as the program benefits agriculture to an extent that it can be called definitely beneficial to the defense effort, I urge that you lend vigorous support to enacting this report into law and getting it initiated at the earliest moment possible.

Joseph B. Bates (1893-1965), rural schoolteacher and high school superintendent in Kentucky for sixteen years; Greenup County clerk (1922-1938); member, United States House of Representatives (1938-1952); candidate for United States Senate nomination (1956); born in Republican. *Who's Who in America, 1950-1951,* 26th ed. (Chicago, 1950), p. 163.

OHIO VALLEY ATOMIC ENERGY PLANT
Letter / August 28, 1952

[To David Aronberg, Ashland]

AN earlier reply to your August 18 letter was impossible due to a week spent in western Kentucky. The importance of the matter which you discussed, however, was not left unattended to.

Immediately following the announcement of the Atomic Energy Commission that a decision had been made to locate the much-sought-after plant in Ohio, the two Kentucky Senators were contacted relative to the possibility of securing Kentucky locations for the power plant development that would accompany construction of the atomic energy works in Ohio.[1] As was the case with the promotional work that was done in the state's effort to secure the big plant, every facility of state government possessing data and information upon which these important decisions are reached was made available to both the senators and the federal agencies involved. On the state level we shall make just as concerted an effort to acquire one or all of the talked-about power plant projects as was made earlier in our efforts to induce the commission to locate its primary plant within our borders.

Recognizing the all-out Ashland effort made in this regard, and being personally dedicated to further increasing industrial employment and activity in the state through new and expanding manufacturing and industrial plants, I share with you the same keen disappointment which you indicate. Nevertheless, I cannot believe the fact that due to the interest of the people of several Kentucky communities and the acknowledged suitability of several sites hampered our overall bid to get the new plant to locate in our state, nor can I conceive that these factors were primarily responsible for our failure. As a matter of fact, had our efforts been successful, I would be convinced that the merits of the two above-mentioned considerations were primarily responsible. In practically every instance of a new plant taking residence in Kentucky there are a host of interested communities vying for favorable consideration. This, in my opinion, represents a healthy and desired attitude on the part of the citizens of each of those cities.

The role of the Kentucky Agricultural and Industrial Development Board is that of furnishing facts and figures on available manpower, kind and extent of natural resources, adequacy of transportation facilities, and the many other pertinent factors that are taken into account before a final site determination is made by the men charged with the success and destiny of the great industrial concerns that have already and are continuing to settle in our midst.

In the future, as in the past, we shall continue to work untiringly toward Kentucky's economic growth and industrial development. The success that we meet, however, will be accomplished without favoritism to one area at the expense of another.

---

1. The Atomic Energy Commission announced that a plant would be built near Portsmouth, Ohio. Governor Wetherby believed that the decision of the AEC not to locate in northeastern Kentucky was due to its inability to find suitable level ground. See speech from November 20, 1952, in the Economic and Industrial Development section.

David Aronberg (1894-1967), mayor of Ashland (1952-1956, 1960-1964); national vice commander, American Legion; born in Manchester, England. *Louisville Courier-Journal,* February 12, 1967.

ROUGH RIVER DAM CONSTRUCTION
Letter / November 7, 1952

[To Major General Lewis A. Pick, Washington, D.C.]

OVER an extended period of time detailed studies and surveys have been made by the Corps of Engineers for the desirability of constructing a dam on Rough River as part of the Green River Flood Control program. During recent months there has developed widespread citizens' interest in such a project and public endorsement and promotional activity have been given the project by the Green River Valley Citizens League as well as a majority of the people of Hartford, the county seat of Ohio County, who would benefit from low flow control and the clearing of the river channel.

In addition to submitting my impressions of the public's general attitude toward the dam and who would be most directly affected by its construction, I wish to extend herewith the official approval and endorsement of the proposed project by the Kentucky Flood Control and Water Usage Board. As you may recognize, the board functions as a principal public agency concerned with the extensive flood control and water resources and utilization problems with which we are confronted.

Attached herewith is a report from the Flood Control and Water Usage Board to Henry Ward, Kentucky Commissioner of Conservation. It may be considered as the state's approval and recommendation. As chief of the Corps of Engineers you are urged and requested to secure funds for the early initiation of work on this project.

TVA BENEFITS FOR SOUTHEASTERN KENTUCKY
Letter / July 21, 1953

[To Gordon R. Clapp, Knoxville, Tennessee]

YOUR letter of July 3 and the booklet, *Working with Areas of Special Need,* were read with interest and a sense of sadness. It almost confuses me to realize that the present national administration has sought to curtail and discourage, rather than cheer and expand, the magnificent work of the Tennessee Valley Authority.

The benefits created by the TVA in Kentucky are monumental and have meant much to our citizens, industry, and agriculture. Hope has been expressed here that somehow TVA would make a special survey in southeastern Kentucky, which is fast becoming an economic wreckage. The coal industry is suffering sharply in that section and much of the land needs rehabilitation. What is most disturbing, of course, is the vast number of Kentuckians, particularly young ones, who are abandoning this area in search of a future in other states. This is a fact of life none of us are proud of.

I have confidence that the next administration will restore the full vitality of TVA and permit it to move forward vigorously in the quest for a better way of life for our people.

For more information on TVA see speech from June 1, 1954, in this section.

Gordon Rufus Clapp (1905-1963), director of admissions and assistant dean of Lawrence College (1927-1933); assistant director of personnel, director of personnel, general manager, chairman of the board of the Tennessee Valley Authority (1933-1954); department city administrator, New York (1955-1956); born in Ellsworth, Wisconsin. *Who's Who in America, 1954-1955,* 28th ed. (Chicago, 1954), pp. 483-84.

STRIP MINING LEGISLATION
Letter / October 28, 1953

[To Mrs. T. K. Bippus, Louisville]

AMONG the recommendations I will make to the 1954 General Assembly will be a proposal providing for the rehabilitation of the scars left from strip mining operations. Attempts to enact legislation of this kind at the last two sessions of the General Assembly have been unsuccessful. The discouraging results of past efforts, however, in no way deter me and my strong desire to secure favorable action in the forthcoming 1954 session.

Mrs. T. K. Bippus (1912-), retired from general office work in a furniture store and assistant to her late husband, a doctor of chiropractic; born in Evansville, Indiana, and resides in Greenville. Letter, December 9, 1980.

STRIP MINING REGULATION
Letter / December 11, 1953

[To R. L. Stearns, Jr., Stearns]

YOUR opposition to strip mine legislation is acknowledged. I am completely familiar with the serious economic situation in southeastern Kentucky due to the downfall of the coal industry.

Ever since first observing the ravages strip miners have inflicted on western Kentucky, I have been strong for some type of regulations that will require these operators to restore the soil damage they have committed. The face of the earth belongs to the people for their use. Enough damage is being done to it without permitting any more while it can be placed under some sort of control.

Strip miners in other states are regulated and are still in business. A bill to regulate strip mining will be introduced in the coming session of the legislature with my endorsement. The legislature, of course, will make the final decision. The bill will not be brutal, but will indicate that this administration is trying to do positive things for the welfare of the general public.

Governor Wetherby did introduce a strip mining bill. The struggle was intense over its enactment. The governor, when informed that one member of the General Assembly whose vote was needed was deserting his bill, called that person into a private meeting. As a result, the legislator voted for the bill and it passed. Wetherby's support of strip mining regulation was evidence of a love of the land stemming from his activities as a sportsman.

The act said unregulated strip mining of coal caused soil erosion, stream pollution, stagnant and contaminated water, floods; destroyed the value of land for agricultural purposes; counteracted conservation efforts; destroyed property; caused fire hazards; and in general constituted an imminent and inordinate peril to the welfare of the Commonwealth. It created a Strip Mining and Reclamation Commission that had power to supervise, administer and enforce this act. It required a permit to strip mine, and a plan for reclamation had to win the approval of the commission. A fine of not more than $5,000 could be imposed for violation. See *Acts of the General Assembly of the Commonwealth of Kentucky,* 1954, Chapter 8 (S. B. 45), pp. 19-28.

Robert L. Stearns, Jr. (1903-1965), with Stearns Coal and Timber Company (1926-1962); president, Kentucky and Tennessee Railway (1940-1962), chairman of the board (1962-1965); director of the National Coal Association, B. R. Campbell and Sons, Inc., and of McCreary Motors; born in Ludington, Michigan. *Louisville Courier-Journal,* May 9, 1965.

INTERSTATE AIR POLLUTION CONTROL

Letter / December 6, 1954

[To Charles N. Howison, Cincinnati, Ohio]

THIS is in response to your November 30 letter in which you recommend the establishment of an Ohio River Valley Air Sanitation Compact.

Louisville and our cities in northern Kentucky are also greatly interested in learning of new ways to fight air pollution and methods might eventually be found or created by research teams sponsored by an interstate compact.

We have in the state government an agency known as the Legislative Research Commission which carries on numerous research projects at the direction of the legislature. This agency was commanded by the 1954 session of the legislature to bring out the facts on a large number of ideas and suggestions which would benefit the members of the legislature in writing new laws. Also, the commission's present budget holds down the possibilities of taking on new ventures in public welfare.

The next session of the Kentucky legislature convenes in January, 1956. It would be my suggestion that the Smoke Abatement League consult the leadership of the legislatures in Kentucky, Ohio, Indiana, and perhaps West Virginia when their next sessions convene and present the importance of the interstate air pollution problem. Interstate compacts require legislative approval and, if approved, will require legislative appropriations.

I have a letter from Mayor John J. Moloney,[1] of Covington, Kentucky, and his message also bespeaks of the seriousness of this situation.

The 1956 session of the General Assembly did nothing about air pollution.

1. John J. Moloney (1905-1966), mayor, Covington (1951-1955, 1959-1964); candidate for secretary of state (1963); head of state Bureau of Municipal Affairs (1964); member, Kentucky Senate (1966); candidate for the United States House of Representatives (1966). *Louisville Courier-Journal,* November 7, 1966.

Charles N. Howison (1902-), affiliated with foundry and power shovel companies in Marion County, Ohio (1922-1935); contracting officer for the National Park Service (1935-1941); manager of the Government Contracts Division of the Crosley Corporation (1941-1945); executive secretary,

Air Pollution Control League of Greater Cincinnati (1946-); member, Sons of the American Revolution and Air Pollution Control Association; born in Marion County, Ohio, and resides in Cincinnati. Letter, December 8, 1980.

WILDLIFE CONSERVATION SUPPORT
Letter / May 13, 1955

[To Jimmy Betts, Lewisburg]

BEFORE being elected governor of the state, I was an ardent sportsman and my interest during the past five years has not waned. One of the real pleasures I have enjoyed, and I hope it might in some degree be considered one of the real services I have rendered, has been the close cooperation that has existed among the Fish and Wildlife Resources Department, the Conservation Department, and myself. It is through this kind of cooperation that our overall conservation program has been advanced more rapidly than during any similar period in the history of soil, water, fish, and wildlife practices.

During his tenure as governor, Wetherby frequently hunted and fished throughout the state, particularly in western Kentucky. This activity received wide publicity and resulted in an impression held by some that the governor did not take seriously enough his duties as chief executive. However, Governor Wetherby was encouraged by many within state government to continue to draw nationwide attention to Kentucky's sporting opportunities in the interest of tourism.

Jimmy Betts was president of the Coon Range Fish and Game Club.

AGRICULTURE

SCOTT COUNTY FARM BUREAU
Georgetown / January 18, 1951

I KNOW of no challenge as great or as important to the welfare and security of our country as that offered in the field of agriculture. The basic resources of food, clothing, and shelter must be provided through agriculture for an ever-increasing population. These needs must be met both in our time and in all generations to come.

Farming today is no ordinary occupation. It is a business that prospers in direct proportion to the special skills that are employed. The successful farmer utilizes every skill he can learn and employs every tool at his command. He uses wisely the great variety of services offered to him by federal, state, and local agricultural agencies.

On the middle level your state government has achieved outstanding success in carrying out a series of programs designed for the improvement of Kentucky agriculture initiated three years ago.

The state Department of Agriculture through its livestock sanitation program, vaccinated more than 40,000 calves for bangs disease in 1950. The true value of this work will be evidenced for years ahead. Within the same department an aggressive weights and measures inspection service has been expanded to cover most of the scales within the state. This feature alone has already saved the buying and selling public many thousands of dollars.

Just over a year ago a centralized surplus commodity distribution system was inaugurated within the Agriculture Department which has made available to schools and institutions food surpluses supplied by the federal government, valued at more than two million dollars.

This was accomplished at an administrative cost of only $30,000 to the state.

There are other special and significant projects now being carried out by the department on an experimental or testing basis, an example being a sorghum molasses cooperative selling arrangement centered in Hancock County and a poultry-egg producing-selling cooperative embracing several southeastern counties.

There is another agricultural endeavor on the state level that is successfully blending the practical aspects of the dirt farmer's experience with theoretical and scientific knowledge of the College of Agriculture specialist. This program involves the rehabilitation of state-owned institutional farms and has greatly increased the productive capacity of the land, livestock, and poultry. During this rehabilitation 2,341 acres have been purchased. This additional land, together with the land already owned, totals approximately 11,000 acres. It has been cleaned up, a soil test made, treated with a basic application of fertilizer as indicated by these soil tests, and converted to a rotation suitable to its inherent capabilities. Most of the land on these institutional farms was formerly used without regard to its capabilities and, as a result, was eroded and seriously depleted of its fertility. The institutional gardens have been shifted to the most level land on the farms to reduce erosion.

A fertilizer program based on soil tests and the needs of the crop has been instituted, better varieties are planted, and irrigation systems have been purchased where an adequate water supply is available. Improved canneries and root cellars have been provided to enable the institutions to process and store the increased production.

A beef cattle program has been initiated at Kentucky State Penitentiary and Kentucky State Reformatory to take advantage of the increased pasture acreage that has resulted from the improved land use. Kentucky State Penitentiary owned 69 head of beef cattle, 329 head have been purchased, and we now have a total of 681 head on all institutional farms. Kentucky State Penitentiary has not purchased any fresh meat since July 1949, and beginning January 1, 1951, Kentucky State Reformatory and Kentucky Houses of Reform will be self-sufficient for the remainder of this fiscal year.

The average daily egg production in 1948 was 818. The average for 1950 was 1,620 with all pullets not yet producing.

Fifteen new laying houses have been constructed, four prisoner-of-war barracks at Kentucky State Hospital have been converted to laying houses, and five new brooder houses have been built. This gives the institutions adequate housing for 18,000 laying hens and an annual brooder capacity of 53,000 baby chicks.

The dairy enterprise was better managed than the poultry enterprise. However, inadequate housing, low producing cows, and poor records seriously hampered efficient milk production. Dairy Herd Improvement Association records are now being kept on all institutional herds, low-producing cows are culled and replaced with higher-producing cows. Milking machines have been purchased and installed at all institutions except Central State Hospital. Machines have been purchased for this institution and will be installed upon completion of the milking parlor now under construction. Dairy barns have been remodeled and facilities are being provided for calves and heifers.

Swine numbers have been reduced to comply with the reduced row crop acreages. Improved housing has been provided. Five new farrowing houses have been completed. Eleven hog shelters and twelve feeding slabs have been constructed. The mixed breeds, common on most institution farms, have been generally replaced with a bacon type hog so that a higher percentage of lean meat in relation to lard can be obtained.

Increased productivity of the land and livestock has resulted in a more adequate diet for the patients and inmates and is reflected in the improved health of the wards of the state. While the state's institutional population has increased substantially, the farming operation has furnished an abundant and steady food supply, resulting in a saving for the taxpayers of Kentucky, and at the same time elevated the custodial standard of our institutions to the highest point in the history of the Commonwealth.

Agriculture in Kentucky and the nation is faced with both a challenge and an opportunity for service. As never before our social, religious, economic, and political freedoms are threatened. The full might of America's physical, moral, and intellectual capacity has been committed to the cause of democracy. In fulfilling this task, the demands that will be made on agriculture will equal or even exceed those faced during World War II. Through a well-planned and coordinated effort our state's and nation's farmers will meet this challenge and agriculture will attain heights yet unscaled.

CHRISTIAN COUNTY FARM BUREAU
Hopkinsville / February 5, 1951

It is a pleasure to be here with you members and friends of the Christian County Farm Bureau and to visit with you and your neighbors. I am sure Mr. Allen and Mr. Stanford, like myself, appreciate being permitted to look in on a great Christian County farm family in its new home.[1]

Not too far back in history it was traditional for the family with a new home to invite its neighbors and share with them the pleasure of its new house. They killed the fatted calf and, spreading corn meal on the floor, polished the newly laid boards as they danced to fiddling music. The floors have all been polished, Mr. LaMotte,[2] before we gathered here. But after eating the wonderful meal the homemakers have provided, I know that fine cooking is still a tradition for a Kentucky housewarming.

It is an honor to participate with you in the dedication of this splendid new agriculture center. This building is the high point of attainment in the work of your farm bureau. It is eloquent proof of the industry and enthusiasm that have brought to one of the greatest agricultural counties in our Commonwealth, and you fifteen hundred members, the distinction of being the largest country farm bureau unit in the state.

This center testifies to the foresight and able leadership directing the affairs of your farm bureau. It is also evidence of a progressive and forward-looking bureau membership, conscious of the advantage of being part of a great farm organization and confident of agriculture's ability to meet the demands and cope with the problems that these critical times have thrust upon it.

I understand that there are several here tonight who have been active in the Christian County Farm Bureau since its beginnings more than thirty years ago. They, I am sure, particularly understand the meaning of the saying that, "We cannot expect the harvest the day after the seed is sown."

A few minutes ago Mr. Garnett[3] told us some of the history of the Christian County Farm Bureau, and he brought home the fact that this building stands as the culmination of many years of working, managing, and planning on the part of Christian County farmers.

As your new agriculture center is put into service, Christian County becomes the first county bureau in the state to have its own headquarters housed in a building designed and constructed solely for the benefit of the community's farm family.

Kentucky's agricultural eminence has been recognized for many years. This standing was achieved through proper utilization of our abundant farming resources. In addition to these essentials of successful farming, Kentuckians have come to realize the merits of a general and diversified farming program. Formerly the success or failure of many a Kentucky farmer rested almost completely on a single crop. Noticeable change took place, however, in the late thirties and early forties when the demands of the Second World War emphasized the need for increased agricultural production.

Here in western Kentucky the past fifteen years have wrought impressive change and improvement in farm and agricultural practices with respect both to production and the procedures followed in reaching that production. The most progressive changes made followed the widespread seeding of winter resistant grass strains and marked increases in grass and hay production of the common varieties through extensive use of fertilizer. Following in the path of more abundant forage, Kentucky's beef production experienced marked increase.

The specialists of the college of agriculture have long favorably compared Kentucky's dairying possibilities with such firmly established states as Wisconsin and New York. The farmers of Kentucky took the cue, and if we compare the number of dairy cattle, the milk routes, the number of milk processing plants turning out butter and cheese, we can see that in a short time dairying has become one of our state's major industries.

Kentucky's sheep industry reversed its course and is making a comeback as a major cash income source. Kentucky finished lambs are recognized as a delicacy in the industrial eastern markets and, as a consequence, command premium prices.

Diversified farming pointing toward greater income has manifested itself in other ways. Through a program of marketing assistance furnished by the State Department of Agriculture egg and poultry production have been greatly expanded. Recognizing the superior quality of our old-fashioned sorghum molasses, Kentucky farmers have developed a thriving business and placed this fine product on grocery shelves across the country. Another growing farm undertaking in western Kentucky, which is a novel addition to the list of Kentucky's substantial money crops, is the raising of popcorn. The plantings now run into thousands of acres and its full potentials are not yet realized

Just as healthy diversification and increased farm income are the proper concern of the progress-minded farmer, so also is the addition to everday life of the services and conveniences which government provides at the people's request.

Transportation and year-round road and highway facilities are the keys to the realization of improved consolidated schools, to church attendance on Sunday, and to a market for your produce during the week. This administration is willing to take credit for handling your road program in as efficient mannner as any since Kentucky's present road program was begun about the time your farm bureau was formed.

Possibly of a deeper personal interest to you and Farm Bureau members throughout the state is the rural road program, which during the past three years has made unparalled progress. During those three years there have been built and maintained more miles of farm-to-market roads than were built since the inception of state responsibility for Kentucky's rural roads.

I know you not only have the present interest of rural roads at heart, but will concern yourself, as I will, with the preservation of the present program and its continued expansion. I want to say to you folks here at this meeting that so long as I am in a position to influence legislation, every resource at hand will be mustered to oppose those who would by crippling legislation attempt to destroy the rural road act. Any insidious charge which directly or indirectly threatens the administration of this progressive program designed for the welfare of every rural Kentuckian, and for the greater development of our state, will find an opponent in me and, I feel, in every farmer with an improved road from his house to the market, the store, the school, and the church. Any opponent of the rural road program must reckon with the thousands who know we are nearer today than ever before to completing the task of putting Kentucky's road system in year-round travel condition.

I am also proud of the record that the Rural Electric Co-ops have made in their effort to furnish electricity to every rural home in Kentucky. During the past three years not a single application for extension of lines and service facilities by either private or public utility has been denied by the Kentucky Public Service Commission. Immediately upon becoming governor I urged that determination be made as promptly as possible on the application of the Eastern Kentucky Rural Co-op to construct and operate a generating plant. That application was subsequently approved, clearing the way for a substantial increase in the electrical power to meet the needs in the territory served by the Eastern Kentucky Co-op.

The people of Kentucky have the right to expect that all agencies of their state government will work as efficiently as possible. In visiting a community where state agencies and institutions are located I have the feeling that the people of that community are particularly interested in the operation of that facility.

I know you people are especially interested from the farming standpoint in the operation of Western State Hospital.[4] Here, as at all other state-owned institutional farms, important strides are being made in improving the productive capacity of the land, livestock, and poultry. Two weeks ago, an additional thirty head of good milk cows were bought for Western State Hospital, putting the dairy project in good shape. Two dairy type barns have been approved and, barring material restrictions, will be under construction soon. The present herd is on a paying basis and supplies at least a pint of milk per day for each patient. The hog and chicken projects are also greatly improved. Necessary construction of laying houses is complete and plans are well under way for annual production of twelve to fifteen hundred eggs per day. In addition, this will assure a meat supplement of an estimated thirteen tons of poultry for consumption each year. In the hog division two new shelters and a sixteen-pen farrowing house have been built and placed in use.

Production of green vegetables at all of the state mental hospitals has been greatly increased. Here at Western State Hospital more than 400 tons of vegetables were produced last year and more than 17,000 gallons were canned. At present, there is being installed in the cannery equipment sufficient to take care of all surplus vegetables.

Like you members of the Christian County Farm Bureau, the state is doing all possible to be a good farmer. As the custodian of the good earth on which we all depend, we can do no less if we are to keep faith with those generations which will follow. A strong healthy America is dependent on agriculture meeting in both quantity and quality the needs of all our citizens.

More than 300 people attended the dedication of the new $40,000 structure located on West Ninth Street. Governor Wetherby was accompanied to Hopkinsville by Dr. H. L. Donovan, president of the University of Kentucky, and Henry Ward, commissioner of conservation. *Kentucky New Era,* Hopkinsville, February 6, 1951.

1. Mr. Allen, no vita available. J.E. Stanford was executive secretary of the Kentucky Farm Bureau Federation.

2. Golladay LaMotte was the Farm Bureau president who presided over the dedication and introduced the speakers.

3. Holland Garnett was a charter member of the Christian County Farm Bureau that began in 1912 or 1913. He presented a brief review of the organization's history at this dedication.

4. Western State Hospital for patients with psychological disorders is located at Hopkinsville. The institution was approved by an act of the General Assem-

bly in 1848, and the first patients were admitted in 1854. See Charles M. Meacham, *A History of Christian County Kentucky from Oxcart to Airplane* (Nashville, 1930), pp. 296-98.

KENTUCKY GREEN PASTURES PROGRAM
Frankfort / March 17, 1951

IT is a real privilege to appear on the first program of radio station WGRC devoted to the Kentucky Green Pastures Program.[1] This planned series of twenty-six broadcasts will do much toward informing the people of our state on the important work now being carried on for the advancement of Kentucky agriculture.

I know of no challenge as great or as important to the welfare and security of our country as that offered in the field of agriculture. The state-wide promotional plan known as the Kentucky Green Pastures Program has been a significant factor in the agricultural prosperity our Commonwealth is now enjoying. The continued cooperation of Kentucky farmers in this program will assist materially in every phase of our agricultural advancement.

It is impossible to enumerate all of the benefits or to estimate the value accruing from the 1950 Green Pastures Program, in which over 2,600 farmers in 118 Kentucky counties participated. These farmers have recognized that the soil is a heritage all of us must protect. From our land, food, clothing, and shelter must be provided for an ever-increasing population of Americans and hungry millions in sister nations throughout the world. These needs must be met both in our time and in all generations to come.

Farming today is no ordinary occupation. It is a business that prospers in direct proportion to the knowledge and skill employed. The successful farmer uses wisely the great variety of services offered him by federal, state, and local agricultural agencies, and the Green Pastures Program is fast becoming one of the greatest and most widely backed agricultural programs Kentucky has ever had.

A good grassland farming program along with a livestock program to effectively utilize the abundant forage produced insures the production of cheaper milk, butter, meat, and eggs, the basis of our diet. It reclaims for productive use millions of acres of unproductive land now wasting from erosion. It permits the farmer to use Kentucky weather and climate advantageously. It profitably utilizes labor the year round and can, to a large degree, mean economic stabilization for our state.

Continued education, cooperation, and coordination can prove that the general welfare of all Kentucky's citizens is safely rooted in a sound, progressive agricultural program. Agriculture in our state and nation can attain heights yet unscaled if all of us do our part and encourage our neighbors to do their part to make each farmer the best farmer, employing the best farming practices of any farmer who has yet tilled the land.

---

1. The Green Pastures program was conducted under the auspices of the University of Kentucky's agricultural department. Its purpose was to sow grass and to build up the state's beef industry. The program did its work by means of speeches, of which this is one example, and by conducting tours. It achieved its greatest successes in western Kentucky. As a by-product of its work, fescue grass was developed and used extensively in the state.

STATE FAIR PLANS ANNOUNCEMENT
Louisville / April 21, 1954

My interest in the Kentucky State Fair dates back much further and is much more of a reality than most of you know. I have been kidded many times since becoming governor about my farming experiences as a youngster in the raising of red hogs on a share basis. It was then that I, with an overdose of pride, took my best shoats to the Kentucky Fair to compete against many hog raisers who worked at the business a lot less hard than I did. From those times on I have been keenly interested in the operation of the Kentucky State Fair.

As lieutenant governor and as a member of the State Building Commission in 1948, one of our first considerations was the development of a State Fair program for Kentucky commensurate with its people and its products. During the middle forties there was little incentive to support the fair. The plant itself was in a very bad state of repair, with much of it being used for defense purposes. Our fair had become a dumping place for bad shows and practices that brought about much more glaring press headlines than do the better operated fairs of today. It was during this period that the customary annual loss from the holding of the fair had risen to an amazing figure of $90,000. In 1947, Jack Matlick[1] had been asked to act as manager. He did a magnificent job under the most difficult circumstances. It was at about this time that the Kentucky State Fair Program entered a long-range improvement plan, as designed by the Clements administration. The first step in the reorganization plan was to regulate and improve the method of selecting State Fair board members, who were charged with the responsibility of operating the fair. Legislation was passed during the 1948 session so that one-half the appointed board membership would be filled from a list of recommended persons by state agricultural organizations of unquestionable repute.[2] The governor is then directed by law to name three members of his own choosing, who must be from opposing political parties, from those recommended by the organizations.

In addition to the appointment of these six members, three Democrats and three Republicans to the board, two of which are appointed annually and the terms of office running for four years, the remaining membership is made up of three ex officio members, the governor, the commissioner of agriculture, and the director of the Experiment Station at the University of Kentucky. Other legislation has been passed at subsequent sessions of the legislature to properly guide and govern an efficient and commendable operation of the state fair, with particular emphasis being placed on a general plan covering the needs of the new fairgrounds. It might be said here that from this early date, to the present, remarkable progress has been made. The attendance at the fair has doubled; the net profits have jumped from a deficit to an accumulated total at the close of the last fiscal year of nearly one half million dollars.

Governor Clements was greatly interested in the agricultural development of the state, which included a long-needed and overdue adequate state fair plant. Without knowing the politics of Jack Matlick, then or now, he was persuaded to act as manager for at least a period until the new organization could take over. His activity and ability in the organization of the affairs of our state is clearly shown in these reports tonight. With competent fair managership determined, the appointment of members to the board under the new program was at hand. The first choice went to Smith Broadbent, the chairman of our board. Other new blood brought onto the board includes Ashby Corum, and Tom Ballantine, who worked well with the old-timers, Clarence Miller, Onie Cook, and Scoggan Jones.[3] These early plans called for an entirely new fair plant in a new location of such size and design to embody in a practical way the varying needs and recommendations of the many fine organizations that make for the betterment of our state. There was just no question in the minds of any of us that the new plant was necessary, not only because of the inadequacy of facilities and space at the old grounds, but actually for the very health and welfare of our people, as evidenced by continual warnings from the state Health Department and the city and state safety and police departments.

With the decision made to proceed with the new fair program, the Kentucky Chain Stores Council was asked for a loan of Ivan Jett[4] for part-time service to act as consultant to the fair board. Ivan has rendered a great and valuable service to his state through his excellent recommendations to the board for various decisions from time to time.

Approximately 400 acres of land was acquired for the new location here in Louisville. You might be interested to know why it was felt that this was the best location within the state. Within a radius of seventy-five miles of Louisville is found 30 percent of the land area within the state, which comprises 32 percent of all the farms within the state. Within this area there is over 48 percent of the cattle and calves, 37.5 percent of the hogs, nearly 40 percent of the horses and mules, and even a higher percent of sheep. Here is located the foremost industrial center of Kentucky; here is found our greatest number of people. So you can see, actually this is the central spot of our state, agriculturally, industrially, and in density of population. Of added importance is the fact that almost 20 percent of the farms in Indiana lie within this same radius. The location of the new state fair becomes more unique with time. It presently is bounded on the south by the new Inner Belt Highway, on the east by the proposed North-South Expressway, on the west by Crittenden Drive, which is among the streets set up for widening and general improvement, and is bounded on the north by a railroad. Just to the south and across the Inner Belt Highway is Standiford Airfield. All of these important travel ways will add greatly to its accessibility and multiuse. This location can be reached easily from any part of town or country without traveling through the congested traffic of the downtown area.

An allocation of the State Building Commission from the 1950-1951 appropriation made available the funds for taking care of the expense involved in the completion of contracts for grading, drainage, and road surveys. The remaining funds in this grant by the state are helping substantially in meeting present demands for the overall financing of this program.

Plans for the construction of this project have been interrupted many times. During the early part of my tenure as a member of the Building Commission funds were available for the construction of this project, but they were gladly yielded to pressing defense needs for building materials. A couple of years later, when materials became less critical, a priority rating was given this project by the NPA in Washington, but there were then no state finances remaining that could be applied to this program. Efforts were made in many directions for possible loans, including the RFC, but none bore fruit.[5] During this interim of time the architect, Fred Ellswick and Associates, proceeded with the plans and specifications. I am now informed that these plans can be completed within a matter of days.

The State Fair Board employed about a year ago Parsons, Brinkerhoff, Hall and McDonald, engineers of national reputation, to make a feasibility study of the proposed project. As recently as last week their report was handed us. I am pleased to say to you, my friends, that the report is highly favorable, which fact leads me to make the following announcement, one which I am sure that you have been invited here to hear. The State Building Commission at its last meeting allocated $825,000 to be used in the construction of this project. We further complied with the report by setting aside funds to take care of any underestimate of the construction cost that the architect may have made. By far the largest of these additional considerations is the safety fund, constituting some half million dollars. We are confident, however, that no part of this fund will be needed since recent experiences from construction bids are more competitive and are expected to be actually lower than the estimate. Then too, in the three previous contracts let on this project the bids have averaged better than 10 percent below the architect's estimate. We have reason to believe that the original allocation for construction may not be entirely needed.

The total cost of this project is estimated at $15,400,000. The feasibility report states that the income from the activities held at the new Fair and Exposition Center will retire the necessary bonds to complete the financing of the project in twenty-five years. There are many sources of revenue planned in this new operation, such as the holding of the annual Kentucky State Fair, farm equipment shows, industrial and trade shows, sports shows, ice shows, horse shows, farm meetings and conventions, basketball, boxing, wrestling, rodeos, and the like. You might be interested in the number of livestock that it will accommodate for showing: 1,848 cattle, 2,500 sheep and hogs, 541 horses, and many thousands of poultry. These needs are in line with the trend of the participation in our recent fairs, in that each year we have broken previous records in the number of livestock shown at the fair. The coliseum is the hub of the entire structure and actually will be one of the largest inside arenas in the entire country. For the horse show available seats number 14,500; for basketball games, 16,600; and for boxing and wrestling, better than 20,000. The restaurant and cafeteria together can accommodate an even 1,000 for conventions. The exposition building can easily be converted into a dining room with a capacity for better than 2,000. The stadium is actually the roof over the horse barns. Presently it will have 21,000 permanent and 10,000 temporary seating capacity. Provision is made in the initial foundations for an expansion, when and if it becomes necessary, to a figure higher than 60,000. It is the plan of the State Fair Board to sell the old fairgrounds in order to obtain additional revenue needed in the construction of the new fair.

The Fair Board proposes to immediately prepare for the sale of revenue bonds and the advertising for construction bids to interested contractors. The feasibility report states that completion should be made in two years or less. We hope that all of you as well as all other supporters of our fair program will continue your patience with the inadequate facilities at the old fairgrounds while construction proceeds as rapidly as possible at the new plant.

I am deeply grateful to all of you for every contribution that you have made toward this project as well as to our Commonwealth in general. It is a great pleasure to serve such a great state made up of such wonderful people. I believe, with you, that the new Kentucky State Fair and Exposition Center, when completed, will contribute additional greatness to our beloved state.

---

1. John O. (Jack) Matlick (1911-), circulation department of *Kansas City Weekly Star* (1930-1933); Coppers Publications (1933-1936); circulation director, *Kentucky Farmer* (1936-1940); became editor and general manager of *Kentucky Farmer* (1940); manager, Kentucky State Fair (1945, 1947-1948); chairman, Kentucky Agricultural Council (1952-1953); commissioner, Department of Natural Resources (1960-1968); born in Scotland County, Missouri, and resides in Louisville. *Who's Who in America, 1954-1955*, 28th ed. (Chicago, 1954), pp. 1741-42.

2. The State Fair Board was now composed of nine members including the governor, commissioner of agriculture, dean of the College of Agriculture of University of Kentucky, and six members appointed from the state at large with due consideration given to geographical distribution throughout the state. The term of the appointment for the six members was four years. Article two of the act outlined specifically how the six appointments were to be filled by the governor. See *Acts of the General Assembly of the Commonwealth of Kentucky*,

1948, Chapter 62 (H. B. 255), pp. 120-22; 1948, Chapter 222 (S. B. 297), pp. 539–40.

3. Smith Dudley Broadbent, Jr. (1914-), president, Kentucky Seed Stocks, Inc. (1948-1951); chairman, Federal Reserve Bank of Louisville (1953-1955); department chairman, board of directors, Federal Reserve Bank of St. Louis, Missouri (1965-1972); director, Pennyrile chapter of Rural Electrification Administration; born and resides in Cadiz. *Who's Who in America, 1974-1975,* 38th ed. (Chicago, 1974), 1:376.

Marshall Ashby Corum (1887-1968), road contractor; farmer; business manager; president, U.C. Milk Company; president, the Mid-State Company; President, Kentucky Highway Contractors Association; member, Kentucky State Farm Board (1952-1956); born in McLean County. Letter, December 8, 1980.

Thomas A. Ballantine, Sr. (1902-1975), attorney; became president of the Louisville Taxicab and Transfer Company in 1945; president of Louisville Chamber of Commerce (1950-1953); joined the Kentucky State Fair Board in 1949; became a member of the Commission on Education in 1952 and of the Board of Trustees, University of Kentucky, in 1952; resided in Anchorage. *Who's Who in Kentucky* (Hopkinsville, Ky., 1955), p. 18.

Clarence L. Miller (1912-), performance supervisor Agricultural Adjustment Act, Department of Agriculture (1937-1940); farmer (1940-1950); chairman of Kentucky Agriculture Conservation Service, Department of Agriculture (1953-1954); director of tobacco division C. S. S. (1954-1956); vice president, Commodity Credit Corporation (1956-); director, Kentucky Fair Board (1947-1954); director, vice president, Kentucky Farm Bureau Federation (1951-1953); born in Louisville. *Who's Who in America, 1960-1961,* 31st ed. (Chicago, 1960), p. 2003.

Onie Cook was from Henderson. No other vita available.

Scoggan Jones, Sr. (1900-1962), farmer; member and president of Kentucky Farm Bureau Federation; born in Louisville. Telephone interview, Scoggan Jones, Jr., December 3, 1980.

4. Ivan L. Jett (1911-), teacher of vocational agriculture, Stamping Ground (1931-1940); director of marketing, Kentucky Department of Agriculture (1940-1941); director, Kentucky Chain Stores Council (1941-1947); became director of the Kentucky Agricultural Council (1947); member of State Fair Board, Agricultural and Industrial Development Board, Green Pastures Program, and director of Kentucky Educational Council; born in Jackson and resides in Georgetown. *Who's Who in the South and Southwest, 1956,* 5th ed. (Chicago, 1956), p. 458.

5. NPA was the National Planning Association and the RFC was the Reconstruction Finance Corporation.

FORMATION OF AN AGRICULTURAL COUNCIL

Letter / May 20, 1952

[To Ivan Jett, Georgetown]

As you know, agriculture is the major industry in Kentucky, and a higher percentage of our people are engaged in and dependent upon agriculture for their livelihood than any other single enterprise. Much interest has been manifested in utilizing and developing our agricultural resources to the fullest extent, to the end that the economic status of our people will be raised and rural life will be more attractive and fruitful.

Numerous persons, both individuals and those representing organized groups, have discussed with me the possibility of an agricultural council as a constructive agency in terms of dealing with our agricultural problems and opportunities here in our state. We have a rather large number of agencies and organized workers in the agricultural field, and I believe they can be more effective if the work of these respective agencies and groups is coordinated and integrated in terms of one overall program.

Agricultural councils have been organized and are now functioning in a number of other states, and it is my belief that such an organization has a distinct contribution to make here in Kentucky.

I am taking the initiative in calling together a group of people representing the various agricultural interests and agencies in Kentucky for the purpose of determining the possibility of an overall agricultural council in our state. After discussing the opportunities and functions of such a council, the group will then make a final decision as to whether or not an agricultural council in Kentucky should be formed.[1]

This is a cordial invitation to you and a personal request that you meet with us at the Pendennis Club, Louisville, at twelve o'clock noon DST, Monday, June 2. An early response would be helpful in making luncheon arrangements, and I shall be looking forward to seeing you on that occasion.

---

1. An agricultural council was formed out of this meeting, and Ivan L. Jett became its president. For a biographical sketch of Mr. Jett see speech from April 21, 1954, in this section.

KENTUCKY & THE NATION

HOMECOMING DAY
Louisville / December 15, 1950

"THE Sun Shines Bright in My Old Kentucky Home." The thought expressed in Foster's immortal song has lived with us down through the years and today, as Kentucky is taking spectacular steps forward in every field of endeavor, these imperishable words become more and more impressive and meaningful.

Those Kentuckians who have traveled the road home during the 1950 Mid-Century Homecoming are, I am confident, keenly aware that our state is on the march and rapidly going forward. We are proud of the Kentucky that is described in song and story, the Kentucky which is the "home that our feet may leave, but not our hearts."

We point with pride to accelerated industrial development in our communities. An effort has been made to create a healthy climate for industry, with sound and workable laws intended to meet existing requirements of government and, at the same time, provide an incentive for industry to make orderly expansions. During the last three years more than 250 new industries, employing 40,000 people, and with an annual payroll of $60 million, have located in Kentucky. This development is the result of a great deal of work by state government agencies, by private organizations such as the Kentucky Chamber of Commerce and many community chambers throughout the state, and by many firms and unselfish individuals who have devoted time and effort to building a greater and more prosperous Kentucky.

Our basic and important agricultural program has kept pace and compares favorably with the progress made in the industrial field. Recognition accorded the agricultural phase of our state economy is evidenced by the dual purpose of practically every development organization in the state. Typifying this is our Agricultural and Industrial Development Board.

Important strides are being made in the health and welfare of the citizens of our Commonwealth. We are experiencing an accelerated highway construction and maintenance program and a concentrated effort is being made, through the cooperation of the state chamber and your state government, in publicizing our scenic and historic attractions.

We cannot rest on our laurels completely on the basis of what has been accomplished. Government and private citizens alike must look forward, determined to explore new fields in the promotion of a better economic balance between agriculture and industry. The job is never finished for those who have the will to succeed. We have that will. We shall succeed.

Although we are justly proud of our strides of progress, in some quarters of the world where Kentuckians are engaged shoulder to shoulder with fellow Americans, the sun is not shining so brightly because of the dark clouds of aggression that shadow the rays of freedom. We are humbled by the spirit and determination of our boys on foreign soils, fighting against tremendous odds for our free way of life.

An old tale that has long appealed to me is that of the French drummer boy in one of Napoleon's Legions who was ordered to beat a retreat during a period when the outlook was dark and gloomy for the success of the troops of that leader.

"Sire, I know not how to beat a retreat," said the drummer boy. "My master only taught me how to beat a charge."

"Then beat a charge," the officer commanded the boy. The drummer boy complied and another great victory was added to the list.[1]

Our American boys are possessed with the same volition as Napoleon's Drummer boy. Victory will be ours, for we know that right, in the end, will prevail. The full might of America's physical, moral, and intellectual capacity has been committed to the cause of freedom. Whether the pursuit of this noble cause leads us down the turbulent road to war or down the thoroughfare to peace, Kentucky, as in the past, will make her full contribution. As we gird ourselves for whatever effort of sacrifice is required the call to duty will find our Commonwealth prepared.

This task is too great for human strength alone. None of us have sufficient wisdom to provide answers to all the complex prolems that confront us. It is fitting, therefore, that we close Kentucky's Mid-Century Homecoming Year with a note of prayer, a prayer of thanks, and a prayer for peace.

I humbly beseech every Kentuckian to go to the church of his choice next Sunday and, as we look to the star of Bethlehem for strength, my prayer is that the Prince of Peace may endow each of you with an abundance of peace and prosperity, and we may, with God's blessing, continue to enjoy a greater Kentucky on which the sun will always brightly shine.

Homecoming was a year-long recognition of Kentucky's progress. More than 100 communities held homecoming observances. It was believed that the Korean War had tempered the gaiety of the celebration. Governor Wetherby spoke at a dinner held at the Brown Hotel to mark the end of the activities. He was made an honorary citizen of the city of Louisville. *Louisville Courier-Journal,* December 16, 1950.

1. The story of the French drummer boy is an old one with many versions. In 1963 Parnassus Press published Ruth Robbins illustrated story, *The Emperor and the Drummer Boy.* This book bears a good parallel to the story that Wetherby related.

KENTUCKY PRESS ASSOCIATION
Louisville / January 26, 1951

I APPRECIATE the opportunity of sharing with you tonight the privilege of paying tribute to a man who has rendered outstanding service to our state. It is an honor to join in this undertaking the group which contributes perhaps more than any other professional society to the molding of thought and public opinion.

The Kentucky Press Association, now in its eighty-second year, is recognized in the Commonwealth for its never-failing support of worthy public movements. Within your membership are the talent, knowledge, and leadership capable of pointing the approach and solution to the many social, moral, and economic problems facing our civilization.

Although I am numbered among those who realize the great contribution the press makes to our way of life, it would be presumptuous for me to attempt a discussion with you of the responsibilities of the press or of the difficult problems of your profession. Each of you can call to mind at this moment some incident in your own experience where many working together have accomplished what an isolated few could only dream of doing. You know the importance of having many spokes in a wheel and of each of the spokes to a wheel. In the printing plant the composing room is as essential as is the editorial department. On the football team the line and backfield are of equal importance for the success of the team.

Teamwork and unity of purpose are essential in every field of human endeavor. They are needed now as never before at all levels of government —national, state, and local. They are needed in the production lines of our nation's industry. Our victories in World Wars I and II stem from the coordinated efforts of our men on the battlefield and of our production mobilization on the home front. In the present conflict, this same unity is of immediate and absolute importance if we are to resist the destructive forces bent on conquering or annihilating the free peoples of the world.

I am confident that Kentucky's Fourth Estate will continue to render superior public service through the advancement of individual liberty and a democratic way of life.

In some places there may exist the belief that to be in public service one must hold a civic office or political position. Fortunately, such is far from being the case. We are grateful that ours is a land in which merit it recognized wherever it be found. There are countless fields where distinguished public service may be rendered by the individual citizen.

Among the community's greatest contributors, to mention just a few, are the family doctor and nurse who in times of illness attend our needs. The minister who endeavors to point a better way of life. The jurist whose ideal is to seek the true course of justice. The editor as a molder of public opinion for the general welfare of all. The combined efforts of these, and every other profession and interest, are necessary if each community in our state is to realize its greatest growth and civic potentiality.

There is not one among you who is unaware of the value of teamwork. In the field of athletics teamwork is the very essence of success. Fresh in our minds is the teamwork of the Wildcats, evidenced by each player contributing his skill and effort to win the coveted Sugar Bowl.[1] Coach Paul Bryant[2] is the synthesis of the spirit which won that victory. We honor him for teaching young men to develop themselves in such fashion as to reach the top rung on the athletic ladder. The recipient of the 1950 distinguished citizenship award has brought fame to the university, recognition to the football team, and glory to our Commonwealth.

Paul Bryant has directed a group of fine young men who have often won and occasionally lost. But all in all he has taught the value of clean competitive sports, the foundation on which all college athletics must rest.

For when the One Great Scorer comes
To write against your name
He doesn't write whether you won or lost
But how you played the game.

I want to say at this time, it is my hope that all members of this famous team will find within the bounds of our state the opportunity to pursue their chosen careers and contribute to the success of our state, just as they did as members of the 1950 university football squad, in order that the whole state may share in the reflected glory of their individual achievements.

Recently, I had the pleasure of bestowing on Coach Bryant the highest honor which the governor can give—the commission as a Kentucky Colonel. He also received from the atheletic department of the university the longest coaching contract at the time in football history. And now you have seen fit to bestow upon him the highest honor of your association—the Kentuckian of the Year Award.

---

1. On January 1, 1951, the University of Kentucky defeated the University of Oklahoma by a score of 13 to 7 and ended that team's 31 game winning streak. *Louisville Courier-Journal,* January 2, 1951.

2. Paul Bryant (1913-   ), assistant football coach, University of Alabama (1936-1940); head football coach, Vanderbilt University (1940-1941); head coach, University of Maryland (1945); head coach, University of Kentucky (1946-1953); head coach, Texas A & M (1954-1957); head coach, University of Alabama (1957-   ). *Who's Who in America,* 1978-1979, 40th ed. (Chicago, 1979), p. 450. Governor Wetherby was a close personal friend to Coach Bryant, and the two men hunted together. The governor was an ardent sports enthusiast who attended many games in collegiate athletics, but he was particularly fond of University of Kentucky football. In 1952, Coach Bryant was offered a job at the University of Arkansas, but Governor Wetherby helped to persuade him to remain in Kentucky. In 1953, when the athletic department at the University of Kentucky did not fulfill certain agreements with the coach, Governor Wetherby accepted his decision to leave.

DEDICATION OF GENERAL BUCKNER'S PLAQUE

Frankfort / February 21, 1951

THIS is a day of remembrance when all those assembled here do honor to one of Kentucky's most distinguished soldiers, General Simon Bolivar Buckner, Jr.[1] This occasion is dedicated to the memory of one who paid the supreme sacrifice in defense of freedom, justice, and right. It is a privilege to welcome those who pay tribute to him today.

General Buckner was an illustrious son of a great Kentucky family. His grandfather fought in the War of 1812.[2] His father, a West Pointer, scholar, poet, statesman, gentleman, newspaperman, Mexican War veteran, gallant officer, and governor of Kentucky, rendered dauntless and invaluable service to the South in the cause of the Confederacy.[3] His handsome log house, tucked away under the trees at "Glen Lily" in Hart County, is the Old Kentucky Home of that section of the state.[4]

The soldier we are honoring today typifies the spirit demonstrated by Jackson's Kentucky Volunteers in the Battle of New Orleans and the heroism of the Kentucky soldiers displayed on the field of battle in every war in which our country has participated. No post was too advanced for him to pay an unexpected visit. He was a leader rather than a director, as is evidenced by the restless spirit and relentless courage of his front line activities in World Wars I and II. The brilliant career of the defender of Alaska, liberator of the Aleutians, and victor of Okinawa was cut short by enemy artillery fire at Okinawa in 1945 while the general was at a forward observation post.

Memorable chapters in the blood-stained history of war have been and are being written by men and women whose noble deeds present dramatic stories of loyalty, courage, and heroism. Time has not dimmed their records of gallantry and sacrifice.

The immortal story emanating from the late war and written into the history of warfare is that of the four service chaplains in whose memory a chapel recently has been dedicated in Philadelphia. As an enemy submarine torpedo struck their troop ship in the bleak North Atlantic the four chaplains—a Catholic, a Jew, and two Protestants—gave up their own life jackets after the available supply was gone, joined arm in arm and with prayer on their lips for safety of others were swept under the billowy waves.[5] One of these heroes, Clark Poling, was the son of an eminent clergyman and author, Dr. Daniel Poling,[6] whose life has been devoted to the service of God and man.

In an address at the University of Kentucky this past summer, Dr. Poling said he is often asked: "What did your boy get by dying?" His inspiring reply gives us a glimpse of the meaning and value of the sacrifice of every man who has died in the service of God and our country. Dr. Poling said: "Why sir, he and all the others who died, and those of that vaster number, thank God, who challenged death and lived, he and they got for us the chance to keep on talking, got for us the chance to hold and cherish all our freedoms, the chance to pass them on unimpaired and strengthened to our children and our children's children. Sir, they got for us the chance, the fighting chance, to win the peace."

And so fellow Kentuckians, General Simon Bolivar Buckner and the dead have not died in vain unless we the living live in vain. It is the least that we the living may offer if we would be worthy of these who gave the last full measure and whose memorial we dedicate.

---

1. Simon Bolivar Buckner, Jr. (1886-1945), instructor, United States Military Academy (1919-1923); instructor, Command and General Staff School (1925-1928); executive officer, Army War College (1929-1932); assistant commandant and commandant, United States Military Academy (1932-1936); commanding general, Alaskan Defense Force (July 1940); commanding general, Okinawa (1945); killed in action June 18, 1945; born in Munfordville. *Who Was Who in America, 1943-1950* (Chicago, 1966), 2:89.

2. Aylette Hartswell Buckner (1806-1869), member, Kentucky House of Representatives (1842-1843); member, United States House of Representatives (1847-1849); born in Greensburg. *Who Was Who in America, 1607-1896* (Chicago, 1967), H:83.

3. Simon Bolivar Buckner, Sr. (1823-1914), served in Mexican War (1846-1848); instructor, United States Military Academy (1848-1850); inspector general of Kentucky (1860-1861); brigadier general, CSA (September 1861); prisoner of war (February-August 1862); major general (1863); lieutenant general (1864); governor of Kentucky (1887-1891); member of the constitutional convention of Kentucky (1891); Democratic candidate for vice president of the United States (1896); born in Hart County. *Who Was Who in America, 1897-1942* (Chicago, 1968), 1:162.

4. Glen Lily was a two-story, twenty-two-room house built in 1819 by Aylette Hartswell Buckner. Situated seven miles east of Munfordville, it was surrounded by a three-thousand-acre tract of virgin forest. The property was named for the daughter of Simon Bolivar Buckner, Sr. Robert A. Powell, *Kentucky Governors* (Frankfort, 1976), p. 133.

5. The story of the four chaplains, all first lieutenants, is told in Robert L. Gushwa's *The Best and Worst of Times: The United States Army Chaplaincy, 1920-1945* (Washington, D.C., 1977). Clark V. Poling and George Fox were Protes-

tants; John P. Washington, Catholic; and Alexander D. Goode, a Jew. The army transport ship *Dorchester* carried 751 army passengers and a large cargo when it left St. John's, Newfoundland, for Greenland under escort. On February 3, 1943, the ship was hit by a single torpedo. It took only twenty minutes for the ship to sink in the freezing waters.

6. Daniel Alfred Poling (1884-1968), Prohibition candidate for governor of Ohio (1912); pastor, Marble Collegiate Church, New York (1922-1930); pastor, Baptist Temple, Philadelphia (1936-1948); chaplain, Chapel of the Four Chaplains (1948); wrote many books on the theme of World War II; born in Portland, Oregon. *Who Was Who in America, 1969-1973* (Chicago, 1973), 5:575.

FRED VINSON DAY
Louisa / July 11, 1951

SINCE the original thirteen colonies united in defense of human freedom our nation's strength and greatness have rested on the individual and collective contributions of the states composing the union. The early history of our republic is replete with accounts of great deeds by great Americans.

Although our mother state, Virginia, was acclaimed as the "Mother of Presidents" during the first quarter century of the United States, a representative share of these immortal patriots may rightfully be claimed by each of the original thirteen states.

As explorers and settlers moved westward to claim the vast expanses of rich farmland, state after state was admitted to the union, and with the addition of each star to our flag new and invigorating chapters of history were written by Americans whose names are revered by a grateful people.

During every critical period of our national existence men of strength, vision, and fortitude have come forth to assume leadership roles. In time of war the brilliance of American military leaders has proven equal to the tasks necessary for victory. In times of great social, economic, and political strain and uncertainty leadership of matchless quality has appeared upon our nation's stage to allay fear, instill confidence, and point the way toward stability, progress, and happiness. During the long intervals of peace with which our nation has been blessed, we have been guided by men whose boundless energies, leadership capacity, and constructive genius have provided Americans with the highest standard of living on earth. As this great epic is recounted the dramatic role of each state may be pointed to with pride. The banner enumerating unselfish contributions made by the citizens of each state is worthy of being flown from the highest masthead.

In making this acknowledgement the brilliant rays of light that have emanated from Kentucky during every generation have served our nation as a beacon. Kentucky's sons and daughters have distinguished themselves in the service of our state and nation. In every emergency her people have rallied to the forefront in defense of decency and justice. In times of peace her citizens have been loyal to the principles that make our country great and have taken on willingly obligations to make more secure the blessings of a free land.

I only wish I could unroll today the full and colorful tapestry of Kentucky's revealing and mighty contribution of our republic since 1792. The roster would bear an array of names of men whose recognized eminence would stretch across the land and beyond the seas. The list would include intrepid explorers and pioneers, dauntless soldiers, brilliant scholars, surgeons and inventors and wise statesmen and political leaders.

Kentuckians are a proud and appreciative people. Colorful pageants, historical assemblies, and memorable events have been crowded into the chronicle of Kentucky's development. Many of these occasions symbolized a community's love and esteem for a native son, reflected commendably on the character and civic virtues of the community and exemplified flowers to the living rather than to the dead.

Today's program demonstrates that you people of Louisa, Lawrence County, and this area, are adding luster to our noble heritage. This impressive crowd, graced by the presence of many nationally prominent leaders, is indeed fitting tribute to the distinguished Kentuckian we honor today.

Fred M. Vinson,[1] chief justice of the United States, and head of the judicial branch of our federal government, began his career of public service as Louisa city attorney in 1911. Through the years he has won the respect and complete confidence of the public and impresses all those with whom he comes in contact with his wisdom, courage, and capacity for leadership. His versatility has carried him to the pinnacle of success and prominence in all three branches of government. As a member of Congress Fred Vinson was recognized as one of the outstanding authorities on tax and fiscal matters as well as an able and fearless legislative leader. After leaving Congress for a period on the federal bench in the District of Columbia, President Roosevelt placed this great Kentuckian in charge of some of the most important emergency programs during World War II. As economic stabilizer he was the acknowledged "assistant President" of the United States.

During those perilous war years and the critical reconversion days that followed, our honored guest demonstrated a breadth of judgment and range of knowledge seldom seen. A grateful president and nation, acclaiming his record of service in the mobilization program, rewarded his efforts and superb qualifications by appointment to the high post of Secretary of the Treasury. Handling the vast and complicated treasury operations with the same masterful touch as had characterized his previous administrative work, he stood in line for even greater recognition and responsibility.

The next development was the crowning point and fitting climax to a series of promotions unique in the annals of American history. In June 1946[2] the president appointed and the Senate confirmed Fred M. Vinson, the first Kentuckian as chief justice of the United States. With his stature and eminence already established, he follows the same pathway of service and protector of human freedom that has led him to greatness and to be personally esteemed by all America. I am proud to have a part in paying tribute to *our* chief justice.

As Kentucky has shared him with the nation, I know the nation now shares with Kentucky the joy and pride that is ours as we celebrate Fred Vinson Day.

Mr. Chief Justice, Associate Justice Reed, Associate Justice Minton of New Albany, Indiana, almost a part of Kentucky, Governor Patteson, distinguished guests, I welcome you all.[0]

---

1. Frederick Moore Vinson (1890-1953), city attorney, Louisa (1913); commonwealth attorney (1921-1924); member, United States House of Representatives (1923-1929, 1931-1933, 1935-1938); associate justice, United States Court of Appeals (1938-1943); Office of Economic Stabilization (1943-1945); federal loan administrator (March-April 1945); director, Office of War Mobilization (April-July 1945); secretary of treasury (1945-1946); chief justice of the United States (1946-1953); born in Louisa. *Who's Who in America, 1952-1953*, 27th ed. (Chicago, 1952), p. 2496.

2. President Harry Truman made the nomination on June 20, 1946.

3. Stanley Forman Reed (1884-), member, Kentucky General Assembly (1912, 1916); general counsel to Federal Farm Board (1929-1932); general counsel to Reconstruction Finance Corporation (1932-1935); solicitor general of United States (1935-1938); associate justice of the Supreme Court of the United

States (1938-1957); born in Mason County. *Who's Who in America, 1952-1953,* 27th ed. (Chicago, 1952), p. 2008. Justice Reed Spoke at the dedication of the plaque to Vinson.

Sherman Minton (1890-1965), public counselor of Indiana (1933-1934); member, United States Senate (1935-1941); administrative assistant to the president of the United States (January-May 1941); judge, United States Circuit Court of Appeals (1941-1949); associate justice of the Supreme Court of the United States (1949-1956); born in Georgetown, Indiana. *Who's Who in America, 1954-1955,* 28th ed. (Chicago, 1954), p. 1875.

Okey L. Patteson (1898-), president, Fayette County court, West Virginia (1935-1941); Fayette County sheriff (1941-1944); state campaign manager (1944); assistant to Governor Clarence Meadows (1945-1948); governor of West Virginia (1949-1953); born in Mingo County, West Virginia, and resides in Mount Hope, West Virginia. Charles Ambler and Festus Summers, *West Virginia, the Mountain State* (Englewood Cliffs, N. J., 1958), pp. 486-88.

INTRODUCTION OF HENRI BONNET AT TRANSYLVANIA COLLEGE ANNIVERSARY
Lexington / April 23, 1954

WITH pride and pleasure I introduce to you today a gentleman who has devoted so much of himself to the promotion of better understanding among nations in intellectual and spiritual matters.[1] I am sure you know of his distinguished career, and I feel privileged to provide a little of the biography of our illustrious guest.

In the universities of France he received high honors. His further studies were interrupted by World War I. At the close of the war he was discharged with the rank of captain, embellished with citations for bravery and incredible courage. Returning to civilian life, he became foreign editor of the Paris newspaper, *The New Era.* His grasp of foreign affairs led to his appointment to a post in the secretariat of the League of Nations, and in 1931 he left Geneva to become director of the International Institute of Intellectual Cooperation, a division of the League of Nations.

Early in World War II he and his wife[2] escaped to England before the Nazis conquered most of France, and while in Great Britain was an inventor of Free French strategy. He came to the United States to assume a post on the faculty of the Free School for Higher Studies. He also served on the editorial board of the magazine *Free World.*

Much of his time was spent in Chicago as a special adviser to the World Citizens' Association. His books and dissertations on cultural subjects and foreign politics are numerous.

On December 25, 1944, his country honored the United States by appointing him ambassador.

He has some firsthand observation on the government of our Commonwealth for, in 1952 on a visit to Frankfort, he entered the chambers of the Kentucky Legislature and won the avid acclaim of both houses.

Ladies and gentlemen, may I present His Excellency the Ambassador from France, Henri Bonnet.

---

1. Henri Bonnet (1888-), professor of history, University of Paris (1912); foreign editor of *Ere Nouvelle* (1919); member of secretariate, League of Nations (1920-1931); director, International Institute of Intellectual Cooperation; secretary general, Permanent Conference Hautes Etudes Internationales; vice president, Center of Studies of Foreign Policy in Paris (1931-1940); minister for information, Provisional Government of France (1944); ambassador to the United States from France; born in Chateauponsac, France. *Who's Who in America, 1954-1955,* 28th ed. (Chicago, 1954), p. 267.
2. Halle Zervoudaki Bonnet.

REGULATION OF COLLEGE ATHLETIC PROGRAMS
Letter / December 27, 1951

[To J. Morton Williams, Beaver Dam]

THIS is to acknowledge and thank you for your letter of December 19 concerning the subject of college athletics.

As a result of the wide ramifications involving basketball fixes and point-shaving and the closeness to home that the sinister influence of underworld gamblers has had on young men playing on University of Kentucky teams, there is much interest now evidenced by both educational leaders and the public generally toward strengthening regulations governing the conduct of college athletic programs. It was this venture of suspicion that has been cast on the University of Kentucky that prompted my appeal to the New York authorities urging that prompt and effective steps be taken toward clarifying a situation that could only lead from bad to worse with each day's delay.

While complete success was not attained through our efforts in this regard, it is felt that the atmosphere has improved considerably with the most recent action of the university, and I trust that the whole affair can be brought to the speediest possible conclusion so that the name of the university and of its loyal and honest athletes can again be free from the doubt and confusion that has existed for the past several months.

The University of Kentucky became involved in a gambling scandal on the night of October 20, 1951, when investigators from the New York district attorney's office seized Dale Barnstable, Alex Groza, and Ralph Beard. The three basketball players were accused of being paid for going over the spread in a game played at Madison Square Garden in New York City. Seven colleges were involved. Later Bill Spivey admitted being approached by gambling interests, and he was suspended by the university's Athletics Board. In late 1951 a New York grand jury charged Walter Hirsch, Dale Barnstable, and James Line with accepting bribes to shave points. The judge who heard the case dealt a suspended sentence to Ralph Beard, Dale Barnstable, and Alex Groza. Judge Streit said that the University of Kentucky placed an inordinate amount of emphasis on basketball and football. Adolph Rupp, basketball coach, was accused of aiding and abetting in the immoral subsidization of players. In Kentucky there was an adverse reaction to the judge's statements and the decision because there was no reference to organized gambling in New York and to those who produced the scandal. It was noted that there had been no fixed games before they were featured at Madison Square Garden. Governor Wetherby held these criticisms of the situation. See Russell Rice, *Kentucky Basketball's Big Blue Machine* (Huntsville, Alabama, 1976), pp. 226-34.

The NCAA fined the University of Kentucky $100,000, and the team was suspended from Southeastern Conference basketball for one year. See *Louisville Courier-Journal,* August 12, 1952.

UNIVERSITY OF KENTUCKY BASKETBALL SCANDAL

Letter / May 15, 1952

[To Curtis G. Benjamin, New York]

DURING recent months the name of our great state university has been publicized from coast to coast because of indictments that were returned in New York involving six Kentucky basketball players. As a result of the banner headlines that have been devoted to this situation and the innumerable press releases and lengthy statements that have been issued, serious and damaging reflections have been cast on our university's athletic department and, for that matter, the entire university administration. While there is evidence that possibly a degree of laxity in the university's control of athletics contributed to the unfortunate point shaving in which these young men participated, though that is open to question and cannot be proved or invalidated with a clear-cut answer, the sensational publicity has far overshadowed the actual guilt of the players or of the school's board of trustees and its administrative officials in correcting whatever policies that need changing and the steps that have been taken to insure as far as humanly possible, that similar occurrences will not again arise.[1]

As a member of the board of trustees of the university, I cannot overemphasize our determination to take every conceivable precaution to insure that present and future athletes will not become similarly involved. However, it is of more than a passing coincidence that the contamination of these young men occurred in New York.

---

1. In 1952 the Kentucky General Assembly passed an act relating to bribery of participants in professional or amateur games, sports, contests, horse racing, and horse shows. Anyone who gave, promised, or offered any valuable thing to an athlete or coach, owner, etc., with intent to influence him to lose or try to lose or cause to be lost or to limit a margin of victory was guilty of a felony, punishable by imprisonment for not less than one year, nor more than ten, and by a fine of not more than $10,000. Recipients were punished in like fashion. It is interesting that the penalty for this offense was greater than for the 1954 strip mining law. Yet, as the act stated, there was an imminent danger to the existence of sports activities in the state; and in Kentucky that is stating a great deal. See *Acts of the General Assembly of the Commonwealth of Kentucky, 1952*, Chapter 1 (S.B. 1), pp. 1-2.

Curtis G. Benjamin (1901-), director, Community Theatre, Tucson, Arizona (1927); McGraw-Hill Book Company (1928-1966), president (1946-1960), chairman of the board (1960-1966); member, National Academy of Science (1967-1969); born in Providence. *Who's Who in America, 1974-1975*, 38th ed. (Chicago, 1974), 1:222.

LABOR UNREST AT CENTRAL CITY
Letter / August 14, 1952

[To Claud D. Edwards, Mayfield]

THIS acknowledges your scolding communication of August 8 in which you deplore the Central City situation.

Please let me advise you that Kentucky State Police are on duty, and have been so for several weeks, at Central City maintaining law and order. For such a tense situation, there has been little violence and injury. The problem at Central City is novel and must be handled in a most temperate manner, preferably in the courts or at the conference table.[1]

I presume from your letter you desire me to order armed troopers into the city and to attack the labor element with gunfire. This is not the way to settle this situation which now has nationwide attention. If we reacted as you indicate you want us to, Kentucky would be denounced as a pocket of Hitlerism and un-Americanism by all the liberal forces in the world.

District No. 50 knows what it wants. The citizens of Central City know what they want. It is their crisis, and I trust time and mutual good judgment on each side will reconcile the issue in a democratic way.

The mayor of Central City[2] and all of the merchants have advised me they are highly pleased with the actions taken so far by this office.

May I inform you also that I am as aware as you are of my duties under the constitution and statutes.

---

1. Without publicity Governor Wetherby sent the state police to Central City to keep the peace. This was a novel use of the police force stemming from its reorganization by the General Assembly in 1948. The disturbances there resulted from the efforts by the United Mine Workers to organize in the area. It

was the merchants who persuaded the governor of the need for a peace-keeping force. Indicative of the situation, on August 5, 1952, a small building owned by a merchant who had been resisting the UMW efforts was dynamited. Two union men were arrested and charged with the act. That month merchants were able to win a temporary injunction against picketing, coercion, and violence. *Louisville Courier-Journal,* August 6, 26, 1952.

2. Albert P. Harding.

Claud D. Edwards (1899-), merchant, born in Marshall County and resides in Mayfield. Letter, December 8, 1980.

NEWSPAPER MICROFILM PROJECT

Letter / June 1, 1955

[To Felix Joyner, Frankfort]

THE Kentucky Press Association, in cooperation with the University of Kentucky, has developed a proposed microfilm project. It is designed to assist in preserving the history of the Commonwealth as recorded in our newspapers. There have been numerous meetings and discussions held preliminary to the final conclusion that the program should and could be launched. I have participated either directly or indirectly in these discussions. President Donovan, W. C. Caywood, president of the Kentucky Press Association, Victor Portmann, secretary-manager of the Kentucky Press Association, and Fred Wachs are the responsible people in promoting this idea.[1]

After setting the program in motion, there is definite belief among these people that it could be maintained on a self-sustaining basis. To get it launched, I have agreed to support it through an allocation from the Emergency Fund to the university in the amount of $20,000. May I suggest that you take preliminary steps to effect the transfer of this amount upon further notice from me within the next few days.

---

1. Herman Lee Donovan (1887-1964), superintendent of various public school districts in Kentucky (1910-1921); professor of education, George Peabody College (1925-1928); president, Eastern Kentucky State Teachers College (1928-1941); president, University of Kentucky (1941-1956); president, Ken-

tucky Education Association (1948-1949); born in Maysville. *Who's Who in Kentucky* (Hopkinsville, Ky., 1955), p. 95.

William Curtis Caywood, Jr. (1908-), *Winchester Sun* (1930-1963), editor (1938-1963); joined the faculty of University of Kentucky School of Journalism in 1963; born in Madison County. Hambleton Tapp, ed., *Kentucky Lives: The Blue Grass State Who's Who* (Hopkinsville, Ky., 1966), p. 79.

Victor R. Portmann (1892-), Department of Journalism, Universiity of Arkansas (1927); assistant professor, Department of Journalism, University of Kentucky (1927-1962); member, secretary-manager of Kentucky Press Association (1936-1966); born in Jackson, Minnesota, and resides in Lexington. Letter, December 23, 1980. Mr. Portmann writes: "Appalled by the damage to state newspapers and few libraries having complete files of any state papers, Portmann was named chairman of a group, backed by the state Department of Safety, and through the wonderful assistance of Governor Wetherby, from his emergency fund, granted the press association and university the $50,000 to buy cameras and necessary equipment in the University library. With the cooperation of the newspapers, we believe that all historical valuable yesteryear files, as all current issues, are now on film."

Fred B. Wachs (1897-), general manager, *Lexington Herald* and the *Sunday Herald-Leader;* recipient of many awards and member of numerous organizations; resides in Lexington. *Who's Who in Kentucky* (Hopkinsville, Ky., 1955), p. 348.

Leon Felix Joyner (1924-), member, Kentucky budget staff (1948-1955); member, field staff of Public Administration Service, Chicago (1955-1960); Kentucky commissioner of personnel (1960-1962); health and welfare administration (1962-1963); commissioner of finance (1963-1967); vice president, University of North Carolina (1968-); born in Savannah, Georgia, and resides in Chapel Hill, North Carolina. *Who's Who in America, 1978-1979,* 40th ed. (Chicago, 1978), 1:1698.

REORGANIZATION

SHOULD KENTUCKY GOVERNORS SUCCEED THEMSELVES?

Frankfort / January 1953

SINCE the beginning of recorded history man's social organization and political concept have afforded a rich and most interesting field for study and scholarly enterprise. Varying with climate, geography, time, and national origin, civic society has found expression in many different ways. As each has existed, it is possible to compare the difference between communism and private enterprise, hereditary rulers against elected magistrates, a dictatorship as contrasted with a democracy.

With the brief mention of these opposites, it is apparent that continual change and adjustment through the ages have characterized our political development. While conflict and bitter wrangling have had far-reaching influence on the world's great political systems, it is comforting to reflect on the even greater effect reason, tolerance, and judgment have had in fashioning American democracy. Upon these anvils of eternal moral strength and political endurance, the federal Constitution was framed. The charter has remained, with remarkably few changes, our basic guide in constitutional government since 1789. It has prescribed the form and general content of all forty-eight state constitutions, and been closely followed by many foreign republics.

In tracing the evolution of the prohibition in the Kentucky Constitution against the governor succeeding himself, it is proper to note that no such restriction was imposed by the original federal document. While much evidence exists that many of those participating in writing the federal Constitution felt great uncertainty about the masses governing themselves with wisdom and stability, there can be no doubt that the proponents of popular self-government prevailed in including certain specific provisions, the absence of which would have made it designed for autocrats instead of democrats. Equally impressive are the omissions that have prompted thought and speculation during the decades. The silence of the founding fathers on a president succeeding himself testifies to the belief of the Constitutional Convention that that question should best be left to the electorate of the new union. Dire prophecies of usurpation and dictatorship were voiced from the beginning, but there is nothing in the record that lends credence to the thought that the absence of a direct prohibition of a president succeeding himself has diminished the fruits of democratic government or bred executive tyrants. The presidents from Washington to FDR, either through personal choice or the people through the ballot, maintained themselves in office for eight years or less. Of course, it is impossible to say with any degree of finality upon what each of those men based their decision not to attempt a second or a third term. But it is not too much to assume that the foremost consideration was whether they could again get elected. No man in public life relishes an unsuccessful race. Neither is one in a position to run for high office unmindful of the habits of voters to oppose and kick out those already in power. This latter thesis has been demonstrated and repeated many times in American political life.

So the discretion permitted by the nation's basic law was vitiated by the more compelling force of the peoples' will. This so-called two-term tradition, however, was dramatically altered in 1940. In the case of FDR the nation had a leader willing to assume the burdens of the presidency in excess of two terms, and subsequent elections showed overwhelmingly that the people endorsed this past known performance as chief of state. Therefore, in contravention to the above proposition, the people's free-will expression was exercised as decisively for an individual, his policies and program, as it has been against others lacking their support and confidence.

In completing the cycle, suffice to say that the adoption of the Twenty-second Amendment now limits the president to a maximum of eight years in office. While its proponents undoubtedly included many well-meaning, yet unsuspecting, people, the real basis of its sponsorship was a newly victorious opposition party in control of Congress, still smarting from the sting of four successive presidential defeats and vengefully determined to destroy the political magic of his name.

As the constitutional ladder is descended to the Kentucky rung, mention should be made of the four constitutions and the provisions made by each for the succession of the governor: Under the first constitution there was no prohibition to the governor succeeding himself. Under the second constitution the governor was ineligible for the succeeding seven years. Under the third constitution the governor was ineligible to succeed himself for four years. The fourth constitution in 1890 and the one now in effect prohibits all nine statewide elective officials from succeeding themselves.[1] There were one hundred members in the 1890 constitutional convention. While a bitter fight raged on the question of the governor succeeding himself, when the final vote was tabulated only six members of the convention voted for the governor to immediately succeed himself in office.

Carrying the general discussion of the federal aspects of this subject to more concrete examples, it might be said that the framers of our state constitution were in 1890 more prone to suspect and be afraid of the people's prerogatives than were those writing the federal Constitution one hundred years before. While meaning to protect the people of the Commonwealth from political bosses, machines, and unscrupulous officials, the extensive and detailed directives and prohibitions in the constitution evidence their melancholy attributed toward the ability of future generations to safeguard their domestic heritage. These gentlemen seem to have been oblivious to the "kick the rascals out" psychology of Kentucy voters. The idea of the great silent mass that rises on election day never entered their thinking.

A Kentucky governor is elected under our constitution for four years without legal opportunity, regardless of how acceptable his program has been, to put it before the public for approval or rejection. In practical application he must successfully run the legislative gauntlet during the first hurried ninety days he is in office if he is to adopt a program and have an administration worthy of history's harsh pen. The remaining general assembly two years hence is invariably plagued with vicissitudes common to "lame duck" tenures. By then the governor is on the down-hill side of his term and political tension is already mounting in anticipation of the next gubernatorial contest.

Turning away from what is to what might be, let it be assumed that a governor could offer his finished product of service to the voters for their endorsement or rejection after four years. Time could then be taken to plan and program carefully and expertly and still not be confronted with harassing problems of what gets done will have to be finished in the first two years of his term.

The public deserves the right to be able to re-elect an able, popular governor if his record merits their approval. On the other hand, a man that serves his state ably, honestly, and courageously as governor should have the legal opportunity to stand for re-election.

In addition to the precedent established by our earlier state constitutions and that of the federal Constitution, there are many states in which the governor can succeed himself. Brilliant public service records have been made by some states' chief executives resulting from their continued periodic re-election to office. Where there are free and honest elections it is inconceivable that a legal barrier is necessary to avoid the selection of an incompetent, a crook, or a despot.

It is the duty of all citizens to insure honest and fair elections. If a governor is elected under these circumstances and meaning exists in the term "popular self government," who has the effrontery to oppose the right of that governor to seek re-election?

Through the orderly process of change and adjustment previously mentioned, added dignity and importance should be given to majority rule. If a majority of citizens be willing to elect a Kentucky governor to succeed himself, there should not be an artificial barrier to the exercise of this privilege.

It appears that this speech was prepared for delivery at an agricultural conference that was canceled because of a snowstorm. The speech was then released to the press in order to initiate reform.

In 1961 Governor Wetherby was a delegate to the convention to revise the Kentucky State Constitution. The new document did allow a governor to succeed himself; however, voters rejected the constitution.

Subsequently, Governor Wetherby preferred a single term of six years for a governor.

1. For the 1792 Constitution see Article II, Section 3. It granted a four year term and makes no mention of succession. See Bennett H. Young, *History and Texts of the Three Constitutions of Kentucky* (Louisville, 1890), p. 21.

For the 1799 Constitution see Article III, Section 3. This section stated that the governor shall be ineligible for the succeeding seven years after the expiration of his office. See Bennett Young, p. 40.

For the 1850 Constitution see Article III, Section 3. This section stated that the governor shall be ineligible for the succeeding four years after the expiration of his term. See Bennet Young, p. 65.

For the 1890 Constitution see Section 71. This constitution continued the four year ineligibility period. See *Constitution of the Commonwealth of Kentucky* (Frankfort, 1981), p. 18.

PUBLIC RELATION AND STATE PUBLICITY REORGANIZATION

Letter / December 27, 1951

[To Bill Ladd, Louisville]

As your December 16 note was not considered as a part of the record, I trust you will accord my response likewise.

It is good to know that you and several others from whom I have heard who are in the newspaper and public relations field concur in the general state publicity administrative reorganization that is currently being put into effect. I think, by drawing into one centralized agency the sprawling and unwieldy public relation and state publicity jobs now being done by the various departments, it will insure a much more efficient and effective job than could otherwise be done.

On the matter of personnel, I should like to say that it is the state department heads that I must hold accountable for the success or failure of the programs which they direct and for which all of the people hold me accountable. If I am to keep their accountability to me on an uncompromised basis, I cannot pass judgment on or in any way interfere with the discretion they exercise in the selection or utilization of the employees to whom they must look in seeing that their department's responsibilities are carried out in the most effective and harmonious manner.

This is the policy I have adhered to strictly during the past year and to which I shall subscribe during the next four. It reflects my attitude in the case of every personnel change that is made by one of the department heads.

William W. Ladd (1902-), worked for the *Louisville Courier-Journal* in a number of positions including reporter, sports reporter, news editor, desk man, and was a radio and television critic for WHAS in Louisville (1927-1967); born in Madison, Wisconsin, and resides in Louisville. Telephone interview, December 28, 1980.

CONTROL AND SALE OF ALCOHOLIC BEVERAGES
Letter / December 4, 1952

[To Charlie Friedman, Louisville]

IT is indeed encouraging to read some cogent observations about the whiskey business from one who deals in liquor. I can give you first-hand knowledge that the liquor trade is one of the most discouraging problems confronting state government. Applicants for licenses are well screened yet every time one of them violates the law, gets investigated and publicized, it seems that his background is damaging to the industry and horrifying to the public and the government. Much thought has been devoted to the ways of administering the Alcoholic Beverage Control laws but much more is needed.

I am pleased to know that you have brought this issue to the attention of distillers and others in the business. May I suggest that you meet with the people in your trade and carefully prepare legislation barring the issuance of a license or the opportunity of working in a liquor store to anyone convicted of one felony or three misdemeanors. The General Assembly is considerate of matters tightening control over the sale and handling of distilled spirits, although it seems to be very difficult to write clearly defined and easily understood legislation on the subject of alcoholic beverages. You and your cohorts have more than a year to produce some constructive bills and ideas on the subject.

Putting the Alcoholic Beverage Control Board members under civil service is an interesting thought, but I imagine it would be met with strong legislative adversity.

SHORT BALLOT AMENDMENT
Letter / April 7, 1953

[To Mrs. John T. Barriger, Louisville]

THANK you for your letter stating the Crescent Hill Woman's Club is supporting the short ballot amendment which was endorsed by the

1952 legislature and will be subject to voter action in the November general election.

There is not a great deal of research material available here on this question, but it has long been discussed by students of government, most of whom favor it.

As you know, every four years the citizens elect nine state officials —governor, lieutenant governor, attorney general, auditor, superintendent of public instruction, treasurer, commissioner of agriculture, secretary of state, and clerk of the court of appeals. The amendment, if approved by the people, would provide for the election of the governor, lieutenant governor, attorney general, auditor, and clerk of the court. It further provides that the legislature shall regulate the appointments of the commissioner of agriculture, treasurer, secretary of state, and superintendent of public instruction. The amendment was drawn so as not to lodge the appointive power with the governor, although the legislature, if the amendment passes, may do this.

The theory behind this amendment has two major aspects. First, it would eliminate the possibility of nine unfriendly persons being elected to office and disturbing the operations of orderly government. Secondly, it would encourage the naming of persons having technical training and esteemed ability to these four posts which require skills not in rich abundance among "politicians." This is in no way a reflection upon the present elected officeholders. I am merely reciting the academic theory behind the movement.

The amendment leaves to the people their right to elect their chief executive; his lieutenant; the attorney general, who will defend the Commonwealth in law suits and prosecute those who violate state laws, including persons working for the governmental agencies to insure they remain honest and upright in financial transactions and in the render ing of service; and the court clerk, who in addition to keeping appellate records also serves as chairman of the State Election Commission and the Registration and Purgation Board. The legislature may have shown considerable wisdom in retaining the clerk in his position of being responsible to the people due to these two chairmanships.

Efforts exerted by your club in behalf of this amendment will be appreciated by all those interested in progressive government.

On November 3, 1953, Kentucky voters rejected the constitutional amendment calling for a shortened state office ballot. A second amendment, revising the method of distributing state school funds, passed. *Louisville Courier Journal,* November 5, 1953.

Mrs. John T. Barriger (1900-), school superintendent, Board of Education, Louisville (1920-1930); member, Crescent Hill Women's Club and the Walnut Street Baptist Church, Louisville; born in Henderson and resides in Louisville. Phone interview, December 4, 1980.

CONSOLIDATION OF COUNTIES

Letter / July 23, 1953

[To Herbert R. Kohler, Louisville]

THERE are 120 counties in Kentucky, with 120 courthouses, 120 teams of office holders who fear the 120 teams of aspirants, 120 county governments, and 120 political situations. Each county is proud of itself, jealous of its history.

Legislators hesitate to contemplate the abolition of even one county, for they conclude that if the General Assembly can abolish "X" county, it could abolish "Z" county, and so on. A legislator whose home county was abolished by the General Assembly would rather join the Foreign Legion than return to find his people stripped of their traditional local government.

These are the hard facts confronting those advocating a reduction in the number of counties. The constitution gives the legislature full power to abolish counties, but it is a privilege never exercised.

To be watched with interest is the fate of the "short ballot" amendment to the state constitution, which will be voted upon in November. In that amendment we seek to lower the number of statewide elective officials from nine to five. Advance word is that the county courthouses are not in favor of this amendment on grounds that if the people favor a reduction in the number of statewide elective officials, the people may be in favor of lowering the number of county elective officers. The courthouse crews would never be sympathetic to this. If the amendment fails, it will indicate that most of the people are in favor of the present state and county elective offices.

About the only recourse you have at hand is to help promote the calling of a constitutional convention to rewrite and modernize the entire charter. One of the reforms that could be written into a new constitution might be a limit of perhaps sixty counties in Kentucky. This might be accomplished more easily by a constitutional convention than by the legislature.

At the 1952 session of the General Assembly, a measure was introduced with maps asking for, I believe, forty-seven counties. The press handled the news stories enthusiastically, which was distinctly not the reaction among the legislators. The measure died at birth.

Governor Wetherby's support for the consolidation of the counties may in part have been due to his being from Jefferson County where attachment to that governmental unit is less than in the rural areas of the state.

In 1961 a constitutional convention drew up a new document that subsequently was rejected by the electorate. It did not have a provision for the consolidation of the 120 counties.

Robert Ireland has written cogently of the strength of loyalty Kentuckians feel for their county units in *Little Kingdoms: The Counties of Kentucky, 1850-1891* (Lexington, 1977) and the *County in Kentucky History* (Lexington, 1976). For more information see letter from July 15, 1953, in the Legislative Messages and Statements section.

Herbert R. Kohler (1886-1973), educated at Princeton University; special agent with North Western Mutual Life Insurance Company; born in Louisville. Telephone interview with Mrs. H. R. Kohler, December 3, 1980.

EDUCATION

EASTERN HIGH SCHOOL COMMENCEMENT
Louisville / May 22, 1951

It is graduation time across the nation. From thousands of schools this week countless young men and women will walk the last time as high school students. Although the ceremony we are enacting is everywhere the order of the day, commencement, and these who graduate here tonight, are special to me.

As a youngster I went to grade school in the old green schoolhouse at Middletown. Twenty-six years ago I was a member of the graduating class of the Anchorage High School. Through the years I have been closely associated with the school program. My son graduated from Anchorage, and last year Suzanne graduated as a member of the last class of that school.

Tonight marks the first commencement of a new and larger school that includes students from Anchorage and other Jefferson County communities.

Anywhere else it would be natural to enter without pause upon the observations that I have in mind. But because Eastern is our home school, being with you on this occasion is a very personal privilege which gives me greater pleasure and at the same time greater humility than I would experience at any other commencement. I have lived as a neighbor and personal friend of many of you who are parents of this group, and you and I together have watched them grow up. With this understanding of my feeling toward this group and this occasion I am sure you appreciate the fact that it would be more natural for me to sit as a listener, possibly to one of you, than to stand here as speaker.

I share your pride in the accomplishment of this group. I likewise share the pride of all in the splendid school plant, the outstanding training and educational facilities which Eastern offers. Eastern has the kind of facilities, teaching staff, and student body that can make it one of the great Kentucky high schools.

In my talk tonight I shall not attempt to follow the lines of the traditional commencement speaker. Each graduate knows that he stands poised on the threshold of new responsibilities and new opportunities. What I shall try to say will be recognized as a practical interpretation of the business of living, working, and learning from experience. Not by any means do I propose to reminisce, for it is the future with which you and all of us are concerned.

Your high school days have undoubtedly been glorious and profitable ones. They have not been an end unto themselves but have instead been the designs fashioned during youth for the years of your adulthood.

As memorable as your commencement week activities have been, climaxed by tonight's diploma as testimony of your attainment, the real importance of this event lies in the transition which you as individuals are making at this time. Up to this point you have been closely guided by devoted parents. Your teachers have served as good counselors. Everywhere you have been offered helpful guidance. Your presence in the graduating procession demonstrates both your ability in the classroom and your willingness to accept guidance.

I do not mean to say that you are about to be set adrift or that your connection with these anchor points will be severed through high school graduation. Your parents will always be as concerned with your welfare. Your pastor will be as interested in you in future years as he is today. Your teachers will follow your progress with deep personal interest, and I know they stand ready at all times to help you. But following this commencement you will have a change in schedule. Replacing geography, algebra, and English 4B, will be exericses in judgment, initiative, and responsibility. These are basic subjects and important chapters in daily living.

You are already confronted with the necessity of choosing the path you will follow after graduation. This may be one of the most critical decisions you will ever make. The course you select this summer may be the course you follow a lifetime. In making this choice you will have the accustomed advice, but the decision must be yours. This choice of a vocation or a field for further study will be one of many demands for good judgment for which your background and training have been intended to equip you.

Through twelve years orderly classroom assignments of required work have been outlined to you. But there have never been restrictions against voluntary study and exploration beyond that expected of you. The student who has read another chapter, solved another problem, and conducted an additional laboratory test has developed the requisite habit upon which success is founded. In school assignment has been to you like the "Alpenstock" to the mountain climber. In years ahead individual initiative must be substituted for the stimulus and work plan your teachers have furnished you.

If any common quality were sought among the figures of America's fabulous success stories it would be found to be the drive of initiative. A study of fifty of the foremost business, industrial, and financial leaders of this country shows that twenty-four were born poor, seventeen were born in moderate circumstances, and only nine were born wealthy. The high attainments and honored stations of these men who began life as errand boys, coal miners, and shoe cobblers is proof that in America neither birth, nationality, religion, heredity, nor environment are barriers, or for that matter passports, to success. Here worth alone counts, and the only caste which we Americans have ever tolerated is merit. Through preparation, initiative, and work each demonstrates his merit and his worthiness of being numbered in the group where his abilities place him. There is no way by which you can get something for nothing. The capacity for work is the individual's bargaining commodity. It may be that the good work habits you carry with you will be the most valuable and sustaining benefit received during your years in school. Initiative has been the spark that started every upward climb. But long years of just plain hard work have been the fuel by which each great man has powered his climb to the mountaintops of success.

Behind every great enterprise and every great social movement has been some unselfish and tireless man with foresight, courage, and faith. Thomas A. Edison possibly contributed more to the progress, enjoyment, and benefit of mankind than any American. Except for the inquiring mind of this single man and his great faith that accomplishment would reward his endless toil, we might yet be limited to a flickering light.

We cannot all be Edisons. But regardless of our inherent abilities it is nonetheless incumbent upon us to apply diligently whatever talent we have and can develop. We each have an obligation to render the maximum contribution we can make both to ourselves and our communities.

As each of you finds your place in business, industry, agriculture, as housewife or college student you will become in your own right a member of a community, the reflection of which mirrored and multiplied becomes our state and nation. Progressive states and healthy nations are but composites of many communities. Their strength is a summation of the financial, educational, and moral fibre of their citizens. You will have a hand in determining the quality of your community and thereby your state and nation. The character of that community will depend to a great extent upon the calibre of leadership your generation provides.

Your country and your state have made a considerable investment in preparing you for assuming the responsibilities of citizenship. If you intend to continue your education, I hope you will seek out one of our many fine Kentucky colleges or universities. If you plan to seek employment or go into business, I hope you will pick a location within the Commonwealth. Kentucky has made remarkable strides in developing and expanding business opportunities, to the end that our citizens need not become rolling stones but can find here at home the opportunities they deserve.

Some years ago there appeared a book called *Acres of Diamonds.* [1] The story goes that a man seeing little in his immediate surroundings sought riches far and wide, but after an extensive and futile search he returned home to discover that there were diamonds in his own backyard. The undeveloped riches of this man's backyard are not unlike those of our own Commonwealth. Our possessions, both human and material, await only the direction of trained minds, capable leadership, and constructive use.

Kentucky is marching under a banner of progress and prosperity. You can become a bearer of this standard regardless of what specialized field of endeavor you select.

Kentucky is a land of opportunity and you as Kentuckians can find here a place within your chosen field. Your parents, your teachers, and all Kentuckians will appreciate your remaining within your native state and making the contribution for which you have been so well fitted.

---

1. Russell H. Conwell, *Acres of Diamonds* (New York, 1915).

DEDICATION OF SCIENCE BUILDING KENTUCKY STATE COLLEGE

Frankfort / September 26, 1952

THIS is an historical occasion in collegiate education in Kentucky. As chairman of the state Property and Buildings Commission, a new state agency of sensitive and sensible reaction to the needs of all our people, I am proud, pleased, and sincerely impressed by having the authority to yield, in behalf of the commission, control of this magnificent structure to the new, and the first, Board of Regents for this important institution. I know it shall be well managed.

Your science building has been constructed at a cost of about $450,000. This money was appropriated from a pool of taxes paid by all Kentuckians, from the banks of the Mississippi, to the craggy shores of the Big Sandy at the extreme eastern borders of our beloved state.

I can assure you that most Kentuckians are glad that we have built this accommodation for the betterment and advancement of this student body and those to follow. I know for a fact that the state building commission has received as much satisfaction from its completion as your grand president, Doctor Atwood,[1] has received.

Let me give you a few reports on the encounters met in the construction of this fine edifice. The original contractor, chiefly through bad luck, had to abandon the project shortly after he got it underway. New help was sought and by diligence the new help has this building ready for occupancy. Its laboratories are the most modern. It has the necessary office space for the persons who will make it a living, thriving institution. In the late spring, in the early fall, when the sun is ruthless in its effect upon studiousness, heat absorbent windows, such as are installed in the United Nations building, will make conditions inside pleasant. It represents the best in construction that the state of Kentucky can afford at this time, and I know that the students who ponder within its walls will be surrounded by the newest conveniences. No withdrawl from the aims of fireproofing and safety was undertaken and in terms of these modern factors this building has them all.

President Atwood and your new Board of Regents, I take enthusiastic pleasure in placing this structure in your and their able hands. The Commonwealth of Kentucky is honored to have built this accommodation for your growing curriculum. You, President Atwood, the oldest in terms of tenure as a president of a Kentucky state-supported college, deserve a major share of the thanks of our people, for the facilities and gains earned for your race, not only at Kentucky State College, but in other areas of our state and the South.

The Kentucky Building Commission respectfully entrusts the care and upkeep of this institution with you and your regents.

Kentucky State University was founded as a result of an act passed by the General Assembly in 1886, providing for the establishment of a State Normal School for Colored Persons, as the institution was named. In 1938 the name was changed to Kentucky State College for Negroes. In 1952 the term "for Negroes" was dropped from the title of the institution, and the General Assembly made the college an independent institution under its own board of regents. *Kentucky State University Catalogue, 1978-1979 and 1979-1980,* Vol. 14, no. 4, pp. 6-7. See "An Act Relating to Education," *Acts of the General Assembly of the Commonwealth of Kentucky,* 1952, Chapter 41 (S. B. 113), pp. 67-75.

1. Rufus Ballard Atwood (1897-), director of agriculture, Prairie View State College (1923-1929); president, Kentucky State College (1929-1962); a sergeant in World War I, he was awarded a medal for gallantry in action; born in Hickman and resides in Cincinnati. *Who's Who in America, 1950-1951,* 26th ed. (Chicago, 1950), p. 100.

LINDSEY WILSON COLLEGE GOLDEN ANNIVERSARY
Columbia / May 27, 1954

I AM delighted to be a guest here today of Lindsey Wilson College, and must say that I am greatly impressed by all of this well-organized activity. My thanks go out to you for the honor of participating in the program marking your golden anniversary.

Before coming down here from Frankfort some information about your college was delivered to me and convinced me that Lindsey College is just about the most valuable asset in this section of the state.

This school was established by the Louisville Conference of the Methodist Church, an institution with which I am more than familiar. The school began to move toward activation in 1903 with an administration building which, when completed, cost about $12,000 a figure that is baffling in the light of present-day school construction costs.

This entire plant is located today on nine acres of ground purchased from Mrs. C. S. Harris of Columbia for a modest sum. The money used to launch Lindsey Wilson College was donated by the Louisville Conference, the Columbia district, and the citizens of Columbia. It was money wisely offered and wisely spent.

Your school was named in honor of the deceased nephew and stepson of Mrs. Catherine Wilson of Louisville, one of the more liberal donors to the school. The school's objective was to train students for Vanderbilt University, which at that time was under the control of the Methodist Church.

Your school in those days taught students from the first through the twelfth grades, but by 1923 it became a junior college after dropping most of the elementary grade program. In those days, your institution was well know for its very strong and able Department of Education.

From two buildings, worth $12,000 in 1904, Lindsey Wilson has grown to ten buildings and a financial value of $510,000. This speaks well of the administrative abilities of Dr. Henry[1] and his two presidential predecessors.

Lindsey Wilson has achieved all the accreditation possible. It is a member in good standing of the Southern Association of Colleges and Secondary Schools, the University Senate of the Methodist Church, and the Kentucky State Department of Education. In my time, I have known of some institutions in Kentucky not acknowledged with such complete formal support.

The influence of your institution has continued to have a brilliant impact on this section of the Commonwealth. Practically all of the elementary teachers in Adair County and surrounding counties received their training at Lindsey Wilson. Coming from a family of several medical doctors, I was surprised and pleased to learn that, with one exception, all the doctors in Columbia obtained their premedical work here, and with one exception, all of the dentists. This is a distinguished contribution, one that many other rural areas of Kentucky would desire to claim. Your school is proud of the two Rhodes scholars who absorbed their early academic instruction here—the late Roy Helm, a good friend of mine who died while in service on the Kentucky Court of Appeals, and Strother Hynes, now an attorney for an important railroad corporation in Virginia.[2]

Lindsey Wilson is not a state-supported college. It wants to grow and remain in progressive business. It is ready to expand. It is now in the early stages of another improvement program. Physical improvement for a college requires money. The plans call for a campaign of $300,000 to renovate the girls' dormitory, mens' dormitory, gymnasium, dining hall; and to construct additional housing for the faculty and staff members. Your school deserves this support, and whatever I can do to spread the word of this need will be accomplished.

A college of this type keeps alive the welfare of its nearby communities. Through taxes the state is able to support only a limited number of colleges. I dread to think of the educational disaster that would befall the Commonwealth if private and independent colleges were compelled to leave the field.

I hope through your accomplishments and the few humble words I utter here today, Kentuckians will realize a little more firmly the vital and indispensable role independent colleges play in the progress and welfare of Kentucky.

I am tremendously pleased by the thoughtfulness and kindness you have shown by asking me to visit you today. This is a day my recollections will retain. I take this opportunity to congratulate your college on its fiftieth birthday, to congratulate Dr. Henry for his fine administration, and to wish Lindsey Wilson College another fifty years of contributing to the greatness of Kentucky.

---

1. Victor Percival Henry (1890-1963), ordained a Methodist minister (1919); pastor at Clay (1917-1919); pastorate, Louisville, Kentucky Conference (1919-1921); missionary in Africa and Cuba (1921-1928); pastor in various southcentral Kentucky communities (1928-1942); district superintendent, Columbia (1941-1946); president, Lindsey Wilson College (1942-1956); born in Central City. *Who's Who in the South and Southwest,* 1956, 5th ed. (Chicago, 1956), p. 406.

2. Roy D. Helm (1888-1951), attorney; circuit judge of the Thirty-third Judicial District (1940-1946); member, Kentucky Court of Appeals (1948-1951); born in Cumberland County. Frank Kavanaugh, *Kentucky Directory* (Frankfort, 1950), p. 122.

Strother Hynes, no vita available.

SOUTHERN REGIONAL EDUCATION BOARD
Boca Raton, Florida / November 11, 1954

It is good to have this annual opportunity to meet together and talk about what has happened in southern regional education.

I am glad to take a moment to look both backward and forward, backward to where we've come from, forward to where we're going. When I do I find myself thinking about three fairly simple questions. First, what difference does regional education make? Second, what fears does it create? And third, what promise does it hold? Let me talk about each of them briefly.

I'm becoming more and more certain that regional education has made, and does make, a substantial difference. It has steadily moved in the directions we envisioned back in 1947 and 1948 when the form and structure of the compact and the board were taking shape. Looking back, I recall how high our hopes were. Today, I can see how many of the hopes are being realized.

Let me describe what I mean. We wanted economy. We're getting it. We wanted quality. We're moving toward it. We wanted new programs when necessary. They're being established. We wanted facts for planning. They're being supplied. And, being human, we wanted money from new sources if possible. The flow is starting. Hopes are becoming facts, dreams are becoming realities. I can only mention some of the efforts of the board.

It is working on some twenty-five regional programs, including city planning, petroleum sciences, architecture, chemistry and chemical engineering, educational television, recreation, agriculture, psychology, mental health, and others, all of which we hope will be formalized under memoranda of agreement between the universities concerned and the board.

We wanted economy. I won't try to estimate how much the contract programs have saved the states, for it can run from $30 million to $60 million depending on the basis for your calculations. I know that Kentucky has saved some $5 million by avoiding the construction of a veterinary medical school which would have unnecessarily duplicated established schools elsewhere. Louisiana has just done the same thing.

As the memoranda of agreement programs develop we can expect similar savings there. Probably Fuller Warren,[1] former governor of Florida, overshot the target a bit several years ago when he called regional education "the greatest bargain since manna fell on the children of Israel." But he didn't miss it far.

We wanted quality. We wanted programs as good as any in the United States. We knew that the young men and women of the South deserved no less than the best education we could provide. We knew, as former Governor Gordon Browning[2] put it when he was chairman of this board, "There is no economy in mediocrity." Because of this board the quality of education in several fields is rising. Take statistics, which can lie at times, but which are at the core of modern science. Working with the Southern Regional Education Board, three of our great universities in Virginia, North Carolina, and Florida have joined together to put on a three-year series of summer sessions. The quality of the first was so high that it drew eighty-four students from twenty-two states and three foreign countries. The three universities plan similar ventures for the next two summers, largely for the benefit of young faculty members in the southern states.

The goal of quality also lies before several of the great universities in states along the Gulf of Mexico. These universities are studying the ocean and all that lies therein. Each has a laboratory and equipment for these studies. But none is satisfied that results from research are adequate to the problem and opportunity of using the ocean to its fullest. They have been carefully testing the possibilities of joining their programs to create teaching and research of a quality way beyond the capacity of any single university to support. If they can do it, and the prospects look good, we can give southern students education in marine sciences of first quality.

We wanted economy. We wanted quality. The board's program is helping to get both. But we wanted other things also: new programs when needed; facts on which to plan; and new money. We're beginning to get them too.

We wanted new programs. Take the program of graduate education and research in nursing for an example. You'll remember that the board encouraged this program by a resolution at its 1952 meeting in New Orleans. I'm happy to tell you now that the board's efforts are paying dividends. Six universities, public and private, Texas, Alabama, Vanderbilt, Emory, North Carolina, and Maryland, are working to establish graduate programs to train supervisors and administrators of nursing for hospitals and instructors for nursing schools. Two of these universities have already begun admitting graduate students. All this has occurred in a region where two years ago no university was offering graduate work in nursing, outside of public health, even though over twenty universities in other parts of the country were doing so. Studies which preceeded establishing the programs in nursing showed that the South could easily absorb something like thirteen hundred nurses, with graduate degrees, each year, as supervisors in hospitals and instructors in schools. Without this number nursing service and education will suffer. Because of the compact a needed new program is on its way.

We wanted facts for planning. We were right in those early discussions to be concerned with facts for planning. We knew that planning for education in the region could be no better than the accuracy of our knowledge. We hoped, therefore, that the board would cooperate with the universities to bring together information and ideas on which plans could safely rest. The board has done this with increasing skill.

I'm going to mention only a few of the board studies whose significance is unmistakable: 1) projections of school and college enrollments to 1970; 2) training and research in mental health; 3) veterinary education in the South; 4) training and research in government; 5) doctorate programs in southern universities; 6) training for teachers of exceptional children. There are a number of others. Each of these studies has dealt with a field of major concern to the South. Each can be a guide to planning.

Representative Kenneth H. Cagle[3] of Louisiana, a member of this board, can tell you how one of these studies, the one on veterinary education, has already affected his state. Mr. Cagle persuaded the Legislative Work Conference in 1952 to request the board to undertake a study which would aid Louisiana in reaching a decision on establishing a school of veterinary medicine. After the board study pointed out that the urgent need in the South was not for another veterinary school, but for research, Mr. Cagle courageously proposed to the legislature of Louisiana that it modify its earlier action and authorize that funds be made available for establishing a veterninary research center. The 1954 legislature followed Mr. Cagle's leadership. In the words of President O. C. Carmichael[4] of the University of Alabama, "It seems to me to be about the best illustration I know about ways in which the Regional Education Board can serve the South." This remark has special significance since Dr. Carmichael addressed the first large conference on regional education in March 1948 at Gainesville, Florida.

I won't comment on the usefulness of the other studies except to call attention to the fact that the projections of university enrollments may make it possible to plan now for the expansion certain to come, and that the study of training and research in mental health may help us move in new and fruitful ways to solve an age-old problem. We'll hear more about both these studies today.

We wanted money. We hoped, back in those early days, that the universities could become more adequately supported both from public and private funds. That hope is being realized. Public funds have continued to flow to southern universities from the regional contracts in medicine, dentistry, veterinary medicine, and social work. During the year 1953-1954 these amounted to $1,300,000 which went to nineteen southern universities, both private and public. Under the board's policy, private funds for regional programs have steadily increased. During the past two years almost $275,000 reached programs of higher education in this way.

Foundations have already tenatively committed something over three-quarters of a million dollars during the next four years. Other applications are pending which, if successful, will add a great deal more. We expect these to increase, both from foundations and from industry. Under the regional program in forestry, for example, representatives of the forestry council, composed of industry, government, and education people, will visit industrialists in Memphis, Shreveport, and Mobil during the next week. They will discuss ways of increasing industry's support for forestry education and research. Mr. E. J. Gayner III,[5] president of Brunswick Pulp and Paper Company, will head the delegation. He is convinced that industry has an obligation to assist education, recognizing industry's dependence on universities for personnel and research.

Thus, as best I can judge, the board is achieving the goals we sought. It is making a difference. We're getting economy. We're getting quality. We're getting new programs. We're getting facts and we're getting money. That is an impressive list. It is an accomplishment of which the board may well be proud. The states of the Far West and New England are attempting to do likewise under similar compacts. They are looking to the South for guidance.

Yet, I am aware that the very success of the regional education program has created certain fears, perhaps unfounded. I am not sure whether the fears some people have expressed are grounded on dangers which exist or whether they arise from illusions. But we should look at them carefully to eliminate dangers if they exist or to avoid possible dangers if they are not now present. Some have expressed the fear that the states may have created a regional bureaucracy when they established the board. They fear that the board may develop a life of its own, not subject to effective control either in direction or extent of program. Actually, in my observation, the board has been extremely, almost excessively careful, to avoid either unneeded expansion or "empire building." It has constantly attempted to strengthen universities by collaboration, rather than to weaken them by sponsoring competitive programs. Witness how it has contracted with universities for what could have been staff work in foreign affairs, mental health, marine science, and other projects. Its recommendations have emerged from extremely wide discussions and agreement. In the mental health project, for example, some 2,000 people participated at one point or another.

In fact, I sometimes think that the board is too meticulous in searching for groups which should participate in developing regional programs. A large amount of staff time and money is consumed by these efforts. But I should rather have it err on the side of too much collaboration than of too little. If there is error, I think it lies in the direction of too much. As best I can see, the meetings of this board, the considerations of its executive and finance committees, the Legislative Work Conference, and the multitude of councils, commissions, committees, and conferences which are used for advice and consultation make sure that the program is responsive to the region. Proper methods of guidance are built into almost every step the board takes.

Some of our university friends have feared that the board might compete with universities in searching for private funds from philanthropic foundations or other donors. Universities, like all forms of human endeavor, need money. They are always in need of more money. Some may look with skepticism on an agency such as the board, which also searches for money, often from sources comparable to those to which the university turns. Some conflict may be unavoidable here, although I'd guess that it is minor. Essentially the board has searched for funds which become available primarily because of the regional character of the projects with which it is concerned. The best illustration lies in the newly established program in graduate education in nursing where the board aided universities to obtain grants from foundations. Some $750,000, over a five year period, will go directly to the universities as a result of this regional effort. It is money that would not have been granted except for the regional program. As one foundation representative remarked, when considering the grant, "Actual regional planning and regional cooperation, if that idea can be promoted and developed, we are going to be much more interested in helping at the beginning. We want to stress that point, because it is one of our major points of interest."

My conviction is, therefore, that the fears some have expressed are not caused by present dangers, but we must be alert to make sure that the board continues to avoid dangers these fears imply. What of the future? What promise does regional education hold? The promise of regional education parallels the promise of the South. All of us have watched with growing pride the way in which the South has improved its social and economic situation over the past twenty years. The region has become an area of hope, of activity, of advance. We are no longer captives of a declining agriculture. We have found greater strengths in industry and in a more vigorous agriculture than we have ever known.

Our cities are burgeoning. As population grows, complexity of southern life increases and the needs for highly trained persons multiply. The place of universities and higher education in general becomes more and more crucial. Estimates made by the board, for example, show that by 1970 we will have twice as many college students as we now have, and our graduate schools will have expanded by two and one-half times. These staggering increases are largely a reflection of changes in southern life. Fewer people in the South work on the farm. More work in industry and more in the professions. As a result, the South's needs for education in the professions increases. We can be sure that the numbers of university students will increase. We must make sure that the ingenuity of the South is sufficient to meet the demands of these students for education of high quality so the region can meet its needs for persons of high skill.

From the beginning, the major purpose of regional education has been to help the states to meet their needs for highly trained persons. If we hold steadfastly to that objective, using funds as wisely as we know how, supporting each other, and depending on each other in the development of a South-wide higher education effort, I am confident that we can supply both the demands of southern students and the needs of the southern region. Put briefly, the promise of regional education is part of the promise of the new South.

Beyond education, I think the efforts we have undertaken together across state lines, by joining the political and educational leadership of the region, stand as an example to our states of ways in which we can solve our problems. It brilliantly demonstrates to ourselves, and to others, how our sense of region can be turned to constructive ends. It shows how major problems affecting us all can be worked out together, using the various devices of specialization, concentration, and mutual stimulation and support to create strength. Cooperative efforts like these need not be limited to education, and are not limited to education. But, because we have worked more intensively here, perhaps we have developed patterns and methods which can help to assure the success of similar efforts in other fields. The promise of regional education is a promise of increased effectiveness of our sovereign states. Through it, we may learn of better ways to reach our ends, through our own ingenuity, imagination, and effort.

Lawrence W. Wetherby, as lieutenant governor, helped to organize the Southern Regional Education program in 1948. In 1954 he served as its board chairman, and in that capacity he delivered this address at its annual meeting. Fourteen southeastern states composed the regional program. Among its many purposes was a sharing of educational resources in order to avoid the costly duplication of offerings. A reciprocal arrangement admitted Kentucky students to graduate and professional schools in the region. The fact that the consortium saved revenue funds for each state appealed to Governor Wetherby's fiscal conservatism. For an example of how the program worked see letter from February 26, 1951, in this section.

1. Fuller Warren (1905-1973), member, Florida State Legislature (1926-1928, 1938-1940); member, Jacksonville (Florida) City Council (1931-1937); governor of Florida (1949-1953); born in Blountstown, Florida. *Who's Who in America, 1954-1955,* 28th ed. (Chicago, 1954), p. 2790.

2. Gordon Browning (1889-1976), member, United States House of Representatives (1923-1935); governor of Tennessee (1937-1939, 1949-1953); born in Carroll County, Tennessee. *Who's Who in America, 1954-1955,* 28th ed. (Chicago, 1954), p. 348.

3. Kenneth H. Cagle, no vita available.

4. Oliver Cromwell Carmichael (1891-1966), instructor and principal in Alabama schools (1919-1922); dean, assistant to president, and president of Alabama College (1922-1935); dean, Graduate School and Senior College, Vanderbilt University (1935-1937); vice chancellor and chancellor of Vanderbilt University (1936-1946); became executive associate of Carnegie Corporation (1946); president, University of Alabama (1953-1957); with the Ford Foundation (1957-); born in Goodwater, Alabama. *Who Was Who in America, 1961-1968* (Chicago, 1968), 4:155.

5. E. J. Gayner III (1903-), with Foreman Scott Paper Company, Chester, Pennsylvania (1924-1929); vice president, general manager, president of Nova Scotia Wood Pulp and Paper Company (1929-1938); director, vice president, general manager of Brunswick Pulp and Paper Company (1938-1951), president (1951); born in Salem, New Jersey. *Who's Who in America, 1954-1955,* 28th ed. (Chicago, 1954), p. 970.

KENTUCKY STATE COLLEGE
Letter / December 15, 1950

[To the Ford Foundation, Detroit]

AFTER reviewing the application of Kentucky State College soliciting support for a project through education designed to promote the social, economic, and moral welfare of the Negro citizens of our state, and being impressed with the comprehensive and objective planning that the application evidences, I am pleased to lend my full endorsement to the program.

For the past three years I have been rather intimately acquainted with the administrative skill, the operation of the Kentucky State College plant and facilities, and the leadership role that Dr. Atwood has exercised. I have been highly impressed with his approach to the affairs and problems which naturally gravitate for his determination as one of the leading Negro citizen-educators both within Kentucky and this area of our nation.

As one profoundly interested in the promotion of education for the advancement of any segment of our people, I entertain every hope that this apparently worthy undertaking might enjoy the favorable consideration of the Ford Foundation.

FINANCIAL SUPPORT FOR PUBLIC EDUCATION
Letter / February 2, 1951

[To R. Jack Reynolds, Mt. Sterling]

WITH the hope that it might be of assistance in the preparation of your talk before the local PTA group, I am enclosing a memorandum prepared by the senator at the time of the 1950 KEA-General Assembly contest, from which may be obtained factual information on school legislation since 1944.

Recently, the KEA Board of Directors, with the president and secretary of the group, met with me, and detailed discussion was devoted to the entire school finance problem. At that meeting it was agreed that the KEA would select a committee to work on a cooperative basis with the Functions and Resources of State Government Committee, the thinking being that the needs of education could be extensively and expertly studied in this manner, and possibly point the direction that might be traveled in reconciling those needs with the state's resources and ability to meet them. This, in my judgment, could be considered a straw-in-the-wind approach to the difficulties with which education is faced in Kentucky.

Robert Jackson Reynolds (1910-), civil engineer with Kentucky Highway Department (1928-1941); with Bechtel, McCone and Parsons, Stone and Webster, and Mason and Hanger Company (1943-1945); became engaged as a general contractor and manufacturer of concrete products, as well as a radio broadcasting executive (1946); vice president and director of Capital Broadcasting Corporation, Frankfort; member, Kentucky Senate (1950-1958); worked with R. J. Reynolds General Contractor; born in Joplin, Missouri, and resides in Mt. Sterling. Hambleton Tapp, ed., *Kentucky Lives: The Blue Grass State Who's Who* (Hopkinsville, Ky., 1966), p. 449.

COMMITTEE ON EDUCATIONAL DEFENSE PROGRAMS
Letter / February 9, 1951

[To Carl D. Perkins, Washington, D.C.]

THE Southern Regional Education program, in which Kentucky is one of the fourteen states cooperating to improve higher education, has named a Committee on Defense Programs. Its purpose is to find out what are federal government needs from educational institutions in connection with the defense mobilization, and how resources of our institutions in the South can be used most effectively in helping to meet those needs. A more detailed memorandum is attached.

The committee will concern itself with federal needs in scientific research, training, civil defense and other areas. I am sure you are aware that prior to and during World War II, federal contracts with educational institutions were concentrated at a comparatively small number of universities. I understand the federal government is committed to a policy of dispersal and decentralization in the current program, and we are, of course, anxious that the institutions in our region make the greatest contribution possible.

I am convinced that this committee of educators, serving higher education in all states in the region, can help reach that goal. I believe the committee from time to time may be helpful to you. It will maintain an office and executive officer in Washington. I am asking the board, in Atlanta, to send you full information on this project and where its Washington office is to be established.

DESIGNATED COLLEGE SCHOLARSHIPS

Letter / February 26, 1951

[To Boswell B. Hodgkin, Frankfort]

As a result of conferences between university officials and recognized farm groups and agricultural leaders of the state, I have agreed to underwrite the costs of a scholarship program whereby a number of eligible Kentucky students could attend a veterinary college participating in the Southern Regional Education program.[1] In setting up the program, I shall make available from the Emergency Fund the sum of $10,000 to cover scholarships for ten Kentucky boys who might be admitted to southern institutions offering veterinary training. Each of the scholarships will be in the amount of $1,000.

It is also my understanding that two Negro students will be accepted at Tuskegee. Inasmuch as there is now available $2,000 in the College Tuition for Negroes appropriation, I wish to suggest that this sum be made available to meet the scholarship needs of these two students, and I recommend that this account be encumbered for this purpose.

Dr. Donovan, at the university, and the Department of Finance have recommended, and I concur, that the Council on Higher Education be designed as the administering agency of the scholarship plan and, to this end, I have directed the Department of Finance to have prepared the necessary executive order and to take the required steps to effect a transfer of $10,000 to the council and further to arrange with the

Department of Education for the transfer of the $2,000 from the College Tuition for Negroes account to the Council on Higher Education.

---

1. For an explanation of this program see speech from November 11, 1954, in this section.

Boswell D. Hodgkin (1908-1962), rural and urban schoolteacher, superintendent of Clark County schools (1932-1935); superintendent of Winchester schools (1935-1947); state superintendent of schools (1947-1951); director of research and statistics, Department of Education (1951-1956); assistant director, Department of Education (1960-1962); born in Winchester. Frank K. Kavanaugh, *State Directory* (Frankfort, 1950), p. 120.

TEACHERS' SALARIES SPECIAL LEGISLATIVE SESSION

Letter / March 7, 1951

[To Edward H. Weyler, Louisville]

APPRECIATING the interest and concern voiced in your telegram relative to the salary problems in the education field, I assure you it was the same feeling of concern and acknowledgment of responsibility that prompted my calling the General Assembly into extraordinary session to consider legislation appropriating available funds that might be used in improving the teachers' financial status and other benefits that might accrue through increased appropriations to the state's aged indigents, child welfare recipients, those in the needy blind category, and those housed in the state's institutions; however, the legislation which was introduced in the House specified that the appropriation to education was to be allocated on the school per capita basis and earmarked exclusively for teachers' salaries.

It was the desire of all concerned to effect an improvement of the teachers' relative position in this time of inflation and to meet the emergency condition that has arisen among the teacher rank. Any other method of state appropriation would have gone through the equalization channel, which would immediately place the increased funds available for uses in paying teachers and all the other expenditures required in the operation of the district school systems. Considering this factor, and the acknowledged emergency, the problems of employees of the various school districts in the noninstructional field should be directed to their respective school boards.

I am sure that you and all employees in the various school districts who are not now enjoying a retirement program of their own are cognizant of the broadened federal Social Security program on which I have asked the General Assembly to adopt enabling legislation whereby state, city, county, political subdivision, and agency employees might enjoy the benefits in securing the passage of this and the other legislation which the General Assembly has been called to consider. I feel it represents a forward step that will rebound in substantially advancing education and social welfare in the Commonwealth.

For Governor Wetherby's call for an extraordinary session of the General Assembly see speech from February 21, 1951, in the Legislative Messages and Statements section. The legislators approved the requests from the governor mentioned in this letter.

Edward H. Weyler (1901-1976), carpenter, organizer, American Federation of Labor in Louisville; executive secretary, Kentucky Federation of Labor (1937-1954); president, Brotherhood of Carpenters and Joiners (1954-1955); representative, Brotherhood of Carpenters and Joiners (1955-1975); born in Louisville. Telephone interview, Lily B. Weyler, January 12, 1981.

TEACHERS' SALARIES SPECIAL LEGISLATIVE SESSION

Letter / April 30, 1951

[To Lynn Mays, Corbin]

THIS letter is written in response to your April 23 communication with reference to my intention towards the use of funds appropriated by the special session of the General Assembly for teachers' salaries.

I should like to say that in recommending the emergency appropriation of $6 million to the legislature, the economic plight of the teachers of the state during this inflationary period was uppermost in my thinking. Guided by the apparent needs of the teachers and their extremely unfavorable position in this regard, it was my intention at the time the legislature passed and I signed this appropriation bill, and it remains my hope and desire, that salaries of the public school teachers of Kentucky be increased beginning July 1 to the maximum amount which is allocated to each of the school districts in Kentucky.

Lynn Mays (1911-1965), Baptist minister for fifteen years; schoolteacher at Lynn Camp High School for twenty-six years; a businessman interested in politics, sports, and civic leadership; born in Tinsley. Letter from Mrs. Bertha Mays, December 18, 1980.

CAMPAIGN STATEMENT ON EDUCATION
Letter / September 29, 1951

[To Kentucky Education Association, Louisville]

THIS will acknowledge your recent letter in which you invite me to send a picture and a short statement.

I appreciate this opportunity to make a statement for your *Journalette* so that the members of your association may know my general attitude about the educational needs of Kentucky.

Through the years, both as a citizen and as a public official, my record demonstrates my continued interest in the youth of Kentucky. I have served as a member of the school board of Anchorage. I have served as attorney for the Juvenile Court for a period of six years. I also served as judge of the Jefferson County Juvenile Court for four years.

Immediately upon assuming the office of governor last winter, I discussed with the educational leaders of Kentucky the additional needs for education. In March of this year I called a special session of the legislature and requested appropriation be made of $6 million, additional funds to be earmarked solely for teachers' salaries. This recommendation was immediately enacted into law without a dissenting vote.

In my platform as a candidate for governor in the primary, I announced that I advocated and am pledged to support the further improvement of our school system to the maximum of available resources.

I made this announcement taking into consideration the fact that the 1950 legislature created the Committee on Functions and Resources of State Government, which committee is now making a thorough study of the needs of Kentucky and how best to meet those needs. This committee will make a report for submission to the 1952 session of the legislature.[1] This report will be used by me as a yardstick in making future recommendations to the legislature.

The youth we educate today are the leaders of tomorrow, and I propose to continue my interest in their training and development.

---

1. It was proposed and the 1952 General Assembly recommended a constitutional amendment that changed section 186 of the Kentucky Constitution to read, "All funds accruing to the school fund shall be used for the maintenance of the public schools of the Commonwealth, and for no other purpose, and the General Assembly shall by general law prescribe the manner of the distribution of the public school fund among the school districts and its use for public school purposes." See *Acts of the General Assembly of the Commonwealth of Kentucky, 1952*, Chapter 89 (S.B. 225), pp. 245–46. For more information see speech from January 12, 1954, in the Legislative Messages and Statements section.

STATE TEACHERS' RETIREMENT FUND
Letter / March 5, 1952

[To Mrs. Kate S. Brown, Lexington]

I AM most appreciative of your March 3 letter, and in response should like to submit the following in the nature of a report with respect to the overall teacher retirement program. However, I should like to say in the outset that as a part of my platform for governor, and as I have repeatedly said during this session of the legislature, I am not advocating the enactment of any additional tax increases.

Of course, it is recognized by all that additional revenue would be required if further appropriation increases are to be made to the retirement fund or any other state program. Nevertheless, should the General Assembly, through enactment of a new or increased tax law, provide additional revenue, you may be assured that the teacher retirement fund will receive its proportionate share of the money.

May I recite the very substantial monthly payment increases that have been made as a result of the teacher retirement legislation passed during the four-year period in which I have had a direct hand in the affairs of state government. As late a date as 1948, the entire teacher retirement fund was in serious trouble. The fund had not kept pace with growing demands that were made on it and much doubt was entertained as to its future solvency. In that year a $2.5 million supplement appropriation was made which placed the fund on a sound actuarial basis.[1] In addition, further and substantial increased state allocations were made, thereby allowing the average monthly retirement benefits to be increased from $25 to $40 per month per teacher.

Until January, 1951, the school teachers of Kentucky were the only category of public employees covered by any kind of retirment program to which the state allocated matching moneys, and at the same time have received very substantial increases, considering the percentage claimed of the total general fund revenue available.

This background is submitted for your information and I assure you that the welfare of Kentucky education and the teaching profession, including those both in active and retired status, are receiving the largest possible appropriation which the present tax structure allows.

---

1. The regular amount appropriated by the Kentucky General Assembly for the teachers' retirement fund in 1948-1949 was $1,475,975. The increase came out of a surplus in the General Education Fund and amounted to $2,439, 606.64. See *Acts of the General Assembly of the Commonwealth of Kentucky* (Frankfort, Ky., 1948), p. 19.

Governor Wetherby proposed for the fiscal year 1952-1953 a sum of $1, 916,000 to the teachers' retirement fund, and an additional $168,000 over that amount the next year.

For more information on the Teachers' Retirement System see letter from February 19, 1954, in this section.

CRUSADE AGAINST ILLITERACY
Letter / February 27, 1953

[To the Reverend Mother Mary Columba, Louisville]

A GROUP of citizens and educators conferred in my office February 25 to explore the possibilities of launching a crusade against illiteracy in Kentucky. The idea was generated initially by Grover Sales, a Louisville attorney, and retired Rear Admiral Ion Pursell, of Owensboro.[1]

While the conference was not specifically called by me, use of my office was permitted. The discussion was provocative enough to warrant further exploration with a larger and more representative group. It was decided that a meeting will be held in the Senate Chamber of the state Capital on March 18 at 11 A.M., CST.

I am glad to invite you or your representative to attend this conference. All state and private senior and junior colleges, officials in the department of Education, and KEA officers are being urged to attend this pioneering event.

---

1. Grover G. Sales (1887-1967), educated at Columbia College and Harvard Law School; admitted to the bar in 1911; chairman, Louisville Labor-Management Committee (1967); born in Louisville. *Kentucky State Bar Association* (Louisville, 1967), p. 335.

Ion Pursell (1896-), investment adviser, educator, astronomer, owner of Pursell's Investment Service, and retired as a rear admiral from United States Navy in 1950. In 1953 he was Governor Wetherby's executive director of the Commission on Adult Education. He found that 40,000 adults in the state did not know their ABC's, and 250,000 had no higher than a fourth grade education. He started his "Good Samaritans for the Three R's." Children with a few years of schooling would teach their parents or grandparents, other relatives, or friends how to read. He developed a teaching method that cut a year's learning to three months. It became an international organization. He helped over 5,000 learners in fifty states and foreign countries. Hambleton Tapp, ed., *Kentucky Lives: The Blue Grass State Who's Who* (Hopkinsville, Ky., 1966), pp. 426–30.

The Reverend Mother Mary Columba Ishanski (1900-), date of perpetual profession to Ursuline Sisters, April 23, 1921; second councilor, Ursuline Motherhouse, Louisville (1947-1950); general superior of Motherhouse (1950-1956); chairwoman of the Board of Trustees of the Ursuline Society and Academy of Education. She has taught and administered at schools in Nebraska,

Maryland, Pennsylvania, and West Virginia. Born in Cumberland, Maryland, and resides in Louisville. Information supplied by Sister M. Concetta Waller, OSU, archivist, Ursuline Sisters, Louisville.

SCHOOL SEGREGATION
Letter / March 24, 1953

[To Rufus S. Stout, Louisville]

On the TV program of March 18, over WHAS, I answered in the neighborhood of eighty-five questions in twenty-eight minutes, and I feel that I can be forgiven for an occasional mistake.

As I recall, I said the Day Law prohibits Negroes and whites from eating in the same room. I think I backtracked to say that the Day Law applies to the school system and is the only law imposing segregation on Kentuckians. There is no law in Kentucky forbidding Negroes and white people from eating in the same room, but you, as am I, are aware of custom. The state government now operates two cafeterias in Frankfort. They are basically for the convenience of state employees. Use of these cafeterias by white organizations and clubs has frequently been denied.

The 1950 and 1952 legislatures enacted laws which are gradually eliminating the problem of segregation,[1] and I am confident that as the months go by we shall continue to make progress in equalizing opportunities and rights in the field of human relations.

I appreciate your comments on the TV performance, but again urge you to try to understand that it is very difficult to answer many technical and sensitive questions in so short a period of time.

---

1. *Acts of the General Assembly of the Commonwealth of Kentucky,* 1950, Chapter 155 (S.B. 100), pp. 615–16; 1952, Chapter 41 (S.B. 113), pp. 67-75.

Rufus S. Stout (1902-1970), personnel manager, National Carbide Company, Louisville (1943-1967); named to board of directors, Louisville Community Chest (1962); named to state Personnel Board (1966); in the 1930s he taught school in Tulsa and Louisville; born in Little Rock, Arkansas. *Louisville Courier-Journal,* October 20, 1970.

EDUCATIONAL TELEVISION
Letter / May 7, 1953

[To Paul A. Walker, Washington, D.C.]

KENTUCKY appreciates the allocation of noncommercial educational television channels by the Federal Communications Commission. It is my belief that this medium of spreading knowledge and techniques will have a most beneficial effect upon our people.

Steps are being taken toward the development of educational television. Representatives of the University of Louisville, the Jefferson County Board of Education, the Louisville City Board of Education and the Louisville Public Library Board have held a series of conferences to plan for the utilization of the TV channel assigned to Kentucky. The University of Kentucky is also showing an interest in the project, along with many educational leaders in the state.

Early indications show that Kentucky will not be able to submit applications for construction permits prior to June 1955. Our present tax structure is being stretched to the very limits in order to carry on the routine services. We need additional time to determine the costs of educational television and to locate the financial sources to support the work.

I join with other leaders connected with the Southern Regional Education Board in requesting the FCC to extend the application date to June 1955.

Enclosed is a copy of a resolution adopted recently by the Kentucky Legislative Research Commission which has been studying educational television.

Paul Atlee Walker (1881-1965), instructor, University of Oklahoma (1909-1912); practiced law in Shawnee, Oklahoma (1912-1915); attorney, State Corporation Commission of Oklahoma (1915-1919); referee, Supreme Court of Oklahoma (1919-1921); special counsel, State Corporation Commission of Oklahoma (1921-1931); member, Federal Communication Commission (1934-1953), vice chairman (1945-1952), chairman (1952-1953); born in Washington County, Pennsylvania. *Who's Who in America, 1954-1955,* 28th ed. (Chicago, 1954), p. 2769.

CUT IN DISTRICT SCHOOL FUNDS
Letter / January 27, 1954

[To O. F. Brown, Louisville]

THE thirty-two school districts in Kentucky discussed in your January 19 letter, in which school terms have been cut due to insufficient funds, are districts whose assessment of property and local revenue-producing effort fall below the requirements of state law. The law governing the allocation of equalization money to school districts is definite, explicit, and precise. All school administrators are acquainted with it in great detail. There is no way to circumvent or obviate the formula governing the distribution of equalization money.

I am frank to say that the unhappy situation which exists in all of these equalization districts, rather than stemming from discriminatory features of the law or lack of proper administration of it by the state Department of Education, can and should be traced to the disregard of the property assessment law by local officials of the county in which the school district is found.

Since becoming lieutenant governor in 1947, I have devoted attentive consideration to the problems of Kentucky education. In my message to the General Assembly on January 12, although most other programs of state government are being continued for the next biennium at present levels of operation, I proposed a $6 million increase in the common school fund. This proposal has since been enacted into law, bringing the biennial appropriation to the common schools to $69,571,000, over $20 million above the appropriation made by the 1950 session. This, I feel, is sufficient evidence of the degree of my concern toward our schools.

I welcome the views of any Kentucky citizen or organized group regarding any subject or public issue in which they are interested and appreciate your writing me.

O. F. Brown was president, Kentucky Elementary School Principals' Association.

1954 GENERAL ASSEMBLY AND EDUCATION
Letter / February 19, 1954

[To Frank P. Hays, Eubank]

THERE are several teacher retirement bills pending before the General Assembly and, if this session is consistent with the past several, there will undoubtedly be additional measures introduced on this subject. I have neither indicated support of nor opposition to any of these pieces of legislation but will, of course, feel it mandatory to oppose in the end, even to the point of vetoing, any bills that appears to weaken or undermine the teacher retirement program.

As far as legislation designed to increase benefits is concerned, I must say that both in principle and in need such a program has unquestioned merit. Nevertheless, the problem of providing the necessary money essential to increasing benefits remains hard and difficult and highly improbable. The budget and revenue measures that I considered feasible and possible to pass, and which at this time have been passed, treated the retired teachers of the state as favorably and sympathetically as was possible.

I point out, though certain of your cognizance of what has been done for the broad field of common school education during this session, that an additional $3 million was appropriated for each of the next two years to the common school fund. This increase was made possible by the enactment of the state income tax withholding legislation and four new revenue producing bills, the passage of which reflects my own interest in education and the good judgment and sound support of a majority of the membership of the General Assembly who withstood strong and incessant opposition to each and all of these tax increases.

Beginning in 1946, the General Assembly enacted several teacher retirement bills. See *Acts of the General Assembly of the Commonwealth of Kentucky*, 1946, Chapter 111 (H.B. 405), pp. 274-78; 1948, Chapter 194 (S.B. 207), pp. 453-55; 1950, Chapter 78 (H.B. 302), pp. 433-34; 1950, Chapter 79 (H.B. 308), pp. 434-35; 1950, Chapter 194 (S.B. 192), pp. 721-22; 1950, Chapter 197 (S.B. 213), p. 726; 1952, Chapter 144 (H.B. 122), p. 381; 1952, Chapter 226 (H.B. 446), p. 664.

In 1954 the General Assembly enacted several bills relating to teachers' retirement funds. It established a minimum allowance based upon service credit times the years of service. It set the percentage of contributions to the fund based upon age and increased the retirement allowance and the maximum. It granted prior service credit to any honorably discharged veteral of World War I who was a member of the Teachers' Retirement System in good standing. It provided for the investment of funds of the Teachers' Retirement System, stipulating where it could be invested. See *Acts of the General Assembly of the Commonwealth of Kentucky,* 1954, Chapter 64 (S.B. 230), p. 154; 1954, Chapter 194 (H.B. 319), p. 525; 1954, Chapter 196 (H.B. 322), pp. 526-28; 1954, Chapter 215 (H.B. 366), pp. 603-5.

Frank P. Hays was chairman, Pulaski County Teachers in Retirement.

MINIMUM FOUNDATION PROGRAM
Letter / March 9, 1954

[To J. W. Gregory, Lancaster]

YOUR remarks concerning the bill providing the initial steps for a school minimum foundation program are acknowledged. This bill has passed the House of Representatives and currently is before the judgment of the Senate Rules Committee. At least it has shown signs of progress.

No one is more aware than I am of the depressing and deep problems harassing Kentucky's elementary and secondary schools. Our people seem to desire a stronger and more modern school system but they have a supply of reluctance when it comes to financing the vast and needed improvements.[1] Be assured that our educational leaders and the officials of this administration are strong advocates of school betterment, as are the legislators. The minimum foundation bill may provide us with the start toward a major redevelopment of our schools.

The present session of the General Assembly has raised taxes in several revenue areas, but I doubt that it will at this time approve new taxes to support educational reformation that has not been brought into precise focus by school experts.

The committee has been advised of your views.

---

1. Governor Wetherby was referring to the vote of November 3, 1953, in which Kentucky voters approved a constitutional amendment permitting the General Assembly to prescribe the manner of distribution and use of public school funds. The Minimum Foundation Program was enacted in 1954 as a

consequence. Governor Wetherby considered its passage together with the establishment of a Department of Mental Health to have been his two most significant legislative accomplishments. For an explanation of the Minimum Foundation Program see speech from January 12, 1954, in the Legislative Messages and Statements section.

J. W. Gregory was superintendent, Lancaster City Schools.

BOOKMOBILE PROJECT
Letter / July 19, 1954

[To Victor Henry, Columbia]

It was a personal pleasure to me to include your name in the list of representative citizens recently appointed to the Advisory Commission of the Division of Library Extension. As you will recognize, all those appointed to the commission have rendered a great deal of public-spirited service to the work of expanding free public library service in Kentucky.

It will be the duty of the commission to meet together at intervals to be set by the commission when it has organized itself under a chairman, and to advise the Division of Library Extension on such matters of policy and community relations as the Director of the Extension Division may bring to its attention. It might be appropriate for the organization meeting of the commission to be held in August at the time of the presentation to the state of the first complement of bookmobiles. You will be notified of that date as soon as arrangements are completed for the ceremony.

At this moment the Division of Library Extension faces a major expansion of its program because of the efforts of the Kentucky Bookmobile Project and the Friends of Kentucky Libraries to extend library service in rural counties by bookmobiles. The resultant problems of the division, especially in the field of public relations in the counties participating in the bookmobile program, will need the attention and concern of a strong group of interested citizens throughout the state.

I anticipate with confidence the service which you and the other members of the commission can render by cooperating with the Division of Library Extension and the Friends of Kentucky Libraries to insure that the bookmobile program meets its purpose of bringing to all the people of our state the privilege and right of free public library service.

Governor Wetherby's administration initiated the bookmobile project. Its purpose was to equalize library service in Kentucky, particularly in the rural areas. A sum of $50,000 was appropriated for fiscal year 1952-1953. See *Acts of the General Assembly of the Commonwealth of Kentucky,* 1952, Chapter 114 (Committee Substitute for H.B. 39), pp. 306-8.

SCHOOL DESEGREGATION
Letter / September 23, 1954

[To Charles Butcher, New York City]

It must be understood that under our constitution, government is divided into three branches, executive, legislative and judicial. The duty of the judicial branch is to interpret the law and direct the executive to activate these interpretations. The Supreme Court is the highest unit of the judicial branch, and its final decisions are binding on every public official and citizen alike.

The whole difficult and complex subject of desegregation can be resolved only after definite policies are formulated following the Supreme Court decision on the matter. I have already selected a small advisory committee to consider the Kentucky school situation as it is affected by both the legal and social impetus given to desegregation. Sound judgment and clear thinking, free of the confusion and turmoil that characterizes the crusaders' spirit, whether they be for or against desegregation, can solve this situation in Kentucky. I shall lean earnestly on the thoughts and guidance of this committee, and you may be certain the group will work for the best interest of all of us.

It must be kept in mind that the early Americans introduced the Negro to our agricultural and economic life. Our forefathers brought the Negro to our shores, and we have shown little inclination to return the colored people to their native continent. Many of them developed intelligence and skills and moved forward in life, always remembering that they should help those behind them. The Supreme Court has partially approved this process by ordering desegregation in the schools.

Governor Wetherby met head-on the issue of school desegregation. Immediately after the publication of the United States Supreme Court's decision in the case of *Brown* v. *Board of Education of Topeka,* he stated publicly his intention to obey since it was the law of the land. Personally, the governor favored the integration of Kentucky's public schools. Many people within his own administration objected to his stand. The governor appointed an advisory commission of four whites and three blacks to help him and the state Department of Education to integrate the schools. Among its members were Allen Trout and Wendell Butler. It was Governor Wetherby's intention that their influence would see that reason prevailed as integration was accepted and implemented. However, the actual process of integration generally took place after Wetherby left office. Yet, by his immediate and public support for it he set a course of peaceful compliance that was generally realized.

Charles A. Butcher (1893-), application engineer of electric railways, Westinghouse Electric Corporation, Chicago (1917-1919); design engineer of automatic controls, East Pittsburgh (1919-1922); general engineer of automatically controlled power equipment (1922-1929); eastern district engineering manager, New York City (1929-1936); eastern manager of manufacturing and repair department (1936-1941); Crocker-Wheeler Electric Manufacturing Company (1945-1950); assistant to president, Worthington Corporation, New York City (1950-1955); vice president of planning (1955-); born in Des Moines, Iowa. *Who's Who in America, 1960-1961,* 31st ed. (Chicago, 1960), p. 430.

SCHOOL TAXATION NEEDS
Letter / February 14, 1955

[To A. B. Arnold, Falmouth]

It is always a pleasure to read your temperate writings on schoolmen and taxation. Were there more A. B. Arnolds, I feel that Kentucky's school program would be much more advanced.

As an outgoing governor who has had his share of warmth for the progress of education in Kentucky and his share of wounds from schoolhouse sharpshooters, my feeling is that the educators ought to designate a group to figure out how much additional money the schools need and then determine the taxes or how-to-tax method necessary to gain the goal. Once this is agreed upon and publicized, the educators should approach the candidates for the legislature for a commitment to the tax program.

The details of the Minimum Foundation Program are difficult for most people to grasp, and this includes the candidates. The lump-sum additional money should be kept reasonable, for I know that the mood of the public, at least those who write letters, steams at the possibility of new taxes. Yet, the average person may be willing to help out a little more than he is at the present time. This is something else that the KEA pollsters should determine. I know of a recent confidential poll where the sales tax lost, but not by a disheartening margin.

Ansel Beckett Arnold (1902-), superintendent of Pendleton County schools (1941-1954); member of the Advisory Council, member of the Council on Public Higher Education under Governor Wetherby; born in Harrison County. *Who's Who in Kentucky* (Hopkinsville, Ky., 1955), p. 11.

SUPPORT FOR INTEGRATION
Letter / March 1, 1955

[To John A. Jenkins, Bloomington, Indiana]

KENTUCKY is one of the states that has met the Supreme Court's integration decision with general impassivity and good sense. We are waiting for the Court's detailed ruling on how best to proceed with integration planning. Negroes in Kentucky made no attempt to enter grade or high schools last fall.

As an attorney, I respect the decisions of the Supreme Court and as a patriotic citizen must comply with them. I am familiar with the agony and discontent the desegregation decision caused in many sections of the country and am hoping fervently that, when the implementation of the decision is handed down, Kentucky will meet the issue fairly and squarely for all. Disrespect of the Supreme Court is un-American and those overwrought individuals slashing at its prestige may eventually find themselves in difficulty.

At the recent Southern Governors' Conference in Florida, an attempt was made to band the states in the conference in a fight against enforcement of the Supreme Court's ruling. This was voted down in favor of an attitude allowing the southern states to meet the nonsegregation procedure to the best of their individual abilities. I was among those favoring this attitude.[1]

---

1. Governor Wetherby chaired this conference of southern governors. If the southern states had presented a united opposition to school integration, it would have slowed the process. Wetherby was joined in his stand against a united front by the governors of Georgia, Tennessee, and Arkansas.

1955 ELECTION STATEMENT ON EDUCATION
Letter / May 25, 1955

[To C. W. Rule, Prospect]

UPON receipt of my reply to your May 23 letter I trust you will not feel that you are receiving more than you bargained for since I am not a candidate for re-election and cannot succeed myself under the constitution. However, I am tremendously interested in the advancement of Kentucky, and for that reason I am vigorously supporting the candidacy of Bert Combs in the Democratic primary.

So that you may have some of the information about my activities in behalf of the school people of Kentucky during the past few years, I supported in every manner possible the adoption of the amendment to the constitution affecting schools in the 1953 general election. This amendment was passed, and as a result thereof we now have a Minimum Foundation Program for schools in Kentucky.[1] In addition to this activity, during my administration the appropriations to the common school fund alone have been increased more than $10 million per year. We have also enacted during this administration a retirement system for teachers. When discussing schools, the colleges and the University of Kentucky should not be overlooked. The appropriations to all of our colleges and the university have been materially increased during this administration, and the most recent thing that I have done for schools was the appropriation out of the Governor's Emergency Fund to the University of Kentucky of $450,000 to start a new building at the university, and $1 million out of the emergency fund to be spent on buildings at the four state colleges.

The appropriation to the University of Louisville Medical School has been doubled since I became interested in state government.

I cite only these few examples of what has taken place in reference to schools during this administration. I could go on and cite many, many more; however, any person who has followed the development of the school program in Kentucky in its entirety would, I am sure, know of my interest in education and its development in the state.

---

1. For more information see speech from January 12, 1954, in the Legislative Messages and Statements section and letter from September 29, 1951, in this section.

RACIAL INTERMARRIAGE
Letter / June 7, 1955

[To Aurora Chestnut, Richmond]

THE citizens of Kentucky are now required to face up to the school integration directive issued by the Supreme Court of the United States. I am confident our people will meet this radical alteration of our society with patience and temperate feelings. We must abide by the Supreme Court's ruling and comply with its requirements with grace, tolerance, and broader fellowship. I pause frequently to hope that Kentuckians will meet their new social obligations, academic-wise, without spite and revenge.

The Supreme Court had nothing to say regarding intermarriage. Marital decisions still will be governed by the emotions of the individuals involved. I don't believe a law can ever be passed dictating descriptions of people who may marry, except in cases involving incest or bordering on incest.

TEACHERS' RETIREMENT BENEFITS
Letter / August 2, 1955

[To Myrtle McClure Brown, Ashland]

UNDER the law which becomes effective July 1, 1955, the active teachers are paying in larger contributions to the teachers' retirement system. The $400,000 recently appropriated from the emergency fund is for the purpose of matching these increased contributions made by active teachers to the system, assuring greater benefits to those teachers retiring after teaching under the new law. Unfortunately, it does not increase the benefits to those retiring prior to the effective date of the new law. However, the minimum annuity for those who taught for many years at a very small salary was raised under my administration, and if the minimum retirement allowance is again increased in the future, you will be eligible to receive greater retirement benefits in accordance with the number of years you taught before retiring.

As the law becomes effective July 1, 1955, the action was taken at this time. There is no connection whatsoever with the matter and the current campaign, but rather it represents my interest in and concern for the welfare of the retired teachers of Kentucky who have done so much for all Kentucky.

HEALTH & WELFARE

LONESOME PINE COUNCIL BOY SCOUTS
Wheelwright / May 7, 1951

SOME few weeks ago I had the disappointment of seeing my plans to attend a Kiwanis meeting here in Wheelwright cancelled because of the weather. As enjoyable as that visit would have been, I feel your scout program tonight and the luxuriant beauty of the mountains in springtime compensate for that disappointment, and make this assignment truly one of pleasure. In addition, it is my understanding that each Kiwanis Club in the Sandy Valley area sponsors a scout troop and is represented here tonight. This program thereby appears to be an expansion of the earlier one, and we definitely have an advantage over the weather conditions that prevailed at that time.

As governor, my duties have been of a varying and multiple nature. Some are difficult, some easy. Some are pleasant, some less so. But I consider none of the duties of a governor so pleasant or any more constructive than those which relate to the welfare of our young folks and the people who guide them toward becoming useful citizens.

I want to commend you for sponsoring this meeting, so appropriately designated as your appreciation dinner honoring the leaders of the Lonesome Pine Council and its trooper membership. Too often the work of civic leaders goes unnoticed and unappreciated, and I join with you in this expression of gratitude to those who are working so constructively with the young folks in the Lonesome Pine Council area.

I have observed scouting from two vantage points, both as a scout and, later, as an assistant scoutmaster. There is no finer way for a boy to acquire good citizenship training and build good daily habits than through obedience to the scout code. Neither is there a finer way in which a citizen can serve his community than through assisting a scout troop in its training.

During the years I served as judge of a juvenile court, I wished many times as young boys and girls were brought before me that they might have had the advantage of some such training as the scouts provide. The scouts, under your guidance, will learn to obey the law, to understand the meaning of friendship and loyalty. They will bear the mark of your influence into adult life.

While your relationship with them has been apparently one of giving, I am sure you have experienced rich compensation and the reward of sharing youthful activities. Your greatest satisfaction, however, will come when you see the boy scout of today become the leader in community, state, or nation a few years hence.

Certainly it is our obligation to design the future insofar as we are able, so that the lives of succeeding generations will be richer and fuller. Your state government is fully conscious of the important role the education of our youth has in assuring a strong and healthy democracy.

As a result of the increased appropriation by the legislature for education two months ago, our state's public school teachers have been placed in the strongest economic position which available funds allow. This problem, which received special attention during the extraordinary session, will continue to command the serious study and consideration which it requires if we are to fulfill our responsibility to the school children of Kentucky.[1]

Allied with that responsibility is the advancement of public health in our state. Public health services on the county level are being expanded. Through a combined financing arrangement in which funds are made available from federal, state, and local governments many new hospitals are being built to bring specialized care and treatment closer to the sick.

There is, I believe, at every level and in every phase of government a healthy sign of America's attitude toward the problems and needs of youth. An indication of this is evidenced by the attendance and interest in the National Conference on Children and Youth last December in Washington. This meeting, held each ten years since 1909, was attended last year by lay and professional people throughout the country interested in developing in America's children the mental, emotional, and spiritual qualities essential to individual happiness and to responsible citizenship.

Kentucky was well represented at that conference by members of her state Committee on Children and Youth. Many of you are acquainted with the work of this state committee and the action program it is developing in the fields of child health, education, recreation, citizenship, and religion. Much of the committee's accomplishment can be attributed to the fact that an interested, effective individual or small committee at the county level has presented the problems with which the state group is chiefly concerned. With the local group rests the recognition and, finally, the satisfaction of the particular needs of each community. I am vitally interested in seeing the possibilities of the Committee on Children and Youth fully developed to the point where it can be a service organization benefitting all the youth of Kentucky.

As an example of what we have in mind, I asked the committee to select four young Kentuckians to compete for the national medals to be awarded by the federal Congress each year to the youth attaining the most outstanding and meritorious record of service to their friends and community, and to those exhibiting unusual daring and bravery in saving life and property. As a basis for their selections the committee asked each county to furnish a candidate for each honor. From those the committee has chosen two Kentucky nominees for the service medal and two for the bravery medal, and certified their names to the Department of Justice to compete with nominees of other states for the national awards. I am sure many of you saw in yesterday's *Courier-Journal* the story of these four fine young Kentuckians. Glen Green, Jr., of Harlan for service to his community. Joyce Zeigler of Lewis County for community service and outstanding work in the 4-H Club activities. Jimmie Smith of Livingston County and Hilton Tomason of Caldwell County, both nominated for lifesaving.

It is felt that the national bravery award will, in future years, become a counterpart of the Congressional Medal of Honor won by America's bravest on the field of battle, and that the national youth service award will become the highest trophy for young America's achievements.

The free world, of which this country is the vital member, and to whom all freedom-loving peoples of the world are looking for hope and security, today faces its supreme challenge. As our nation is placed in this position in the efforts to attain world peace under justice and reason with the Golden Rule as man's measure of moral value, spiritual leadership and world responsibility weigh more noticeably on our individual lives. Every phase of scouting, its work, pleasures, and training, is fitting the members of the scouts to meet the responsibilities of citizenship they will soon be called upon to discharge. Through your work with the scouts you who are honored here tonight are not only helping to round your scouts into capable, self-reliant individuals, but you also are contributing to the moral and spiritual strength that has been America's fortress in every time of need.

---

1. The appropriations were increased by $6 million. For more information see speeches, pp. 14-23.

DEDICATION OF CALDWELL COUNTY WAR MEMORIAL HOSPITAL

Princeton / May 14, 1951

THIS is a great day for Princeton and Caldwell County. It is the culmination of a series of important days that led up to this moment and the achievement we dedicate at this time.

I doubt if Caldwell County has in its history a greater day than the one on which, through the energy and generosity of local people, cooperating wholeheartedly in a fund-raising campaign, over $90,000 in contributions, ranging from one dollar to $5,000, was raised in a single day. That was a day of pride, a giant step in the making of this hospital.

When the voters of Caldwell County approved the first bond issue another significant day was added to the history of the hospital project and $100,000 to your building funds. With the bond issue and private subscription tests successfully passed, other days of importance followed.

Of the funds acquired from the federal government to be allocated by the State Health Department $132,000 was made available for this hospital. In addition, the state Property and Buildings Commission awarded $27,000 of state funds to the purpose.

Today, of course, is the biggest day of them all, for at last Caldwell countians have assembled to dedicate a structure costing $400,000 and to start it toward the endless chain of days and years in service to the people of this county through the care and treatment of their sick.

Any community that can produce a citizen with the spirit and will for service exemplified by Tom Simmons[1] is the community that will have a hospital, a playground, a school building, paved streets, and whatever else is needed to identify it as progressive. Yours is a community that acknowledges its responsibility to all its people. Throughout the state many other communities are showing the same kind of public-spirited thinking and planning which you have shown here and which are necessary to meet our public needs.

Your state government is taking the lead in this respect. In addition to the $6 million that the special session of the legislature last March appropriated for education, $1 million was appropriated to the state Welfare Department to accelerate the care and treatment program for the patients in our mental hospitals. Just a few days ago one of the outstanding psychiatrists of the nation, Dr. Frank Gaines, a native Kentuckian, was appointed Director of Hospitals and Mental Hygiene. For the first time in Kentucky's history a treatment program is being developed that holds the promise of returning victims of mental disease to their homes as useful members of society. The state government is your partner in the work of making medical care available to all Kentucky citizens.

Your money, your energy, and your best talent have gone into the Caldwell County War Memorial Hospital.[2] It is dedicated to a noble purpose and to the heroic memory of those whose sacrifices continue the blessings of a free America. This building and its modern facilities, the result of community undertaking, could be dedicated to no higher purpose than the prevention of human suffering and the saving of human life.

---

1. Thomas J. Simmons (1909-   ), theatre executive (1929-1953); administrator, Caldwell County War Memorial Hospital (1953-1975), director of fund efforts for hospital expansion (1963-1975); past president of Kiwanis, Princeton Forum, County PTA; member of Pennyrile Health Planning Council; president of Twin Lakes Hospital District; born in Conway, Arkansas, and resides in Princeton. Letter, December 16, 1980.

2. When it was dedicated the Caldwell County War Memorial Hospital was a thirty-nine bed health unit and was termed ultramodern. It was Thomas J. Simmons who started a campaign of solicitation for funds in 1946 for the hospital, and in May 1947 a countywide campaign began which netted over $71,000 instead of the $50,000 originally sought. Voters showed their support with a bond issue, passing the issue 3,162 to 489. Letter from Mr. John S. "Chip" Hutcheson III, editor-publisher of the *Princeton Leader*, December 31, 1980.

OWEN COUNTY MEMORIAL HOSPITAL
Owenton / May 30, 1951

THIS is a great day for the people of Owen County and your neighboring communities. In dedicating the Owen County Memorial Hospital, we start towards many years of useful service an institution that is the outcome of earnest and prolonged effort by those it will serve and by your public officials to bring specialized medical care and treatment within close reach.

In approving as you did a $100,000 bond issue for construction, you folks of Owen County signified your awareness of the need for such a hospital in this vicinity and gave approval for your fiscal court and county judge to proceed. Your fiscal court made county funds available, and you citizens of Owenton and Owen County gave liberally to make this public-serving institution a reality. From federal funds allotted to it for such uses our state Health Department allocated two-thirds of the $258,000 used in constructing and equipping your hospital.

All of you have a part in the hospital that we dedicate here today. It will be a memorial to your county judge,[1] your fiscal court, Mr. B. L. Hancock, Mr. John Thomas,[2] your farm bureau, and to all of you who have encouraged and participated in the work that made it possible[3]

---

1. Howard Ellis was county judge 1922-1957. In 1954 Governor Wetherby returned to Owen County and at ceremonies held at the county fair he recognized Judge Ellis as "Owen Countian of the Year."

2. B. L. Hancock served on the Owen County draft board in 1940, was chairman of the Victory Loan Committee during World War II, president of the Peoples' Bank and Trust Company of Owenton, and in October 1950 was elected vice president of the Kentucky Bankers' Association.

John Games Thomas (1888-1961), mayor of Owenton (1930-1953); he was a businessman interested in the growth of his county, and he led the movement to develop a public water supply. See Mariam S. Houchens, *History of Owen County, Kentucky "Sweet Owen"* (Louisville, 1976), pp. 160, 166, 188.

3. The concluding remarks of Governor Wetherby were the same as those found in the speech from May 14, 1951, in this section, and have been omitted.

KENTUCKY LEAGUE OF WOMEN VOTERS
Louisville / October 22, 1951

THE opportunity I have as a candidate for governor to discuss important matters of public policy before a group of citizens whose interests are centered in the program activities of state government is both welcomed and appreciated.

This event in your yearly schedule offers the nominees of the two principle parties a citizen forum which in a nonpartisan manner is concerned with the candidates' position and attitude toward the subjects comprising the agenda.

On any given occasion the limiting factors of time and circumstances prevent a full and detailed discussion of the many phases and program activities of state government. In fact any one of the three topics listed on this discussion could profitably utilize the full sixty minutes of your business session. In looking over the suggested subjects, however, I am impressed by the nature and importance of your selections and want to commend the league's board of directors for focusing the group's attention on timely questions of public concern.

Since early manhood the problems of child welfare and its many sides have held my deep interest and commanded a substantial part of my time and whatever extent of specialized talent I may have acquired through the years while working in this field. This interest developed as a result of the ground-floor participation I have had in both legislative and administrative experiences dealing with the broad problem of child welfare.

Up until 1932, Kentucky had not recognized the special legal, social, and human welfare problems posed by her needy and delinquent children.

Sensing the pressing demands for legislative action, a group profoundly moved by the inadequacy of our state law and judicial setup prepared legislation and sponsored and guided it through the General Assembly. This measure provided for the creation of a trial commissioner of the juvenile court in those counties where the fiscal court approved.[1]

It was my privilege to be numbered among that early group of advocates of a strengthened juvenile court. I actively assisted in drafting the legislation and aided in securing its enactment into law. In 1933, I became attorney for the Jefferson County Juvenile Court and continued to serve in that capacity until 1937. From that time until 1942, while not officially connected with the local court, I utilized my experience and natural desire to serve the unfortunate and underprivileged children of Louisville and Jefferson County through a host of clubs and community organizations having youth program activities of various kinds.

I again served as attorney in 1942 and in 1943 was appointed judge of the Jefferson County Juvenile Court and remained until announcing for lieutenant governor in 1947.

Both as attorney and as judge I worked tirelessly for the benefit and welfare of the youngsters who, through no fault of their own, came within the purview of the court.

While the office of lieutenant governor once more separated me from day-to-day dealing with the problem of destitute children, broken homes, and delinquent minors, I soon found other and broader channels through which my willingness and experience could be most effectively used.

A high point was reached about a year ago in the attention and consideration being given this important subject. Beginning at that time under the direction of the Legislative Research Commission aided and supported by an advisory commission whom I appointed, whose chairman is the capable and experienced judge of the Fayette County Juvenile Court,[2] a careful survey was begun of all child welfare laws, regulations, and state agencies administering the various child welfare programs. This study and report will include the best thinking within the state and will be submitted to the 1952 General Assembly for its information and guidance, looking toward the enactment of a new and detailed child welfare code.

In a preliminary report, I am advised that they will recommend a Youth Administration for the state of Kentucky. These tentative proposals call for the creation of a centralized agency within the Welfare Department.[3] Its functional responsibility will be to offer temporary custodial care for all juveniles who are involved in court. After careful and expert investigation of family background and home conditions—and complete psychiatric examination—each juvenile will be committed to either the Kentucky Children's Home—or Greendale—the decision being made by qualified social workers. I have confidence in the Research Commission and the advisory committee, and expect to support its findings and recommendations.

Within the past few years the spiral of inflation and rising taxes have focused widespread attention on the fiscal affairs of government at all levels. Demands for additional services by the state government for its citizens are increasing. If we are to meet these demands, additional money must be provided. Who should determine what services are to be increased and how best to meet those needs?

As I have said many times before, the answer in my opinion lies with the people. The people will answer those questions through the representatives on the Functions and Resources Committee and through their duly elected representatives and senators in the General Assembly.

Anticipating the manifold problems found in this great debatable area of public policy, the 1950 General Assembly created this Committee on Functions and Resources of State Government.[4] It is composed of twenty-three outstanding and representative citizens and is now making a detailed study of your government. This committee will make a report for submission to the 1952 session of the legislature.

Turning to the third and last question to be discussed, I should like to point out that the state allocates support for education based on a dual formula. Each is prescribed through a constitutional mandate and neither can be altered short of a constitutional amendment.

---

1. *Acts of the General Assembly of the Commonwealth of Kentucky,* 1932, Chapter 61, pp. 342-47.

2. William E. Nichols.

3. *Acts of the General Assembly of the Commonwealth of Kentucky,* 1952, Chapter 161 (H.B. 157), pp. 428-51. For a description of the Youth Authority Act see speech from December 7, 1955, in the Legislative Messages and Statements section.

4. *Acts of the General Assembly of the Commonwealth of Kentucky,* 1950, Chapter 124 (H.B. 449), pp. 541-43.

SPEECH MATERIAL
Frankfort / August 31, 1954

JUVENILES: The 1954 legislature strengthened and clarified the Youth Authority Act, a law which attempts to channel delinquent, neglected, and sick children into institutions best fitted to help and correct youngsters.[1] It set up court procedure for handling these cases and imposed more responsibility on the parents of children coming before the Youth Authority. The technicalities of administering the act are difficult, but this problem is slowly being overcome.

The state Property and Building Commission, headed by the governor, has provided funds for the construction of a Youth Authority Reception Center near Louisville, and once the Youth Authority Board starts operating this center, the program will become more stable and acceptable to the public generally.

Public Health: The legislature rewrote many of the statutes governing the care of mental patients. The ancient and cruel words used in the old law were deleted and the language made more humane and modern. The Department of Mental Health received substantial increases in appropriations, enabling the department to employ competent doctors and attendants and provide improved custodial service.[2]

The Department of Health was empowered to help counties set up health departments and obtain federal aid for new hospital construction.[3] Many counties are now benefiting from the assistance and guidance provided by the state. This department is now one of the largest in state government. One of its new objectives is to attract young people to attend medical schools and practice in Kentucky. Loans for these students are available through the Rural Kentucky Medical Scholarship Fund. Another new law prohibits employees of the Health Department from actively participating in political campaigns.[4]

Education: The legislature adopted a Minimum Foundation Program for public schools, setting in motion a long-range plan to improve Kentucky's often-criticized school system.[5] Incoming legislatures will be confronted with the problem of providing more money for schools, but the support pattern for better schools is now on the law books. Library service, including the bookmobile project, are in better shape than ever to make many more Kentuckians aware of the contentment and enjoyment found in literature.

The Supreme Court decision terminating segregation in the public schools was met with a minimum of resentment and hostile reaction in Kentucky. The Court will elaborate on its decision this winter in an effort to help states meet the problems connected with desegregation. The governor has appointed an advisory commission of four whites and three Negroes to help him and the state Department of Education combine our separate school systems. Complete desegregation is probably another year away in Kentucky. The governor has called for temperate, clear thinking as the Commonwealth moves toward conforming with this new law of the land.

Safety: The state government has continued to advocate programs designed to make the public more aware of the dangers and tragedies that lurk upon the highways. The governor has a genuine interest in promoting highway safety in an effort to reduce the death toll caused by traffic accidents. The State Police Department has been reorganized so that more high-ranking officers have been placed in district offices. Campaigns to check on driver licenses and registration plates have been conducted to eliminate illegal or unqualified auto operators from the highways.

To assist the police in gaining drunken driving convictions, the legislature passed the so-called Drunkometer Bill.[6] This empowers the police to subject drivers suspected of drinking to chemical tests to determine the amount of alcohol in their blood when arrested.

The legislature increased the taxes on malt beverages, cigarettes, wine, and pari-mutuel betting in a plan to better finance state government and its programs.[7] Salaries now paid state officials are commensurate with the economic times and the government is able to attract well-qualified persons for key positions.

The state park program is one of which Kentuckians may be proud. Our park facilities have become nationally prominent and the tourist industry in Kentucky is now one of our most important.

The operations of government depend on the legislature to adopt sound policies and programs. The legislature then must count on administrative officials to carry out the laws enacted. The Kentucky Legislature, considering the fact it is limited to sixty days of work every two years, has not failed to supply the Commonwealth the tools to do the best job possible under a general tax system that has not basically changed in more than twenty years.

There is no indication that this material was delivered in a formal speech; however, the basic ideas expressed here may have been used on occasion.

1. *Acts of the General Assembly of the Commonwealth of Kentucky,* 1954, Chapter 185 (H.B. 296), p. 494.

2. *Acts of the General Assembly of the Commonwealth of Kentucky,* 1954, Chapter 15 (S.B. 58), pp. 36-38; 1954, Chapter 16 (S.B. 59), pp. 38-42; 1954, Chapter 17 (S.B. 60), pp. 42–48. Governor Wetherby increased the assistance to mental health as follows: 1952-1954, $8,716,000; 1954-1956, $9,672,000.

3. *Acts of the General Assembly of the Commonwealth of Kentucky,* 1954, Chapter 157 (H.B. 222), pp. 435-43.

4. *Acts of the General Assembly of the Commonwealth of Kentucky,* 1954, Chapter 157 (H.B. 222), p. 442.

5. *Acts of the General Assembly of the Commonwealth of Kentucky,* 1954, Chapter 214, (H.B. 365), pp. 590-603.

6. *Acts of the General Assembly of the Commonwealth of Kentucky,* 1954, Chapter 74 (H.B. 16), pp. 163-64.

7. *Acts of the General Assembly of the Commonwealth of Kentucky,* 1954, Chapter 75 (H.B. 17), pp. 164-65; 1954, Chapter 76 (H.B. 18), pp. 165-66; 1954, Chapter 77 (H.B. 19), pp. 166-67.

WHAT THE KENTUCKY LEGISLATURE HAS DONE FOR MEDICINE

Louisville / September 22, 1954

1) ESTABLISHED Medical Research Commission in 1948. Commissioner of Health, three physicians, one interested layman. Contracts with U. of L. Medical School for research services. Started with $125,000 a year. Now gets $300,000. Has produced fine results in surgery, blood diseases, radioactive substances and other research services. Appropriations given commission enable this municipal school to channel funds into other departments. Statewide benefit is reflected in the fact that the percent of Kentucky boys attending U. of L. Medical School has increased from sixty to ninety. This is tremendous factor for a state needing doctors so badly.

2) The 1952 session of the legislature completely revised and modernized the Medical Practices Act.[1] This marked the first time in fifty years these regulations had been touched by the lawmakers.

3) The 1952 session also adopted the Hospital License and Inspection Act, giving the state authority to shut down hospitals failing to provide minimum standards of facilities and sanitation.[2] The legislature overcame strong opposition to place this statute on the law books.

4) In 1952, the legislature established a separate Department of Mental Health, and enabled the governor to appoint a well-trained, young M. D. as head of the department. Appropriations to mental hospitals substantially increased. The commissioner has recruited good assistants and doctors, so that we now emphasize cure rather than custody of patients.[3]

5) The 1954 legislature rewrote the laws governing the commitment and care of mental patients to eliminate cruel, medieval language relating to these people. This was a reform hailed by humanitarians.[4]

6) The 1954 session also enacted laws requiring the quarantining of persons having communicable tuberculosis. This may help to stop the spread of a disease that ravages thousands of Kentuckians.[5]

7) Another 1954 act calls for the inoculation of dogs against rabies.[6] You can well imagine the gales of protests against this enactment in a state where most dog owners exercise independent management over their animals. But the law was adopted because controllable rabies has too long been a threat to the health of the public. It is a difficult law to administer, but the outlook is generally bright for success.

8) With the assistance of the Kentucky State Medical Association, the 1954 legislature revised all the laws relating to chiropody, optometry, and optometric dispensing.[7] The clearning up of these laws was welcomed by these professions.

9) The legislature has been generous in its appropriations to the state Property and Buildings Commission, which has given financial help to twenty-four counties for construction of health centers. With help from the Building Commission, two other counties are erecting health centers, four others are ready to start construction, and five other counties have applications pending for commission money, which doubtless will be granted. (An added note to this benefit was written in longhand on the note card for this point. It said: Many hospitals have been made possible from these funds.)

Recent sessions of the Kentucky Legislature have shown willingness and cooperation in the matter of medical and health legislation. Much depends upon the approach the medical profession takes toward legislators. To have gained so much at the hands of the legislature indicates the Kentucky State Medical Association possesses the know-how in getting along with the General Assembly.

10) Doctors are strongly needed in rural Kentucky. To overcome this shortage, the 1954 legislature put up $5,000 to help Kentuckians through medical school in exchange for a contract promising that they will become public health officers for certain periods of time in rural Kentucky.[8] Your state medical association has made available $167,500 for rural medical scholarships. Loans have been made to eighty students, and fifty-nine of them are attending the Louisville Medical School.

11) The doctors of Kentucky have taken a much sharper interest in civic and public affairs. This is marked by their growing presence on school boards and service club committees. They have frequently served in our state legislature.

In 1949 they established the Kentucky Physicians Mutual, a prepayment plan for medical and hospital services. Thousands of Kentuckians are members of this organization.

These are rough notes that Governor Wetherby used to deliver a speech before the State Medical Society.

1. *Acts of the General Assembly of the Commonwealth of Kentucky,* 1952, Chapter 150 (H.B. 137), pp. 384-400.

2. *Acts of the General Assembly of the Commonwealth of Kentucky,* 1952, Chapter 16 (S.B. 50), pp. 15-25.

3. *Acts of the General Assembly of the Commonwealth of Kentucky,* 1952, Chapter 150 (H.B. 137), pp. 384-400; 1952, Chapter 50 (S.B. 140), pp. 93-103.

4. *Acts of the General Assembly of the Commonwealth of Kentucky,* 1954, Chapter 15 (S.B. 58), pp. 36-38; 1954, Chapter 16 (S.B. 59), pp. 38-42; 1954, Chapter 17 (S.B. 60), pp. 42-48.
5. *Acts of the General Assembly of the Commonwealth of Kentucky,* 1954, Chapter 223 (H.B. 401), pp. 614-16.
6. *Acts of the General Assembly of the Commonwealth of Kentucky,* 1954, Chapter 119 (H.B. 139), pp. 360-76.
7. *Acts of the General Assembly of the Commonwealth of Kentucky,* 1954, Chapter 219 (H.B. 383), pp. 609-10; 1954, Chapter 27 (S.B. 104), pp. 67-71.
8. *Acts of the General Assembly of the Commonwealth of Kentucky,* 1954, Chapter 181 (H.B. 286), p. 479; 1954, Chapter 136 (H.B. 178), pp. 399-401.

SOCIAL WORKERS ORGANIZATION
Frankfort / February 8, 1955

THE story of public assistance in Kentucky, from August 1936 through December 1954, is one of steady advancement, both in the number of needy recipients served and in the total annual payments made from federal and state funds.

The public assistance program in Kentucky was launched in the summer of 1936, and first payments were made in August of that year. Payments at that time were made only to the needy aged who, by the end of December 1936, numbered only 4,651. The average monthly payment was $9.73, and the total amount of state and federal funds expended during the five months' period—August through December—was $226,331.15.

During the year 1937 the total number of old-age assistance recipients rose to 31,443 and the total cost—payments only—reached $3,729,716.99. However, the average monthly payment for that year was only $9.88. In 1938 the total number of old-age assistance recipients went to 35,184; the total payments to $3,807,759.60, but the average monthly payment dropped to $9.02. In 1939, the last year of the administration of Governor A. B. Chandler, the total number of old-age assistance recipients was 45,036 and the total amount expended in payments was $4,661,682.25. The average monthly payment, however, sustained another setback by dropping to $8.63, or $1.10 below the average for 1936, the year in which the program was launched in Kentucky.

During the administration of Governor Keen Johnson,[1] which began in December 1939 and ended in December 1943, the total number of old-age assistance recipients increased nearly 10,000—45,036 in 1939; 52,676 in 1943. And it may be pointed out here that, despite the increase in the caseload from year to year—1940 through 1943—the average monthly payment rose from the low of $8.63 in 1939 to $10.96 in 1943. By the end of 1943, when Governor Johnson was succeeded by Governor Simeon Willis,[2] total old-age assistance payments had reached $6,926,758.

In December, 1942, as Governor Johnson began the final year of his four-year term, Kentucky commenced payments to the needy blind. Then in 1943 the state added a third category of public assistance known as aid to dependent children. At the end of 1943, the state was giving assistance to 1,096 needy blind at a total cost of $169,352 and to 1,474 dependent children at a total cost of $419,717. The total number of needy recipients under the three categories at the end of 1943 was 55,246, and the total of state and federal funds paid to that number of recipients during the year was $7,515,827.

During the administration of Governor Willis—December 1943 through December 1947—the total number of old-age assistance recipients decreased from 52,676 on January 1, 1944, to 47,878 on December 31, 1947. However, the total payments increased from $6,926,758 to $9,931,241, and the average monthly payment went from $10.96 to $17.29 during the same period. In addition to payments to the needy aged, there were payments to the needy blind and to dependent children, so that by the end of 1947 the total number of public assistance recipients had reached 59,122 (needy aged, 47,878; needy blind, 1,715; dependent children, 9,529) at a total cost to the state and federal governments of $14,491,622.

When Earle Clements became governor of the Commonwealth in December 1947, the total number of old-age assistance recipients was 47,878. Through increased appropriations during the Clements Administration, the state was able, by the close of 1951, to give assistance to 66,893 needy aged at a total cost of $20,057,801.50. And, despite the fact that the number of needy aged recipients had increased from 47,878 in December 1947 to 66,893 in December 1951, the average monthly payment grew from $17.29 in 1947 to $24.99 in 1951.

This, however, was only one-third of the public assistance load assumed and carried forward by the Clements administration—1947-1951.[3] The number of needy blind recipients grew from 1,715 in 1947 to 2,489 in 1951, and the average monthly payment rose from $18.36

to $28.49 during the four-year period. As in the needy aged category, increased appropriations made by the General Assembly at the request of the governor, provided sufficient state funds to raise the total state and federal payments to the needy blind from $377,862 in 1947 to $850,948 in 1951.

Furthermore, while increased assistance was being given to the state's needy aged and needy blind under Governor Clements from 1947 through 1951, the state's dependent children were not overlooked. When Mr. Clements occupied the gubernatorial office in 1947, he found 9,529 recipients of aid to dependent children, receiving a total of $4, 182,519 in state and federal funds. The average monthly payment in that year was $36.57. During the first year of his administration, the number of recipients rose from 9,529 to 13,852, and the average monthly payment showed a slight increase—from $36.57 to $36.66. There were additional increases in 1949, 1950, and 1951, so that in the latter years there were 22,898 recipients of aid to dependent children, and the total payments from state and federal funds reached $10,936, 945. The average payment for that year was $39.80, the highest figure since the inauguration of the program in 1943.

The recapitulation of the facts and figures given in the several preceding paragraphs shows that, during the Clements administration (1947-1951), the total number of recipients of public assistance in Kentucky increased from 59,122 in 1947 to 92,280 in 1951; and the total state and federal payments increased from $14,491,622 in 1947 to $31,845,694.50 in 1951. And, it may be further stated that, under Governor Clements the General Assembly, in 1948 and 1950, provided an additional $2,921,505.26 for public assistance in Kentucky, so that the total caseload could be increased from 59,122 in 1947 to 92,280 in 1951, and at the same time provide an increased average monthly payment to the needy aged of $7.70, to the needy blind of $10.13, and to recipients of aid to needy children of $3.23.

Since the advent of the administration of Governor Lawrence W. Wetherby in December, 1950,[4] there has been a gradual decline in the number of recipients of old-age assistance and aid to dependent children. The number of old age assistance recipients dropped from 66,893 in 1951 to 55,721 in 1954. However, the average monthly payment increased from $24.99 in 1951, to $30.80 in 1952, to $34.85 in 1953, and to $34.90 in 1954. Total payments to the needy aged in 1954 were $23,334,341, of which $6,671,172.96 was supplied by the state of Kentucky and $16,663,168.04 by the federal government. The total amount of state funds expended for old-age assistance during the third year of Governor Wetherby's administration was $458,427.83 greater than the total amount of state funds expended for the same purpose during the four years (1935-1939) of the Chandler administration.

At the end of December 1950, and within a few weeks after Mr. Wetherby entered the gubernatorial office, there were 22,898 recipients of aid to dependent children who received for that year a total of $2, 734,062.82 in state funds, plus $8,202,882.18 in federal funds, for a grand total of $10,936,945. The average monthly payment for 1951 was $39.80. During 1952 the total number of recipients of aid to dependent children was reduced to 20,042, but the average monthly payment went up to $49.90—an increase of $10.10. The number of recipients was further reduced in 1953, the total being 19,598; but the average monthly payment was increased to $63.35, or nearly three times as much as the average for 1943, the first year payments were made in Kentucky.

Since December 1950 there has been a slight increase in the number of recipients of aid to the needy blind. There were 2,489 recipients in this category at that time and the average payment per month was $28.49. At the end of 1954 the number of recipients was 2,737, and the average monthly payment was $36.82.

During the three years of the Wetherby administration (1952-1954 inclusive) a total of $112,271,254.60 in state and federal funds has been distributed to the needy aged, the needy blind, and the dependent children of Kentucky. This total for three years exceeded the combined totals for the eleven year period—1936 through 1947—which included the administrations of Chandler, Johnson, and Willis, by approximately $36 million.

Finally, it may be noted that throughout the years, since 1936, that public assistance has been available to the needy folk of Kentucky, the administrative costs have been held to the lowest figure commensurate with efficient service. While we do not have figures showing the cost of administration year by year, we are able to show what it cost in 1953 to administer the three programs—old-age assistance, aid to the needy blind, and aid to dependent children. These figures are included in the "Selected Data on Public Assistance" distributed to members of the County Social Service Advisory Committees by the Community Relations Section, Department of Economic Security.

Briefly, it may be noted that the average cost per case for the overall program during 1953 was only $2.08. Only Arkansas with $1.54 and West Virginia with $1.77 were below Kentucky's figure. Forty-five states spent more money—some of them considerably more—per case, than did Kentucky.

Extreme care has ever been exercised by the administrators of public assistance in Kentucky to assure that every dollar made available for assistance to the needy folk of the state should reach them and not be spent to cover excessive administrative costs. There is a great deal of time and hard work involved in processing a public assistance case. During 1953 a total of 77,657 needy men, women, and children received public assistance and the total amount distributed to these recipients was $37,984,479. And this job was done at a cost of only $2.08 per case.

---

1. Keen Johnson (1896-1970), editor of several newspapers (1919-1925); became editor of *Richmond* (Ky.) *Daily Register* (1925); lieutenant governor of Kentucky (1935-1939), governor (1939-1943); director of public relations, Reynolds Metals Company (1944-1945); under secretary of labor (1946-1947); director of public affairs, Reynolds Metals Company (1949-1970); born in Lyon County. *Who's Who in America, 1954-1955,* 28th ed. (Chicago, 1954), p. 1375.

2. Simeon S. Willis (1879-1965), city solicitor of Ashland (1918-1922); member, state Board of Bar Examiners (1923-1927); judge, Court of Appeals (1927-1933); governor of Kentucky (1943-1947); member, Public Service Commission (1956-1960); appointed to state Parole Board (1961); born in Lawrence County, Ohio. *Who's Who in Kentucky* (Hopkinsville, Ky., 1955), p. 366.

3. The use of the chronological limits of 1947-1951 is confusing here when it refers to the Clements administration. Governor Clements left the governor's office in November 1950. The year 1951 is given here because that would ordinarily have been the extent of his term and because the amounts of money listed for 1951 were the result of the financial enactments of the 1950 General Assembly, when Clements was the governor.

4. Wetherby became governor on November 27, 1950.

RACIAL DISCRIMINATION AT HAZELWOOD SANATORIUM

Letter / January 26, 1951

[To John Floyd, Outwood]

As you may have noticed through the press, a delegation from the Interracial Hospital Movement called on me recently with respect to the problems of racial discrimination in the admission and treatment of Negro tuberculosis victims at Hazelwood Sanatorium. It was charged, in fact, that no provision or facilities existed for the surgical treatment of this racial group.

So that I might be fully informed in this regard, it is suggested that a thorough investigation of this situation be made and a report submitted on your findings. In the event there exists inequality of admission rights and care and treatment accorded patients upon admission, I should like to have your advice and recommendations as to the speediest possible manner in which the discrimination and injustice might be remedied.

John Bunyan Floyd, Jr. (1917-), resident in surgery, Lexington Clinic and Ochsner Foundation (1943-1949); individual practice of medicine specializing in surgery (1949-); director, American Cancer Society (1950); director, Cancer Mobile of Kentucky (1955); board of directors, Kentucky Division American Cancer Society (1955); born in Louisville and resides in Lexington. *Who's Who in the South and Southwest, 1978-1979,* 16th ed. (Chicago, 1978), p. 241.

IMPROVEMENTS IN STATE MENTAL HOSPITALS

Letter / February 9, 1951

[To Minnie L. Russell, Paris]

THE welfare of those folks confined in our mental institutions is as near to my heart as any subject with which the state has official connection, and I assure you the situation related in your communication will be taken up with the Welfare Department and every consideration will be accorded this matter.

I am confident you have observed in the press certain initial changes which have been made in administrative personnel in the Welfare Department preparatory to the revitalization of the mental health and welfare program. Full pursuit will be devoted to the selection of a mental hygiene director who can develop and put into effect a treatment program which we are all convinced is possible and will return rehabilitation patients to their homes capable of contributing to their upkeep and of producing goods and services for society as a whole.

In our efforts to make all possible improvements in conditions at our hospitals, I know we have your fullest cooperation and best wishes, and I do want you to know I am most appreciative of your interest and I invite your suggestions at any and all times.

One of Governor Wetherby's most significant governmental changes was the reorganization of the Welfare Department. It began in 1951 when a separate Division of Hospitals and Mental Hygiene was created within the Department of Welfare. Then in 1952 the General Assembly established a separate Department of Mental Health and defined its powers, duties, functions, funds, and facilities. The new department was headed by a commissioner with an advisory council of mental health. The department, divided into a Division of Professional Services and Division of Business Administration, had the responsibility for the care and treatment of the mentally ill. It was supposed to develop a program looking toward the prevention of mental disease and the postinstitutional care of persons released from public or private mental hospitals.

Along with the Minimum Foundation Program, Governor Wetherby considered this legislation to be the most significant accomplishment of his administration. As a judge and lieutenant governor, Wetherby had served on boards that oversaw mental facilities. He was simply appalled by the terrible conditions he saw, and he carried this concern into the governorship. See *Acts of the General Assembly of the Commonwealth of Kentucky,* 1952, Chapter 50 (S.B. 140), pp. 93-103.

HILL-BURTON ACT
Letter / February 21, 1951

[To Mrs. Elmer K. Robertson, Louisville]

THIS acknowledges your further communication regarding legislation now pending in Congress for the appropriation of funds in conformity with the Hill-Burton Act.[1]

Your further indicated interest and concern are appreciated, and I assure you my moral support and official endorsement of the new legislation, making additional funds available for nurse training and hospital building costs, accompany your efforts. While, as you know, I am not in position to directly influence bills pending in Congress, the state's congressional delegation labor under the assurance of my hearty approval and full cooperation, and through this channel my every energy will be exerted in encouraging their work on the measures in question.

---

1. For an explanation of the Hill-Burton Act see Oath of Office speech, November 27, 1950.

Mrs. Elmer K. Robertson was president, Women's Auxiliary, Methodist Evangelical Hospital.

VETERANS' BONUS
Letter / July 31, 1951

[To Harold H. Keith, Newport]

IN direct answer to your inquiry on my position toward a veterans' bonus, I should like to advise that the financial condition of our state government and the taxable resources of the Commonwealth will not support a bonus to Kentucky veterans without placing one in a strained and difficult position and on a dangerous and depleting footing that would lead to dire economical consequences. In addition, considering the compelling needs of Kentucky's education and welfare programs and also that the veterans and their children would be saddled with the debt which would be largely paid by themselves, I consider it to be in the best interest of both the veterans and Kentucky to oppose such a measure.

Harold H. Keith was general chairman, Executive Department, United Ex-Service Men, Inc.

HEALTH SERVICES ORGANIZATION FOR CIVIL DEFENSE

Letter / January 7, 1952

[To W. Clark Bailey, Harlan]

FROM a study of conference reports and other related data on health services organization for civil defense, I am impressed by the showing of those states in which such preparation on the part of the medical profession has been made by the physicians themselves, working through their state and local organizations in cooperation with civil defense officials.

I have noted with gratification the work of your Committee on Emergency Medical Service which has organized and promoted courses on the medical aspects of atomic explosion for physicians in several Kentucky cities, and recommended formation of an emergency medical service committee by each county society. However, I note also that as of October 1, 1951, less than one-fourth of all county medical societies had reported appointment of such committees, and your state committee in its report mentioned "resistance within the profession" to more active civil defense preparation.

Since your association was represented at the recent civil defense conference in Chicago, you no doubt have a report indicating the general agreement among the group panel participants on several points: most mobile support will have to be provided from nontarget areas; medical personnel should be organized into teams on an equitable basis between communities, so that the total mobile support which the state can furnish may be known; physicians who are not members of hospital staffs or medical societies must be included in plans, as their services will be needed; hospital authorities must be urged to plan emergency expansion, and the professional staff must take an active part in such plans. I do not doubt that you will also agree much remains to be done before plans and organization for mass care of casualties in Kentucky may be regarded as satisfactory. Kentucky physicians are busy, and many, together with a large proportion of our people, probably feel that the danger of attack on our civil population is remote. Good civil defense organization can be used in nonmilitary disasters as well, and is in itself a strong deterrent to aggression.

I should like to request that the task of organization of the medical profession of Kentucky for civil defense, on a statewide basis, be assumed by the Kentucky State Medical Association. In this connection, the state Director of Civil Defense and his staff will be glad to assist in every possible way.

W. Clark Bailey (1900-1957), physician; received his medical degree from the University of Louisville; physician in Harlan (1926-1957); president, state Medical Society (1951-1952); vice president, American Medical Association (1954-1955); family doctor of the year (1955); born in Harlan. *Louisville Courier-Journal,* November 21, 1957.

DEPARTMENT OF MENTAL HEALTH
Letter / February 5, 1952

[To Winfred Overholser, Washington, D.C.]

ACKNOWLEDGMENT is accorded your January 28 letter with the expression of interest in the proposed change in our administrative organization directing the state's mental hospitals. Your views in this connection are valued and appreciated.

It is our plan to introduce into the General Assembly the measure creating a new Department of Mental Health, and I trust that we may muster sufficient interest and support to push this bill through the legislature.[1] The present plan and thinking regarding the feebleminded institution calls for its continued operation under the direction of our

Welfare Department. However, a close working liaison relationship will be maintained with the new Department of Mental Health, and it is felt that its progress can be carried out both satisfactorily and successfully under this type of administrative arrangements.

---

1. *Acts of the General Assembly of the Commonwealth of Kentucky,* 1952, Chapter 50 (S. B. 140), pp. 93–103.

Winfred Overholser (1892-1964), physician, assistant to commander of Massachusetts Department of Mental Diseases (1924-1925); director of division for examination of prisoners, Massachusetts (1925-1930), assistant commander and commander of division (1930-1936); became superintendent of St. Elizabeth's Hospital, Washington, D. C. (1937); professor of psychiatry, George Washington University School of Medicine; member, National Board of Medical Examiners (1948-1954); born in Worcester, Massachusetts. *Who's Who in America, 1954-1955,* 28th ed. (Chicago, 1954), p. 2046.

HOSPITAL INSPECTION ACT

Letter / February 27, 1952

[To Frank H. Moore, Bowling Green]

YOUR communication following final passage of the hospital inspection measure is deeply appreciated.[1]

Since first serving as presiding officer of the Senate in 1948, I have been impressed with the apparent need for an effective inspection and license law covering all Kentucky hospitals. As governor, I am proud to have included in the legislative program a measure as important and constructive as I feel this one to be, and I am greatly pleased that the legislature acted on it favorably.

---

1. *Acts of the General Assembly of the Commonwealth of Kentucky,* 1952, Chapter 16 (S. B. 50), pp. 15-25.

Frank Hampton Moore (1916-), physician, specializes in internal medicine; past director and president of the Kentucky Heart Association; United States Army Medical Corps (1942-1946); born and resides in Bowling Green. Hambleton Tapp, ed., *Kentucky Lives: The Blue Grass State Who's Who* (Hopkinsville, Ky., 1966), pp. 370-71.

ECONOMIC SECURITY FOR UNIVERSITY OF KENTUCKY EMPLOYEES

Letter / June 6, 1952

[To Earle C. Clements, Washington, D.C.]

THE 1951 Special Session of the General Assembly passed legislation enabling officials and employees of Kentucky state and local governments to be brought under the Federal Old-Age and Survivors Insurance benefits.[1] From time to time since the execution of the federal-state agreement, which was necessary to implement the legislative act, various administrative and legal problems and technicalities have been met and resolved. However, in the case of officials and employees of the University of Kentucky, who fall outside of the state-administered teacher retirement system, various and conflicting views and interpretations have been placed on their status with respect to Social Security coverage. Nevertheless, the state Department of Economic Security, Division of Personnel Security, and the Kentucky Attorney General have been and are now of the opinion that these employees can qualify for and are now covered by the provisions of this act and the federal-state agreement.

The latest development is the recent ruling by Mr. A. J. Altmeyer,[1] the federal administrator, that these employees are not eligible to participate in this program.

I am writing you for the purpose of soliciting the assistance of you and your office in the hope that Mr. Altmeyer and the Federal Security Agency might reconsider the reached ruling on this case, thereby allowing this group of employees of our state university to enjoy the protection and benefits of the Federal Old-Age and Survivors Insurance program.

---

1. For more information see speeches from February 21, 1951, March 6, 1951, March 18, 1951, in the Legislative Messages and Statements section.

2. Arthur Joseph Altmeyer (1891-1972), statistician, Wisconsin Tax Commission (1918-1920); chief statistician and secretary, Wisconsin Industrial Commission (1920-1933); second assistant secretary of labor (1934-1935); member, Social Security Board of the United States (1935-1946), chairman (1937-1946), commissioner of Social Security (1946-1953); social welfare adviser (1955-1972); representative at numerous welfare, defense, and labor

conferences; born in DePere, Wisconsin. *Who's Who in America, 1950-1951*, 26th ed. (Chicago, 1950), p. 59.

UNIVERSITY OF KENTUCKY COLLEGE OF MEDICINE
Letter / May 26, 1953

[To T. A. Perry, Owenton]

THIS acknowledges the resolution adopted by the Owenton Rotary Club recommending the establishment of a College of Medicine at the University of Kentucky.

The Legislative Research Commission, with the assistance of an advisory committee on medical education, is hard at work studying this proposal. Their findings will be reported to the 1954 General Assembly. Indications are that the cost of constructing a medical school at the university would be $15 million and it would take $3 million a year to operate it. Our present tax structure, of course, could not bear this expense. However, we shall await the final report of the commission before undertaking extensive consideration of this matter.

Your interest in training more physicians for Kentucky is commendable.

Governor Wetherby did support the construction of the medical school at the University of Kentucky. Completed during the term of his successor, the school was incorporated with the Albert B. Chandler Medical Center in Lexington.

T. A. Perry (1908-), attorney; clerk, City of Owenton (1936–1943, 1946-1980); president, Owenton Rotary Club (1952-1953, 1977-1978); chairman of board, Owen County Historical Society; Owen Countian of the Year (1980); born and resides in Owenton, Letter, December 8, 1980.

TEACHERS AND SOCIAL SECURITY
Letter / October 5, 1954

[To J. R. Whitmer, Bowling Green]

THIS responds to your letter of September 29 in which you request additional information as to how some eighty-five faculty members at Western State College may come under the recently amended Old-Age and Survivors Insurance program.

Mr. Fithian,[1] in his letter of September 8, gave you the very latest information he possesses on the amendment. In November, he plans to attend a national conference of Social Security administrators in Baltimore. Delegates to this conference will be given the latest interpretations and directions concerning the amendment. Mr. Fithian will then be in a much better position to discuss the possibilities in the new law.

Offhand, he believes the teachers in the Kentucky retirement system will have to show they desire to come under the Old-Age and Survivors Insurance plan and certify to me that a majority of the teachers favor a referendum. Mr. Fithian thinks the referendum should be a statewide one. An indication that a referendum is wanted might be obtained at the next meeting of the Kentucky Education Association.

There is one more important consideration. It is estimated that if the members or a majority of the teachers in the Kentucky retirement system vote to come under federal Social Security, the state legislature would have to find $1 million of new money annually to finance the state's employer contribution to the Social Security fund. Under our present revenue-producing system, the legislature would encounter serious difficulty in locating a sum of new money to bring the teachers into the Social Security program.

I believe considerable organizational work will have to be done among the teachers to prepare for a referendum and point out to the legislature where the $1 million could be obtained. The next legislature meets January 1956.

I suggest that you write again to Mr. Fithian on about November 20 to learn of any developments favorable to teachers now under their own retirement system.

Be assured of my sympathy and willingness to cooperate with the teaching profession on this subject.

---

1. Mr. Fithian, no vita available.

WELFARE ASSISTANCE FOR EASTERN KENTUCKY
Letter / February 23, 1955

[To Mrs. B. K. Lawrence, Louisville]

YOUR recent letter regarding the pressing charitable cases with which you are familiar in eastern Kentucky, where the basic essentials of food and clothing are of primary concern to the people involved, discloses an unusual degree of warmth and understanding. I have reviewed your remarks with much care and attention.

The continued and prolonged unemployment in eastern Kentucky coal fields has been the chief factor in reducing the economic status of the people in that area. Remedial action on the scale necessary to solve the pressing economic problem with which the whole area is now afflicted will require the serious attention and vigorous action of the federal government. Officials and agencies of state government are concerted in their action and belief that federal help should be channeled to that region in great volume. Of course, various state programs, such as unemployment compensation, child welfare, and old-age benefits, have been geared to meet as many of the extreme cases as it is possible to do under the law. Then, too, federal surplus commodities have been made available to state agencies and personnel administering the program and making the distributions so that outright hunger has thus far been largely averted.

We shall continue to focus our attention and exert every means at our disposal to improve the economic lot of the unemployed in the eastern third of our great state.

UNEMPLOYMENT COMPENSATION BENEFITS
Letter / April 14, 1955

[To L. C. Robinett, Feds Creek]

YOU have suggested that a special session of the legislature be convened for the main purpose of extending beyond twenty-six weeks the period during which unemployment compensation benefits may be paid. Several persons in eastern Kentucky have made the same proposal and the serious unemployment conditions in that area warrant such thinking.

At the beginning of 1955, twenty-six weeks was the longest period any state in the Union provided unemployment pay. Most of the states held regular legislative sessions this year, but as yet we have not learned whether any of them extended the pay period beyond Kentucky's present limit.

The jobless situation in Kentucky is so desperate that the unemployment fund is now paying out benefits twice as fast as employer contributions are being deposited in the fund. Employers are militantly opposed to this practice and have stated their objections to it in strong language.

There are a few real drawbacks to calling a special session for the purpose of prolonging the time during which jobless pay might be received. Employers who contribute to the fund would express loud, public opposition to the idea, thereby worsening the relationship between employer and worker. The employers also would contend that the current desperate economic times will soon improve.

The state Capitol, which houses the legislative bodies, is undergoing a complete interior reconstruction. At present, the senate and house chambers are dismantled and being made ready for the regular 1956 session. It would be difficult now to find proper quarters for the 138 members of the legislature to ponder the unemployment situation and the extension of jobless pay rights.

I am in hopes that Senator Neely's[1] findings in eastern Kentucky will alert Washington to the seriousness of our problems and induce federal officials to begin thinking about starting some type of public works program, such as we had during the first two administrations of President Roosevelt. The state is unable to institute such programs.

I am sorry that we cannot be of more help to the restless, hungry people at this time.

---

1. Matthew Mansfield Neely (1874-1958), mayor of Fairmont, West Virginia (1908-1910); clerk, West Virginia House of Delegates (1911-1913); member, United States House of Representatives (1913-1921, 1945-1947); member, United States Senate (1923-1929, 1931-1941, 1949-1958); governor of West Virginia (1941-1945); born in Grove, West Virginia. *Who's Who in America, 1954-1955,* 28th ed. (Chicago, 1954), pp. 1966-67.

L. C. Robinett was president, Local Union 8691.

CRIME

GAMBLING IN THREE COUNTIES
Letter / August 27, 1951

[To W. G. Hoagland, Louisville]

THIS is an acknowledgment of your August 15 letter. During the past several weeks I, like you, have been concerned with the unfavorable publicity certain limited areas of our great state have received as a result of investigations made of law enforcement or the lack of such enforcement. As a citizen, a Christian, and a public official, the conditions exposed are reprehensible and constitute blotches on the name Kentucky. However, these conditions are isolated rather than general. They reflect locally rather than statewide.

The fact that these conditions are so restricted in area points to the inevitable question of why gambling has or is now flourishing in three counties in the state with the remaining 117 counties either completely free or nearly so of this acknowledged social menace.[1] The answer is as logical as the question; namely, either a majority of the citizens of the county involved are in favor of this type of activity or at least willing for their law-enforcement officials to condone such practices. In any event, the people of any community get the kind of law enforcement they expect and demand of the officials whom they elect every four or six years.

Law enforcement is almost exclusively a local responsibility. While the state police were given general police authority in 1948 except in incorporated towns and cities, their chief role is the enforcement of traffic laws and the saving of human life on our highways. With a force of only 213 to serve all Kentucky, their law-enforcement duties generally must be limited to the supplemental help which they are able to render local officials. There are several counties, in which those receiving unfavorable publicity are represented, having a law-enforcement complement greater in number than the total state police force. The sheriff and his deputies in every county have full legal authority to rid the community of all open gambling establishments. In any such undertaking the state police will endeavor to lend whatever assistance is requested of them.

It is my sincere hope that the shadows now cast on these communities can soon be lifted through the efforts of an aroused citizenry. I am glad to write you in this regard and assure you that my moral encouragement and full support is lent the citizens of the state who are striving to build law-abiding, prosperous communities in which they and their children can enjoy the blessings of our great state and nation.

---

1. The three counties to which Governor Wetherby was referring were Kenton, Campbell, and Henderson. The governor's initial reluctance to use the state police to conduct gambling raids was set aside, as he ordered the raids to be carried out on the morning of August 31, 1951. These raids on two Campbell County gambling spots resulted in the arrest of sixty-eight persons. The raids were ordered by the governor after the failure of Campbell and Kenton counties to elect reform candidates in the August primary. Police Commissioner Guthrie Crowe accused voters there of being "lax and lackadaisical." Governor Wetherby said he ordered the raids after a newspaper story from Covington stated that gambling was safe in northern Kentucky if operated cautiously. The raids were kept a secret from the local law-enforcement agents. Local residents were upset and placed the blame for the action on politics. Crowe threatened more raids if gambling and prostitution did not end. One observer stated that never in the memory of most residents had gambling been shut down so tightly. *Louisville Courier-Journal,* September 1, 1951.

GAMBLING RAIDS IN NORTHERN KENTUCKY
Letter / September 12, 1951

[To John J. Donovan, Ludlow]

THE action that was taken in northern Kentucky by the state police was done so in good faith and with the hope the bad publicity that area of our state had received in recent weeks can be corrected. This can and will be accomplished if the people who believe in and stand for law enforcement and civic virtues will be as bold in upholding the actions of the police department as the policemen were who participated in ridding at least two establishments of the vice and sordid conditions that were found.

While I am not sufficiently acquainted with the circumstances and details relative to the similarity on one hand, or contrast on the other, as outlined in your letter, between Kenton and Campbell counties, I should like to advise that the state police, prior to their move against gambling in Campbell County, carefully checked places where gambling activities had previously been carried on in Kenton County, and nowhere found open gambling operating. However, as was indicated by Commissioner Crowe immediately following the raids in Wilder, the state will act in the future when local officials show unwillingness to cope with law violaters and to keep the area of their jurisdiction free of vice which undermines, and will eventually destroy, the decency and self-respect of any community in which it thrives.

Gambling became a political issue in 1951. In the Democratic primary, Governor Wetherby accused his opponent, Howell W. Vincent of Newport, of having links to the gambling interests. Vincent denied the charge. Later, Eugene R. Siler, Republican candidate for governor, stated that the gambling raids were a political escapade to help Wetherby. The governor, however, had been uncertain whether the raids would help or hurt him, so entrenched was gambling in certain areas. In retrospect, they seem to have pleased the electorate, and they helped to mitigate the morality issue on which Siler ran his campaign. Governor Wetherby insisted that he took the action because local officials and machinery had dealt unsuccessfully with the problem, while they arrogantly flaunted their breach of law. *Louisville Courier-Journal,* August 1, 1951, September 1, 1951.

John J. Donovan (1873-1969), locomotive engineer with Southern Railway Company; member and officer of the Knights of Columbus; Kentucky Colonel; born in Scott County. Letter, December 10, 1980.

ANTI-GAMBLING LAW
Letter / June 9, 1952

[To Earle C. Clements, Washington, D.C.]

ATTACHED herewith is the correspondence you received from John H. Kinsella[1] of Newport. So that you can reply in a specific manner, I submit the following information with reference to his inquiry.

Since the 1952 General Assembly passed the so-called law on licensed premises, the Alcoholoc Beverage Control Board has adopted a consistent and well-defined policy of processing both new and renewed license applications where the applicant has a federal stamp.[2] This policy is that the application is initially denied or turned down by the administrator charged with the responsibility of issuing licenses, whether they be for either liquor or beer.

Upon the denial by the administrator, the applicant then can appeal to the whole board, following which the case is thoroughly investigated by the department. If upon appeal it is found that, through the use of the stamp, gambling in any form is engaged in or allowed on the licensed premises, the board will affirm the administrator's decision. If on the other hand, it is proved that no gambling is conducted or allowed in or on these premises, the whole board sitting, and assuming that the application is proper and valid in all other respects, will overrule the administrator's decision and grant the license under consideration.

---

1. John H. Kinsella, no vita available.

2. *Acts of the General Assembly of the Commonwealth of Kentucky,* 1952, Chapter 111 (H.B. 22), pp. 304-05. For a description of this act see letter from January 28, 1952, in Legislative Messages and Statements section.

STATE POLICE AND LAW ENFORCEMENT
Letter / November 14, 1952

[To William Branaman, Henderson]

In replying to your October 21 letter, permit me to advise that the attention of Commissioner Shearer[1] has been called to the request made by the group you represent for the removal of one of the department's field men in your area. Inasmuch as you report discussing your group's views regarding the performance of Mr. Lett[2] with Commissioner Shearer, and considering the free hand over matters pertaining to personnel, I feel it sufficient from my own standpoint to report that the commissioner will further review this specific case. After reaching some determination, he will communicate with you about it.

A broader and more important feature of your communication, to my way of thinking, is the reference made to my personnel attitude and the direction that my policy would take as governor toward the menace of commercialized gambling in areas where it has been either condoned or protected by local officials and law-enforcement authorities. There is no doubt that my own purposes and goals are similar and parallel to those of your group as they are applied to the conditions that have so long existed in Henderson County.

In view of this, I do not consider it becoming to measure in terms of a mere pittance the progress that has been made in meeting the total problem. Open and flagrant gambling has flourished in Henderson, as well as in the two northern Kentucky counties of Kenton and Campbell, for years, if not for generations. The opposing citizens, through the machinery of the grand jury, and the local officials, through explicit power and authority contained in the statutes, dealt unsuccessfully with the problem. I am advised periodically, however, that as a result of the police action that was taken upon my orders, widespread gambling activity has disappeared and general lawlessness stemming from the breeding ground of the gambling casinos is at an all-time low.

As I reflect back on my statements or pledges made during last year's campaign and consider them in light of what has taken place, I cannot avoid the conclusion that both the letter and the spirit of those utterances have been met. If my appraisal of the public's reaction is correct, I believe a vast majority of the people most directly affected agree.

I remain a firm believer and strong advocator of local officials, locally elected or appointed, discharging their duties so as to meet one of the basic responsibilities of local government; that is, the protection of life, property and public morals. Nevertheless, I shall continue vigorously the policy of state police participating in law-enforcement activities in those areas that have proven through unwillingness or inability to cope with organized crime.

In closing, I should like to again express both an understanding and appreciation of the role your group is assuming in our joint efforts to make Kentucky a better state. At the same time, I invite your continued interest and cooperation.

---

1. Guy S. Shearer (1909-), probation officer of Jefferson County Court (1934-1936); secretary-treasurer of Board of Barber and Beautition Examiners (1936-1941); justice of the peace of Jefferson County (1943-1946); police judge (pro-tem) of Louisville (1946-1948); member of Kentucky Air Board (1948); commissioner of Alcoholic Beverage Control (1948-1956); assistant attorney general (1972-1980); born in Lancaster and resides in Louisville. Phone interview, December 10, 1980.

2. Mr. Lett, no vita available.

William M. Branaman (1925-), attorney; president, Henderson County Good Government League; born in Barbourville and resides in Henderson. Letter December 6, 1980.

PROBATION AND PAROLE LEGISLATION
Letter / February 18, 1955

[To Ralph H. Logan, Louisville]

It was unfortunate that the probation and parole legislation that was offered the last session of the General Assembly failed to generate more support than it did. While I endeavored to push it along as far and as hard as it seemed advisable, the facts of the matter were that the legislation under question failed to have the kind of legislation foundation support that any substantial legislative subject must have if it is to get very far in our General Assembly.

If those of you with a continuing interest in this problem will furnish me with a list of names from which I might draw to compose another committee, I shall be glad to name them. Of course, it would be understood by the committee membership that another governor and another legislature will be handling such matters and that anything I might do would not be considered binding nor necessarily a part of a legislative program of my successor.

Ralph H. Logan (1910-), chief rent attorney, United States Government (1942-1946); police judge, Anchorage (1950-1951); judge, Domestic Relations Court, Louisville (1952); member, Jefferson Circuit Court (1952-1953); director, president of Southern Savings and Building Association (1947-); Democratic candidate for United States Congress (1948); became member of Governor's Council for Probation and Parole (1956); born in Brownsville and resides in Louisville. *Who's Who in the South and Southwest, 1959-1960,* 6th ed. (Chicago, 1959), p. 489.

CAPITAL PUNISHMENT
Letter / March 11, 1955

[To Mr. & Mrs. Louie Leffew, Louisville]

THE wheels of justice and mercy oftentimes grind slowly. There may be some basis for believing that the long period spent by the Tarrences in death row has inflicted sufficient punishment to satisfy the demands of society for the crime for which they were sentenced. However, this period is the result of a whole series of legal actions and maneuvers all designed to effect their escape from the death punishment to which they were sentenced by a competent jury and trial presided over by a fair and impartial judge.

I appreciate your telegram, as well as your views; however, soon after becoming governor I decided that my responsibility was not to decide that a man should or should not be electrocuted, but rather to assure the doomed individual and satisfy myself that he had been accorded all legal rights and opportunities afforded by law and that, after these safeguards had been carefully observed and he still received the death sentence, there remains no other path for me to follow other than seeing that the conviction is carried out. A set policy of mine before each electrocution is to have the attorney general minutely study the record for any flaw that might exist that would in any way alter the facts of the case or the decision of the court.

Governor Wetherby never opposed the use of capital punishment. He considered it to be a deterrent to crime. As chief executive, the governor was reluctant to interfere with the decisions of the judicial branch of government. Indeed, he did not use the right of pardon given to him except to pardon at the time he left office the convicts who serviced the executive mansion.

VALEDICTORY

VALEDICTORY ADDRESS
Frankfort / December 13, 1955

WE are ready to turn another page toward the future of Kentucky. In the pages of the future we will find sharp and severe challenges confronting the new administration and the citizens it will govern. From intimate experience, I can say the duties ahead are rugged. Your new chief executive[1] will face vast horizons for endeavor and achievement. The progressive aspects of his program deserve the support of all Kentuckians. I wish him well as he takes up the struggle for a better Kentucky.

In recent years, I believe, I know, Kentucky has moved forward brilliantly. I have attended many conferences of governors, and I assure you Kentucky is no longer regarded completely as a colorful but backward state. Many governors have noted our fight to bring Kentucky up the economic, industrial, and welfare scales.

We are making good in the battle to pull the Commonwealth into commercial, agrarian, and cultural balance with our sister states. I plead with you to keep up this pressure. The cartoonists who picture us with straws in our teeth, hayseed in our hair, and mud on our boots will soon be far out of date and way out of line.

As I leave office, with a forgivable reluctance, I desire to say a genuine "thank you" to the officials and employees of the state agencies who served in my administration. The tide of events has brought feelings of anxiety and insecurity to many of the folks who have worked diligently and efficiently for the taxpayers. However, this is a natural state of affairs for a politically minded state like Kentucky, and must be accepted as inevitable. But my admiration for the job you state workers have performed is undiminished.

The command decisions may have been made in the legislature or in the governor's office, but the results must be credited to the thousands of individuals who carried out the orders. If our administration can be praised for its vigorous efforts to improve Kentucky the praise in turn belongs to the department heads and their office and field forces. You will have forever my warmest gratitude.

The city of Frankfort has been a gracious and friendly host during the years we have been at the helm of state government. Many hundreds of our employees have taken up residence within the city and in Franklin County. It has been enjoyable for them and particularly for my family, which has enriched itself with a new son-in-law captured right here within the city limits.[2]

The state government has done something for Frankfort. The magnificent Annex Building behind the Capitol is a structure that would add to the dignity of any city. The exterior of the Capitol Building has been shorn of a half-century of dirt and smoke smudge. The entire interior of the Capitol has been remodeled and modernized. The offices are better equipped. More and better work will be produced in this fresh environment. I can say with reasonable confidence that until some state builds a new one, Kentucky has the most beautiful Capitol Building inside and outside in the nation.

The state-constructed airport nearing completion in West Frankfort will put your community on the air maps and bring commercial airline service to you. This will be helpful in attracting a new industry or two into the city.

As the reins of government are handed over to our successors, I should like to point out that the many programs we have undertaken for the improvement of Kentucky are in manageable shape for continuation. We have attempted to tie up the loose ends of an ambitious construction and renovation project. Building programs at the new state fairgrounds, the University of Kentucky, the state colleges, and our hospitals should be moved onward without delay. These programs would not have been set in motion had they not been subjected to careful study and deemed to be of deep and immediate need.

The Louisville-Elizabethtown toll road should be completed by midsummer. When this turnpike is in full operation, I am sure Kentuckians will be satisfied with our decision to enter this modern phase of highway development. It will protect us against isolation.

Hundreds of small factories and industries have located in Kentucky through the joint efforts of local organizations and state agencies. This has brought economic refreshment to our labor force and to our retailers and banks. Our people should be most grateful to the industries that have expanded into Kentucky. It took time and work to bring them here.

Kentuckians did themselves a great favor in amending their constitution in 1953[3] to provide for a more equitable distribution of state school funds and for a basically stronger school system. The mechanism to put this program into action was written by the 1954 legislature.[4] The number of people who voted for this green light in school improvement is a mandate to find the means to obey the command of the people.

There are a few other items to be mentioned as the curtain on this administration falls. Our state park system has won national recognition. It has made the tourist industry one of the most profitable in the state. Every Kentuckian can be proud of his state parks.

The government is solvent. Its good financial condition will be revealed by a surplus of $5 million at the end of this fiscal year. The new administration should not be troubled by a lack of operating revenues.

The opportunity to serve as governor is rare. I am in hopes that I have asserted the authority of the office to the satisfaction of the majority of the people. I certainly have tried my best to give you a new evaluation of our goals and a new feeling of confidence in ourselves.

The job of governor is a coveted one. There are many days and hours when the feeling is inclined to surrender to futility. But in the flow of the progress we have made on so many fronts, I feel that the past five years have made Kentuckians a little more proud of their state. I have respect for the talents and dignity of our citizens.

Although I have not always been able to say "Yes," I have done my best to make decisions for the common good. There are many times when "Yes" would have been the wrong answer.

I treasure the honors you have granted me, and I trust that your interest in and respect for government have been strengthened. I am now off your payroll, joining you as a free citizen again and looking for a job.

To you, Governor Chandler, my best wishes for a successful administration and one that will carry Kentucky forward and upward.

Good luck to you, the people of Kentucky, and goodbye.

---

1. Albert Benjamin Chandler (1898-), state senator (1929-1931); lieutenant governor of Kentucky (1931-1935), governor (1935-1939, 1955-1959);

member, United States Senate (1939-1946); commissioner of baseball (1945-1951); born in Corydon and resides in Versailles. *Who's Who in the South and Southwest, 1971-1972,* 12th ed. (Chicago, 1971), p. 105.

2. George Bernard Perry married Barbara Juel Wetherby on August 27, 1954, in the Church of the Good Shepherd at Frankfort.

3. Amendment Number XVI repealed Section 186 of the Kentucky Constitution, which had required school funds to be appropriated on a per capita basis, and allowed the General Assembly to prescribe the manner of distribution and use of public school funds. See *Acts of the General Assembly of the Commonwealth of Kentucky,* 1952, Chapter 89 (S.B. 225), pp. 245-46.

4. The Minimum Foundation Program. *Acts of the General Assembly of the Commonwealth of Kentucky,* 1954, Chapter 214 (H.B. 365), pp. 590-603. For more information see speech from January 12, 1954, in the Legislative Messages and Statements section.

APPENDIX

WETHERBY ADMINISTRATION ACCOMPLISHMENTS
Letter / January 27, 1954

[To Buddie Miller, Sadler]

THE road matter in which you are interested is being taken up with the Highway Department officials.

In responding to your statement regarding the accomplishments of Governor Wetherby's administration, permit me to advise that the present governor has been serving as chief executive since November 27, 1950. Following are some chief points to be noted.

In the 1952 legislature Governor Wetherby successfully backed a complete revision of the registration and purgation law designed to rid the voter rolls of ineligibles and to promote more honest elections.

He expressed sympathy in providing authority for the East Kentucky Rural Electric Cooperative corporation to construct a $30 million power plant and transmission lines to serve more than 80,000 rural families now without electric power. The State Public Service Commission and state courts have approved this project, although it is still in some controversy at the federal level.

He won support of a law which made gambling on premises licensed for the sale of alcoholic beverages prima facie evidence for the suspension or revocation of such licenses.

Governor Wetherby brought the annual appropriation to elementary and high schools to a record of more than $30 million.

The recent amendment adoption changing the constitutional restrictions around distribution of the common school fund was hailed by educators as the green light enabling them to improve Kentucky's school system. The governor took to statewide radio and television programs to debate with the opponents of the amendment, which was adopted by more than 200,000 votes.

During his administration the state mental hospital program has been placed in a separate department and is headed by an energetic, well-qualified young psychiatrist.[1] This program formerly was in a department chiefly concerned with penal institutions.

He is the first governor of Kentucky to show an active interest in the construction of toll roads which, in addition to moving north–south traffic rapidly through Kentucky, will take heavy trucks off highways not constructed to withstand constant battering.

He supported legislation in 1952, which needed his help, to reduce the case load of the Court of Appeals by lessening the writing of opinions in small cases. He also backed the writing of a new civil code of practice to replace one clearly outmoded. The new code is now a reality.[2]

Kentucky's park program is now rated one of the best in the United States. The governor has continuously promoted this tourist plan. It has been estimated that tourists left $330 million in Kentucky in 1952, and the 1953 total is likely to be greater.

The general purpose budget for 1952-1953 was $78 million. For 1953-1954 it was $81 million. Faced with unanticipated falling revenues last December, he called his cabinet into a special meeting and slashed the 1952-1953 budget to $74 million and the 1953-1954 budget to $76 million. This was disappointing to department heads but was roundly hailed by the taxpayers.

Governor Wetherby advocated creation of a Youth Authority to handle cases of children found delinquent, neglected, or mentally impaired. The authority now attempts to provide these children with proper care or punishment. Formerly many of them were placed in county jails or the state's juvenile detention institution.

Most legislatures experience complete tumult and stop the clock at midnight on the last night to complete their work. The governor worked closely with his first legislature in 1952 and it adjourned sine die at 2:00 P.M. amid feelings of fellowship and accomplishment.

In August 1951 Governor Wetherby ordered state troopers into Covington, Kenton County, and Henderson to wipe out prostitution and gambling.[3] These successful actions have done much to restore self-respect to the communities. It marked the first time state police were deployed in large numbers against vice and corruption.

This represents some of the accomplishments of this administration. We are attaching a copy of the governor's recent message to the legislature as evidence of additional accomplishments the governor hopes to achieve during the second half of his administration.

This letter was written by Edward A. Farris, Executive secretary to Governor Wetherby.

1. Dr. Frank M. Gaines.

2. See "An Act relating to the appellate civil jurisdiction of the Court of Appeals," *Acts of the General Assembly of the Commonwealth of Kentucky*, 1952, Chapter 24 (S.B. 81), pp. 39-40. See also "An Act relating to rules of pleading, practice, and procedure, and the forms thereof in civil actions and with limited application, in criminal proceedings," *Acts of the General Assembly of the Commonwealth of Kentucky*, 1952, Chapter 18 (S.B. 63), pp. 29–31.

3. This statement is not accurate. On August 31, 1951, Governor Wetherby ordered state police forces into Campbell County only. For a description of this raid see letter from September 12, 1951, in the Crime section.

Edward Allen Farris (1920-   ), chief assistant to Governors Earle Clements and Lawrence Wetherby (1948-1956); active full time in state campaign headquarters of Governors Bert Combs and Edward Breathitt (1959, 1963); private business and legislative representative for consumer finance and insurance industries (1960-1976); distilled spirits administrator and member of the Kentucky Alcoholic Beverage Control Board (1977-   ); born near Cane Valley, Adair County, and resides in Frankfort. Letter, December 29, 1980.

INDEX

www.ingramcontent.com/pod-product-compliance
Lightning Source LLC
LaVergne TN
LVHW040201080826
844660LV00001B/60